Trinity Tales

Trinity College Dublin in the Seventies

Trinity Tales

Trinity College Dublin in the Seventies

Edited by KATHY GILFILLAN

THE LILLIPUT PRESS
DUBLIN

First published 2011 by
THE LILLIPUT PRESS
62–63 Sitric Road, Arbour Hill
Dublin 7, Ireland
www.lilliputpress.ie

ISBN 978 1 84351 191 5

1 3 5 7 9 10 8 6 4 2

A CIP record for this title is available
from The British Library.

Set in Minion with Akzidenz Grotesk display titling by Marsha Swan
Printed and bound in Sweden by ScandBook AB

CONTENTS

FOREWORD

terence brown

TWO SCENES come to mind immediately as I try to recall across the too swiftly accreting decades the Trinity of the 1970s, when I was at the beginning of my professional career as a lecturer in English. In the first, Owen Sheehy-Skeffington, renowned Senior Lecturer in French and public intellectual in the French mode, is strolling with some friends in the public grounds of Howth Castle. He pauses formally, with old-world courtesy, to salute myself and my wife, as we pass on a sunny Saturday, before continuing what is obviously an intent conversation. It was the last time I saw him, for a few weeks later, in June 1970, he was dead and one of the college's most trenchantly liberal voices had been prematurely silenced. In the second scene, later in the decade, I am at the annual provost's garden party on Trinity Monday, in company with the fairly new Professor of French, Francis Higman. At our backs the new Arts Building is all but complete. I say that I hope it will secure the future of the Arts and Humanities in college, in a world still struggling with the aftermath of the first oil crisis (things were bad then too). Higman, who deprecated the globe's wasteful dependence on oil, is not so sure. He is not convinced students will continue to enrol in the courses we have to offer, even in a spanking new building. We raise hesitant glasses to the uncertain future that beckons from Koralek's cast-concrete, post-modernist statement. (When eventually the staff moves in it finds the foyer is dominated by a huge funnel that aggressively suggests the building's inner workings; in fact the heating in my own room gave trouble for years.)

Skeffington, or 'Skeff' as everyone called him in college, as fearless defender of minority causes (Conor Cruise O'Brien, I seem to remember, said he had 'the courage of my convictions') relished the fact that Trinity had been, since the Bishops proscribed attendance at the college by the Catholic faithful, on pain of their immortal souls, a platform from which dissenting opinion could come (not that it often did since few of his colleagues were as outspoken as he). He reckoned the ban did some good in bringing only the most independent-minded of Catholics within its walls, helping to make the college, as it was in the 1960s, a lively bazaar of competing ideas and opinion, where Unionist met nationalist, English Tory met Irish socialist, devout believer met militant sceptic, and the college was small enough for vibrant conversations across the disciplines and for what can best be invoked, as we who were there then to settle for carpet slippers and a glass of something soothing, a variegated social life (see *Trinity Tales: Trinity College Dublin in the Sixties* for the lowdown on the latter).

By the end of the 1970s, with the ban rescinded in the year of Skeff's death, the Arts Building would begin to bulge at the seams, as the children of middle-class Catholic Ireland, especially in Dublin, took Arts and Humanities in Trinity as the hard-earned reward for the rigours of the Leaving Cert. The accents of south County Dublin began to dominate in the narrow corridors of the Arts Building (the redoubtable Professor of Medieval History Jocelyn Otway-Ruthven always insisted it was a 'Building'; UCD had an Arts Block!). Northsiders too were not unknown (it was closer on the bus route, several such students told me, a fellow northsider, than UCD). There were fewer Northern men from such single-sex schools as Inst. and Campbell College, and even students from co-ed Methody were fewer in number (my old school, Sullivan Upper in Holywood, County Down, increasingly sent students to Edinburgh and Glasgow, when in the past some had set their sights on Trinity). The founding of the new University of Ulster helped to break the link with Magee College, Derry, that had traditionally brought Presbyterian ordinands for the final five terms of their BA years. Polite, often quietly brilliant young women from Northern convent schools could be seen as taking some of the places they left vacant. Higman's pessimism had been unfounded but Trinity was no longer the college aslant from Irish life from where the accents of opposition to state power might be expected to issue uninhibitedly. TCD was joining the mainstream. The Arts Building/Block, opened in 1978, was symbol and all-too-concrete expression of that fact.

Trinity, of course, might not have survived the 1960s, and I am not referring to the excesses the Age of Aquarius unleashed even in Ireland. In 1966 Minister of Education Donogh O'Malley had stunned his cabinet colleagues when he announced that free secondary education would be available to pupils from 1967 onwards (many of those students from the Republic of Ireland who crowded the Arts Building by the end of the 1970s and who competed for places in the college's schools of Medicine, Law and Sciences, were the beneficiaries of O'Malley's bold intervention). He followed this bombshell by suddenly announcing that he intended to merge UCD and TCD. (UCD had already taken the decision to relocate to Belfield from Earlsfort Terrace, which would have complicated the proposed amalgamation.) The authorities at UCD rose to the ministerial master plan with a self-confidence that suggested they knew who would rule the roost in the new dispensation. The board of TCD seemed ready to acquiesce. The resulting rebellion by many of the university's staff taught me a lesson that stood to me over the years in college and it was certainly useful in facing the challenges of the transition that would take place in the 1970s.

It's simple enough. Apart from the student body who create and recreate many different worlds as the years run on, there are two Trinitys (oddly numerological as that must sound). The first is the formally constituted college with its board, council, fellows, academic and administrative officers, deans and heads of department and then there is the Trinity of people who know each other, talk and argue with each other, who form friendships built on trust and liking, and develop alliances strategic or otherwise. The two Trinitys are not mutually exclusive, it must be said, but it bodes ill for any policy proposed by the formal college if it does not gain at least the tacit acceptance of the other. Accepting the merger did not, and I remember George Dawson (Professor of Genetics and dedicated connoisseur of Irish and European modern art) chairing with great aplomb a meeting in the Senior Common Room at which it became clear that the settled will of the community was firmly against any merger (it is telling that in the managerial climate currently pervasive in UK universities, many vice-chancellors have closed staff common rooms and faculty clubs, where the 'subversion of mission' can flourish dangerously).

In the event 'the merger' did not go through. O'Malley's sudden death in 1968, government inertia in the face of opposition and controversy, Trinity's rediscovered backbone, meant that by the early 1970s the concept had more or less run into the sand (though TCD did lose its veterinary school to UCD). Later in the decade, though in less seismic fashion, the power of college opinion was evidenced when the initial plans for the Arts Building were revealed. Small staff offices would have no windows. A groundswell of opposition sent the architects back to their drawing boards.

ON A SUNNY late afternoon in May 1974 I was in the National Library in Kildare Street, reading a volume of verse that included poems on the Nazi blitz on Belfast during the Second World War. I thought of stopping and heading to the Lincoln Inn for a drink before setting off home, but decided to take some more notes. About five minutes later a reverberant boom sounded and the dome of the building seemed to take a long breath as it considered whether to collapse or stay intact. The few readers swiftly made for the doors. I went down to where up against the walls of Trinity in South Leinster Street a Loyalist car bomb had exploded. I watched as the human remains were carried away in an ambulance. Getting into college by way of Lincoln Gate I met other ashen-faced colleagues and students desperate to get to phones (no mobiles then) to report their safety. Strangely, the thing I remember most about the terrible evening of the Dublin/Monaghan bombings, in which I might so easily have perished myself en route for that drink, is huge summer blooms in the college's gardens, perfect, fragile in the still, warm air, a rebuke to human waste.

This was not the first time that the college had been affected by the Northern 'Troubles' that took hold so viciously north of the border in the 1970s (though the Dublin bombings brought Northern horrors closest to home). In the week following Bloody Sunday in 1972 the atmosphere in college had been febrile. I remember, for example, Professor Theo Moody leaving a lunch table at the egregious insensitivity of a colleague over what had occurred in Derry and the rest of us at the table following him. Classes were ill-attended as public outrage in Dublin grew. From the college grounds I watched the night sky grow red as the British embassy burnt, fearful of what the future might hold.

In fact, despite these grim events, Trinity, its staff and students, remained largely unaffected by the Northern imbroglio. There were few ready to take hardline stances on the national question, though I recall one student telling me when internment was imposed in 1971 that more RUC officers would have to die. The prospect seemed to excite him. In left-wing circles there was much debate about how the Protestant and Catholic working classes in Belfast could be united, as Provo defenderism tightened its hold on South Armagh. I remember, one night at a party, a left-wing activist student ardently assuring me that the future of Ireland was hanging in the balance in the Belfast shipyards. The truth was, I think, that the southern Irish middle class and the nation's farmers had chosen to turn their backs as far as they could on what they increasingly regarded as an archaic struggle in the six counties. Less than six months after Bloody Sunday in 1972 the citizens of the Irish republic had voted by a large majority to join the EEC along with the United Kingdom. Ireland was voting for modernization not martyrdom.

Trinity itself saw various changes in the 1970s that can be read as part of an effort to align the college with university norms elsewhere. The shortest terms in the known academic world were extended (at seven weeks each they had encouraged an earlier board to consider rejecting Lord Iveagh's generous gift of a bathhouse – 'Why would the young men need it since they were up for a mere seven weeks?'). Honors examinations were moved from the autumn to the more usual June (making postgraduate employment after finals more likely). General Studies with its three subjects (the recourse of many a less-than-studious undergraduate in the 1960s) was abandoned and replaced by the all-honors-level two-subject moderatorship (still extant). Departments adjusted courses to adapt to these new conditions (not without pain, it must be said – the English Department, for example, suffered a version of civil war in the mid to late 1970s, now largely forgotten in a subject area recently deemed fifth in Europe in the international academic stakes). Most noticeable for many of the teaching staff was the marked improvement in average student quality. College had always had its high flyers, even among those in General Studies, but there had been a long tail. From the late 1970s onwards, certainly in English, the majority of students were well-qualified, worked responsibly and produced really very good work. The proportion of upper seconds rose quite justifiably and each year examiners were gratified to encounter quite exceptional work from some of their charges. I often recalled my own tentative undergraduate efforts, as I admiringly read the impressive work of cohorts of accomplished young men and women. Teaching in Trinity in the 1970s, as thereafter, was a privilege and a pleasure – so many gifted students, so much focused enthusiasm.

The election of F.S.L. Lyons as provost in 1974 was a sign that the college was opening out to Irish society. And he was a figure admirably equipped both to represent and effect this transition. Derry-born, but educated south of the border, he had read History in Trinity, where he also lectured for a time. His international reputation as a scholar had been confirmed in England where he was appointed to a chair of History at the University of Kent. His field was Irish history and by the time he was recalled to Trinity to serve as provost his book *Ireland Since the Famine* had established itself as the standard textbook on the subject in all Irish universities. A specialist in Parnell, his biography of 'the chief' would be published during his tenure and he was also contracted to write the 'official' life of Yeats (Lyons's untimely death in 1983 robbed us of this work; the task was admirably performed by another of Trinity's renowned historians, Roy Foster, almost two decades later). So as provost he was known as one whose credentials as an Irishman were unquestionable. This of course had not always been the case with Trinity provosts. In 1977 at the dinner in college to mark the sixth international James Joyce symposium (a signal achievement of David Norris), Lyons told of how when he took up residence in No. 1 Grafton Street in the mid seventies, one of his first acts had been to remove a portrait of a predecessor in the post from his office. John Pentland Mahaffy, redoubtable Unionist and enthusiastic royalist, Lyons told the assembly, was the nightmare from which he was trying to awake.

That awakening involved various acts of good authority as the essentially shy if always elegant provost (whose prowess as former Irish international on the squash courts suggested the competitive steel of the inner man) worked to make it clear that Trinity was taking its place as a university for all. He entertained the Dublin Gaelic Football team in his house. He made overtures as host to key figures in the National University. He committed himself with earnest intent to rapprochement between North and South (I remember him getting together a small group of staff members, of varying outlooks, to meet with a high-level British official to discuss 'the situation' at an especially perilous moment in the ongoing conflict in Northern Ireland). And he took a genuine interest in the cultural life of the country. This accounts for another of my most vivid memories of the 1970s in college. It is of the new-minted Burke lecture theatre in the Arts Building in 1978 filled to the doors as Provost Lyons chaired a reading by Seamus Heaney from his new book *Field Work*. It felt like the new Trinity's coming of age.

Terence Brown (Fellow Emeritus, TCD) was born in Jiangxi, China, of Northern Irish missionary parents. He grew up near Belfast. He took his BA in Trinity in 1966 and was awarded his PhD in 1970. He was appointed junior lecturer in English in Trinity in 1968 and retired as Professor of Anglo-Irish Literature in 2009. In 2007–8 he was Parnell Fellow in Magdalene College, Cambridge. He is a member of the Royal Irish Academy and of Academia Europaea. In 2002 he was made Honorary CMG for his contribution to Anglo-Irish relations. He has published widely on Irish literature and culture, including **Ireland: A Social and Cultural History 1922–2001** (2004) and **The Life of W.B. Yeats** (2001).

INTRODUCTION

kathy gilfillan

THE LILLIPUT PRESS published *Trinity Tales: Trinity College Dublin in the Sixties* in 2009, bringing together thirty-seven contributors from different backgrounds with different experiences of a hinge decade in the history of the college. On foot of the success of that book, the college requested 'more of the same, please'. Here is a snapshot of student life in the seventies, jigsaw-puzzled together by those I could persuade to summon up memories from over forty years ago.

Decades are not neat bundles even if we wished they were for literary or historical purposes. The years bleed into each other; they are ragged and jagged. Some of the contributors straddle both decades, having begun their college careers in the late sixties, such as Elgy Gillespie (1966–73) who 'trooped past the giant Irish elk with bandaged knee into Dr Kennelly's first Theory of English Criticism in the Bear Pit, the Victorian holding-pen in the GMB' with 'a riotous ragbag of straggling, Julie Christie-ish girls in miniskirts with ironed-smooth Looby-Loo hair'. Or Mashey Bernstein (1966–70), who saw himself as a real outsider, 'an Orthodox Jew at the Court of St Brendan'. Many of the Catholic contributors felt they were interlopers in those early days when permission was still required from a bishop to attend the pagan TCD. Ted Smyth, a Protestant, wistfully recalls a 'reasonable amount – though never enough – of sex'.

Politics were certainly to the fore in the lives and minds of many students.

Dr Carol Coulter joined the Fabian Society on her first day in college. The Fabians morphed into the Socialist Society, 'a cauldron of ideological debate among different brands of Marxism'. She and Anne Connolly (1971–5) both ran for presidency of the Students' Representative Council (SRC), won by Anne. Mary Harney (1972–6) made history as the first female auditor of the Hist, 1975–6. It was Kate Cruise O'Brien in 1969 who stormed the male-only Hist during a debate involving her father, Conor Cruise O'Brien. She roped me in as part of the protest. David Ford, the auditor, was in cahoots with the protest along with Conor Cruise and it was under Ford's leadership that women were finally admitted. I note that Patrick Guinness (1975–80) had never passed through Front Gate before his registration day. This was not unusual.

My own first day in Trinity in 1968 began by my having to ask where it was, because I had never been to Dublin before – hard to credit when I had hitchhiked across Europe and often visited the UK. But that was the mindset of many Northern Irish Protestants; we simply ignored the South.

An inspirational English teacher, who was also a graduate, made me choose TCD. I had been accepted by Edinburgh and Aberystwyth and wait-listed by Sussex (my first choice) and in a fit of pique decided to embrace Ireland instead. Oh lucky choice that determined my entire life: I found my husband, Paul McGuinness, and made lifelong friends.

On that first wobble across the cobbles of Front Square in my platform boots, I met Cathy de Hartog who became a wonderful friend. Together we escaped from our separate digs in Whitehall – my landlady, Mrs Anderson, was given to leaving me unintentionally gruesome notes on the kitchen table when I was late for supper, viz. 'Your heart is in the fridge.' We fled southside to share a flat on Waterloo Road.

We were known as the two Cathys or Kathys because we were in the same English year and did everything together. I was in awe of her and she was jealous of any of my other friends. Her grandfather was J.B. Priestley and her father a Dutch writer called Jan de Hartog. Her aunt, Mary Priestley, taught psychody-namic dancing, which was a kind of therapy where the patient banged saucepan lids together in a freeing display of noise and movement – heady stuff for a wee girl from Eglinton in Northern Ireland. Cathy later suffered a breakdown and was diagnosed with schizophrenia, possibly triggered by drug use. I was more of a coward when it came to LSD and too scared to take it but not frightened by the odd joint. How else could you understand Leonard Cohen?

When Cathy left college for treatment, I felt I had lost part of myself. Together we had explored student journalism. I wrote for *TCD Miscellany* and *Trinity News*. After she left I became more political, started a women's lib group, and stood for the presidency of the SRC, encouraged by Shane Ross, John Stephenson and the late Bill Graham who introduced U2 to Paul McGuinness. Eugene Murray won the presidency but we became allies and he appointed me welfare officer. I used this position to write a contraceptive booklet with the help of the Marie Stopes Clinic in the UK that also contained information about sexually transmitted diseases. The SRC published it and I was in some danger of being arrested as it was against the law then to publish any information on contraception. To safeguard me the booklet was credited to the total student population of TCD. Let them arrest every student! When Donnell Deeny read the booklet he looked at me and said with some alarm, 'Kathy, you are so modern.' In fact I just looked modern, staying a virgin until past my twenty-first birthday.

Antony Farrell (1969–73) describes the burning of the British embassy on 30 January 1972 as our 9/11. It was monumentally emotional but I remember the crowd as jocular as well as angry. Nicholas Peck, son of the British Ambassador to Ireland, Sir John Peck, was so overwhelmed by Bloody Sunday that he burnt his British passport. This caused him some difficulty afterwards and no doubt his father some embarrassment.

Students also behaved like students. Nick Mulcahy (1976–80) paints a vivid picture of future president, Mary Robinson, in her nightie on a student trip to Brussels, trying to quell a drunken late-night student binge session. I disgraced myself at Aline Galvin's twenty-first birthday party (at which Horslips played) by taking off my clothes and jumping into the swimming pool, which was private and off limits. I would probably have got away with it had her parents not been placed by the front door to bid goodnight to everyone in person. As I dripped past them, they did not shake hands.

While researching this book I was shocked by the number of students from the seventies who have died since our time in TCD, many of them accidentally and tragically. I especially grieve for Paul Tansey (1949–2008) who graduated in 1972 and was so kind to me as a novice politician. He, of course, was the real thing.

At the beginning of the seventies, the student population was a tiny 4000. Today it is more than 16,000. The cobbles have been tamed by foot-friendly strips of limestone, which Queen Elizabeth II negotiated without a wobble in 2011 to inspect the College Charter stamped with the seal of Elizabeth I. There are exciting new structures such as the Long Room Hub off Front Square, but some things never change, such as the jolt of excitement I feel every time I walk into the Long Room Library with its barrel ceiling and vista of leather-bound volumes stretching the length and height of the lovely wooden space.

As before, royalties go to the Long Room fund of Trinity College.

Kathy Gilfillan (TCD 1968–72; German/English Hons) was research assistant at Blackman Harvey in London,1973–6. She was a copywriter for various Dublin agencies, 1976–90, and a freelance journalist and TV scriptwriter. She is married with two children and lives in Wicklow. A governor of The Rotunda Hospital, she is also a director of The Lilliput Press, and a board member of the Strategic Committee of the Irish Cultural Centre in Paris.

Trinity Tales

Trinity College Dublin in the Seventies

AN ORTHODOX JEW AT THE COURT OF ST BRENDAN

mashey bernstein

WE WERE the same but we were different. Looking at us, people would assume that we all shared the same ideas, values and temperaments. Theoretically at least, we aspired to the same goals, those of a Protestant intellectual ascendancy. After all, we were attending Trinity, a university with a lengthy history of greatness, one of the five oldest and most revered universities in the British Isles. We looked down on lowly UCD with its aura of narrowness and intellectual inferiority. We were – at least in our own minds – a sort of elite.

In those days, the ivied hangover of a glorious past still clung to Trinity's walls, making it a Pale in the midst of the bustling city. Characteristically and symbolically, once one stepped inside those gates onto the cobbled entranceway that faced onto Dame Street, the sounds of a capital city dissipated. Trinity existed in a temporal and spatial warp. It was Irish but outside of Ireland and not English either, even though it liked to imagine that it echoed the best qualities of the Anglo model. It seemed to exist unto itself with its arcane, if not archaic, laws and institutions: Commons, gowns and a sense of snobbery. There were codes, connections and cliques. Its pretensions leaned more to Eton and Harrow than the Christian Brothers' School or the Coombe.

This was all to change in the four years that we were there. We were the last to sample a kind of education that does not exist any more, one that smacked more of the nineteenth than the twentieth century, one that considered any literature written after 1930 and anything outside of England as less than deserving of study. The masters were behind us, relics like the revered Book of Kells. Before we left in 1970, the ban on Catholics had ended with the first official Mass being held: the Old Library, a tiny, intimate gathering place, had been replaced by the gargantuan New Library and the student body had expanded from a cloistered 3000 to double that size. Those who came after simply would not be the same.

But beneath it all, we were as different as could be: hinting at the changes that were about to occur but were not yet fully realized. We were Protestants, atheists, Jews and Catholic. Politically, we ranged from Internationalist and communist to nationalist and royalist. We were rich, poor and middle class. Irish, English and American; the products of public schools and the general school systems; A levels, Leaving Cert. and the Matric.; homosexual and heterosexual.

If I fly over Trinity's portals in October 1966 and swoop down over myself as I walk in those gates for the first time, what do I see? I suppose I seemed like any typical entering Freshman. I had three Leaving Cert. honours under my belt, a healthy attitude to study and was eager to sample what new adventures Trinity would bring me. I was one of sixty accepted to study English Language and Literature.

In truth, I was frightened, alone, intimidated and beset by doubts. In my mind, Trinity was Rugby and I was Tom Brown. I was so scared that I never even went into the Buttery – that watering hole of the college – for the first three months and only then if I knew someone there. If I didn't see anyone I recognized, I would scurry out as quickly as a mole on seeing daylight.

MUCH OF THIS attitude is a result of my background. My experience up to that time had been entirely Jewish and that peculiar brand of Judaism known as orthodoxy. Even though I had grown up in Catholic Dublin and was second-generation Irish, my experience of the city was incredibly limited. Having attended Jewish schools, organizations, summer camps and the like, not only did I not have a single non-Jewish friend, I can honestly say that outside of teachers and my next-door neighbours (who we thought were anti-Semites), I had never conducted an extended conversation with a non-Jew in my life. My life was even circumscribed within the Jewish community itself. Although Dublin had only 3000 Jews, if they did not attend my school, go to my youth group or my synagogue, I hardly knew them. For all intents and purposes, I could have grown up in a metropolis with a population of seventy-five.

To top it off, I had just spent a year in Israel, so all my peers were already ahead of me or scattered into other careers. I was so insular that when I met a fellow student with the first name of Damien I asked him in all innocence where he got such a strange name. It must have struck him as an odd question, especially coming from someone whose own name was the odder of the two! But I only knew 'normal' names like Sammy, Rodney or Norman. In my mind, all non-Jews were called Johnny or Chris. I remember at one of the early lectures, I think on Wordsworth, hearing about the 'prodigal son' and turning to Renée Kingston – daughter of a Protestant minister, as it turned out – and asking her, 'Who was the Prodigal Son?' 'It's Luke,' she said, her mouth open in amazement. 'Luke who?' I asked. As she politely informed me of the parable in the Gospel of Luke and its place in Christian lore, I realized that while I had received a great education, there were some lessons I had not learned in school. That afternoon, I went to Hodges Figgis and bought a New Testament, snuck it into our house (since such a text was considered blasphemy) and read it from cover to cover. (In defence of my upbringing, I should point out that by the time I held my twenty-first party at my house, half the guest list were non-Jews with nary a quibble from my parents and that I got my liberal attitudes from my home more than from any institution.)

To an outsider, my life may have seemed limited but to my mind it was perfectly natural and normal. It was Trinity that was odd. It made every sense that I would not go to classes on even minor religious holidays, that I would not eat in the frightening Buttery because it was not kosher and that I would not attend events if they were held on Friday night or Saturday. I am sure I missed out on some of the advantages of Trinity; I would love to have acted in Players, for example, but it would have been tantamount to my renouncing my faith, my father being a well-respected member of the Dublin Jewish clergy and my elder brother, a Trinity graduate who hated the years he spent there, well on his way to becoming a famous rabbi. Indeed, my friends and family all felt the same way. They were my 'real' world.

Even at eighteen, and although I suspected that changes – which I welcomed and feared – were on the way, I could not imagine a different approach to life. Whatever glories and temptations Trinity offered, they were transitory, illusory compared to the truth of my inner life. I could look at the sweet shop and perhaps nibble at its delights, but it was to be an exotic world that I would only enter at the peril of losing my soul. Yet, perhaps, I was the 'exotic'. Much as I tried to hide it, I must have struck my friends as if I had landed from Mars. For most of my Trinity years, and while I ended up as secretary of the Film Society, assistant editor of *Trinity News* and an active participant in all sorts of college activities, my primary focus was on the Dublin Jewish community. Maybe things would have been different if I had lived away from home, but that was not financially possible, nor was I ready for it. I lived in two camps.

I may have been unworldly but I was not a bad student, though I was beset by doubts as to my intelligence. In comparison to my peers, I seem to have received a rather basic and narrow English education. I had originally wanted to study History but at the last moment, under the influence of my English teacher, who actually cried when he told us of Shelley's death and because I realized that I would have to write essays in english (lower case) whether I wanted to study History or English (upper case), I chose English. I presume others had equally bizarre reasons for the choices they made. Not surprisingly, I felt like a bit of an impostor.

Trinity had a strange system of pedagogy that hardly allayed my fears. On one hand, it treated us like self-sufficient beings but also pandered to us, feeding us regurgitated concepts. We were the elite but treated like peons. In retrospect, what we learned in class was the least significant aspect of our time. Lectures existed in a void. We had seven-week terms with no more than five hours of class a week. And we had signed up to study just one subject for the four years. We would all be together until the end. In both content and style, the lectures, with one notable exception, left much to be desired.

Our first lecture, on Shakespeare, focused on a long discussion on the folios and whether the line read 'too too solid flesh' or 'too, too sullid flesh', as if the play hinged on these picayune ideas. Yet I wrote down their every word slavishly as if I were listening to the oracle. None of us interrupted a lecture to ask if the professor could repeat or defend his idea. We would not ask questions. They would come in, read from notes on paper that had yellowed with age, and leave. But I accepted it as the norm. Why would I think any different? In all the movies I had seen about universities, it was exactly what everyone did. It would be blasphemy to expect change. When, in our senior year, Elgy Gillespie countered David Norris's theory that *Moby Dick* was a comic novel, I was sure she would be kicked out.

As soon as a lecture ended, I scurried off to the bookstore to buy any books mentioned or dove into the Library to figure out what people said. I would study, study. My lecturers intimidated me. I could not confess my lack of knowledge to them or to my peers. I had to keep my sins, my weakness, to myself. Already, the class had stratified. We knew the rising stars, those who in the first few weeks had already stood out from the crowd as the bright lights of the class: Tamsin Braidwood (who would get schols), Paddy Lyons and John Haffenden. They would gather after every lecture to discuss the points raised. They seemed to know the lectures even before they were given and had read the material. While the rest of us were trying to figure out what the material even meant, they were already on to secondary criticism. They would use terms with the familiarity of old friends while I was just getting to know them for the first time – which is as good an analogy as any for my feelings at the time. I was a stranger in a strange land. Everyone was staking their place in the class. Where was mine?

The day of reckoning finally came. Animated, interactive and concerned, Brendan Kennelly was the best of the lecturers. He enthralled and captivated us. His lectures on critical theory sang. He talked about literature not as a dead thing but as something that was alive and vital. Every week Brendan would choose five or six students to address an issue. My turn eventually came. One week, he handed out a poem, 'Speaking of Poetry' by John Peale Bishop, and called on me to talk about its poetic diction. I looked at its free verse and drew a blank. Having feasted on the riches of Keats and Yeats, it seemed rather unpoetic. I was undone – everyone would know that I was a phoney. What was I to do?

I laboured and worried over the piece and decided to confront what I thought were the poem's deficiencies. I wrote a three-page diatribe, ripping the poem apart, complaining of its lack of beauty, comparing it to Shelley and talking about what poetry should be. It was, in my humble opinion, a masterpiece of rhetoric. So armed, I was ready. But as the four other students rose to speak, my confidence drained from me as if someone had placed a literary kryptonite nugget next to my literary soul. They all spoke glowingly of its poetic virtues. They must be right!

Few people in the class knew me at all at this time and here I was about to be unmasked. I slid into the corner, hoping that Brendan would not have time to call on me. He did. As he called out my name, I pondered what to do: say I hadn't completed the assignment, was wrong in my assessment of the poem? What to do? Damn it! I worked really hard on this essay, I am going to read it and read it I did in my best declamatory voice. I began, 'In a work such as this, that speaks about poetry, it is somewhat surprising to find only a few lines which actually contain any poetry' and proceeded to vent my spleen on the poem. I concluded with, 'the poem is a justifiable attempt at non-poetry' and looked up to see Brendan smiling at me. He praised my erudition and delivery and said that I had defended my position vigorously. I remember it all clearly. He caught me on a few points, citing T.S. Eliot's similar use of language. He quoted a line from *The Waste Land* and asked me to compare it to this poet's use of language: something about the 'fag end' of summer. It was enough that I had escaped alive, now he was throwing *The Waste Land* at me, a poem I had yet to read! I confessed as such and Brendan, realizing when to ease up, forgave me. (It turns out after searching for the term that it was from Prufrock.)

After class, I found myself surrounded by those revered intellectual figures who now included me in their ranks, asking me all sorts of erudite questions. I had been tried and not found wanting. That day marked a transition for me. I was in.

Mashey Bernstein (TCD 1966–70; English Language and Literature) teaches writing and film at the University of California, Santa Barbara, where he has taught off and on since 1971. He specializes in Jewish aspects of the media, opera, Norman Mailer and the Vietnam War. He can be contacted at masheyb@aol.com.

IN TRINITY AND BEYOND!

richard fegen

'**WE NEED** more nun sketches!'

We're sitting in a conference room in RTÉ listening to our first-ever notes, James Morris, Andy Norriss and I. We've just delivered another batch of (handwritten) sketches and the producer's dog, a boxer bitch who has her own chair at the table (yes, really) looks well pleased. So she should – we're putting important stuff on the line here. Our finals are a matter of weeks away. It's just we've realized that, however naff the programme will prove to be (and, as it turns out through no fault of our own, it will) it's what we prefer to be doing.

The contributors to the previous *Trinity Tales*, a serious lot in the main, must have been spinning in their new-found classrooms/research labs/City offices when we hit Front Square for the first time. Reading many of their accounts, there is an unspoken feeling (in some cases, definitely spoken) that they were living through the birth of a new order – indeed, going to a lot of trouble setting it up themselves. They must have had such hopes for this new generation of students – we would be the inheritors of the world they had created with their dodging of tear gas and flying cobblestones. We'd take on their mantle and build new, better barricades to carry on the blazing baton they had passed to us in a relay of mixed metaphors.

I'm afraid, by contrast, we were a pretty relaxed bunch – certainly in terms of being radical. Politics was for grown-ups: we were babies revelling in the bright plastic furniture of the crèche, and our fellow kids. We weren't reading Machiavelli or *Mein Kampf*, we were trying to work out which character we were in *The Magic Roundabout*. There's now a TCD Students' Union, with its own natty website, offering advice on exam stress relief and sexual health, but in the seventies we had the SRC run by a forty-year-old man called Bev (probably actually twenty-five years old), who wore brocade waistcoats with a gold watch chain. What he or the SRC did, we had no idea. Most people could have made a wild stab that the acronym concealed something to do with students and representation, or possibly the Rowing Club. So when they held an election (to decide who would represent us?) it passed us by. Where I imagine our sixties forefathers would have familiarized themselves with the issues and canvassed and voted accordingly, the only candidate I can remember (I had his poster in my window) was the creation of Paul Tullio and Chris Davison – a mature, and exotically vowelled student called Mikokis Sturdi, a name carefully designed to sound disgusting from a megaphone. Knowing the two, I'm sure the man stood for the universal adoption of some unspeakably vile practice – and, for all I know, he was quite possibly elected. I certainly voted for him.

Most of us were straight out of single-sex schools, too busy marvelling at our good fortune – 'Gosh, they have girls here and everything' – as we rattled in, often twice in twelve hours, on the bus from our landladies in Clontarf and Booterstown. By day we'd sit around in the Coffee Bar, maturing gently, while the splendid Janet Ball shrieked 'Fried egg!' into the kitchen at the back. Every now and then, someone would make their excuses and head off to a lecture, returning an hour or so later looking virtuous, to find the faces round the table unchanged.

The fact is, we existed in a kind of Trinity bubble and took very little notice of the real world beyond. Perhaps that was inevitable for many of us; certainly, in the early seventies a significant number of undergraduates still came from the UK. They were foreigners, and, like expats everywhere, formed a self-sufficient group. The demographic of the next generation, in the mid seventies, would change dramatically with the ending of the McQuaid ban and students would suddenly come from all over Ireland, many Dubliners becoming nine-to-fivers, living with their parents beyond the walls of Trinity, while others travelled miles down the country to go home at weekends. But earlier in the decade it was all herd instinct: we stuck together in the heart of a city we knew nothing about. When we did venture out, it was into Trinity flats, Trinity pubs, Trinity cinemas – other bubbles.

Easily the most entertaining of these – plus it paid handsomely – was the film industry. Trinity students provided whole swathes of ill-bearded resistance fighters, grotesque peasants and jolly prostitutes for the movies that came to Ireland for the unspoilt countryside and cheap extras. No previous experience was required, you just dropped a photo into Equity and waited for your call. The thing was to keep your face from the camera so you could be used again and again – the pinnacle of ingenuity being Michael Hoey's spending a whole day in a scene of a mental home with his head down the bed and his feet on the pillow. My flatmate Julian Salmon's speciality was being dead bodies in sacks. He also made a lot of money as a model, driving around the Dublin mountains in sports cars showing how good cigarettes were for you. He was into day two of rehearsals for *Country Dance*, then being shot at Ardmore Studios, when word came that his USIT flight to America for the long vac. was leaving the next day. He would clearly never work again if he let them down without a suitable replacement, so set about teaching me every Scottish reel he knew so that I could take his place. We danced until dawn to a 45 of Jimmy Shand, up and down the corridor of our tenement flat until I had the hang of it enough to almost bluff my way if I blended into the background. Unfortunately – and of course he didn't tell me – our Jules had decided to egg his chances and depart with honour by telling the dance coach that his flatmate was, basically, the finest Highland flinger in these islands with a vast experience of every known step and flourish. I can still feel the torture next day of waiting until the entire company of thirty dancers was assembled, to guarantee maximum humilia-tion, and I was called out by a vicious little troll in a kilt, who informed the room, 'Apparently this man's something of expert: watch and learn, everyone.' He knew bloody well. And I didn't disappoint – that scene has become a recur-ring nightmare, as I strathspeyed solo down the centre of the vast rehearsal room and he shook his head. I got the part, much to his annoyance, because the producer said they were desperate and I'd just have to play a person who wasn't very good at Scottish dancing. The job lasted three weeks, I must have earned double figures and I got to partner Susannah York. They probably wanted to make her dancing look good.

We did work hard, just not necessarily in the cloisters of academe. Admittedly, we weren't required to sweat like our children today, as they hand in degree-influencing coursework every couple of weeks. An essay a term was about our level. There was no Ents (entertaintments) officer, so, as our grandparents would say, we had to make our own entertainment. People didn't just talk (actually they did, quite a lot), but they also did things, often the things they'd been talking about. So when someone said, 'Wouldn't it be brilliant if …' it wasn't just an observation, it was a challenge to be put into effect. So they'd joyfully climb into the gorilla suit, grab the banana and be led on a chain up Grafton Street. Or brick up a friend's rooms and hide with a camera till he came back from the weekend. One guy tin-opened the top off a Mini because he thought it'd be cool to have a convertible. All because it seemed entertaining at the time. Paul Tullio (now Paolo) and Chris Davison (now de Burgh) used to stage elaborate brawls in the street. They'd provoke each other loudly until a crowd had formed. One insult would prove too many and a violent mock fight would break out. Having seen all the right movies, they'd pummel away mercilessly, bouncing each other off walls and rolling locked in combat over the bonnets of parked cars. Passers-by tried to talk them down and armlock them apart, until usually a Garda would appear and stop the fight with severe warnings.

This is probably why Players proved such a draw: it allowed people to be silly without the police arriving to stop the fun. Not that there was much competition from lectures for me. I read Ancient and Modern Literature, a course specially designed for people who can't make up their minds: 'Shall I do Latin? Or perhaps French? Or Latin … I know, I'll do both!' The Classics part was deeply dull and I never achieved the standard I'd reached at school. In fact I pretty soon gave up on it, the final straw being when the beautiful Ros Mitchell, who sat two rows in front, shaved her head after joining the Internationalists. So, increasingly I spent more and more time in Players, building sets, attending auditions, failing to get the parts I thought I deserved. If as a child I'd been woken in the middle of the night by a torch shining in my eyes and asked what do you want to be, I'd have admitted instantly, an actor. What a wonderful thing is self-knowledge. Or lack of it.

I can remember falling into the trap of letting someone cast me, for the first and last time, in a part that was anything other than low comedy; as an *ingénue* in John Marston's *The Malcontent*. The serious acting was tricky enough, but I hadn't bargained for my costume. I was put in a sort of nightie, white, short, with lace (I'm sure historically most accurate) and my actor's motivation as I stepped onstage was no more than to stop the audience laughing, or at least keep their guffaws down to titters. Sorcha Cusack (the faithless queen with whom my character had been unwisely making whoopee) would cry something like, 'Save my Ferneze!' and I would run across in my skimpy to shelter in the wings, from where I could see Stephen Remington, staring at me out of the darkness on the opposite side of the stage in a very disturbing and vicious way. Stephen had recently been reading Stanislavski and was hooked on The Method and when he had worked up enough hatred and loathing, I then had to run back, to be skewered on his rapier, hopefully safely under the armpit. Of course it had to happen, because life is like that, but one night he looked so red-misted and psychopathic that I did wonder about changing the plot line and leaving for Verona. However, I set off dutifully, to be spiked … wow! I went down clutching my crotch. He then bleated on about what an awful person the queen was while I twitched painfully at his feet until some kind courtiers removed me to, quite correctly, peals of laughter. It was one of the occasions I began to doubt whether the life of an actor was for me.

But even being in the audience was brilliant, because I wasn't the only one getting laughs in the wrong places. There was a classic moment in one low-budget production when the young hero had to declare his love to the supposedly smouldering heroine. It was a crucial point in the show and, having attended many rehearsals since, I know exactly how it all went wrong. Professionals kiss from the first rehearsal, amateurs always avoid this. 'OK, right, so we've done the kiss,' says the understanding am-dram director: but they haven't and that night when the young man, whose life had been leading up to this moment, swung round for a passionate kiss, she backed away. It was magical, although a bit of a plot turner as from then on it was very hard to believe their passion was all-consuming or that their forbidden love could have had such a devastating effect on so many people's lives. Of course there were other, genuinely wonderful productions and it was Players that proved a springboard after Trinity for Susie Slott, Sorcha Cusack, Susan FitzGerald, Dillie Keane, and many more.

The theatre was also the birthplace of The Jim Flesh Five, the band we took to Wexford for a sell-out residency (okay, perhaps I imagined that last bit). But we did perform twice nightly for the length of the Wexford Opera Festival and we did get money. It was our first taste of life outside Trinity. I can't remember how it came about, but I have a feeling it was the internationally as yet unknown Chris Davison who set it up. The offer was to put on a sophisticated (ha!) Midnight Revue in White's Hotel and play music for the punters in a quasi-nightclub atmosphere afterwards. The band was Chris, James Morris, Julian Salmon and myself and I don't think we rehearsed more than a couple of afternoons. We tended to practise as we played during performances – the arrogance of youth! By the time we hit Wexford we'd really only got as far as naming ourselves The Jim Flesh Five, the joke being that we were only four. Hilarious, and of course we spent many a happy time in the hotel having Jim Flesh paged to come to reception.

The evening would begin with our playing for an hour in a hall smelling of Jeyes Fluid, where we followed a man on a small Casio keyboard with a name like Michael O'Meara-Speciality-Weddings-and-Wakes. He was very patient as Julian had to set up his drums behind him, especially as the little foot thing that stops the bass drum moving forward was broken and Jules had to bang a pair of six-inch nails into the floor instead. He believed it'd be less intrusive if he hammered along with the music: 'Oh we BANG like to be beside the BANG BANG …' We then did our Midnight Revue, the aptly named Baroque Bottom, before assembling to play until the final guests, usually members of the opera company, dragged themselves home, or more likely, into some stranger's bed. Opening night did not go well. Was it the fact that the words of the first number had only been written in White's Coffee Dock that afternoon, or that our stage manager had mistakenly painted the set with oil paint rather than emulsion and we all had sticky white patches on the seat of our dinner-jacket trousers? Whatever, the *Irish Times* critic quite correctly tore into the show under a headline of something like Most Boring Evening of My Life. But hey, school was out and we were professionals.

Everything in Trinity had turned out to be more useful than lectures.

That's what all the sitting around drinking coffee had been about. And the relief that one wasn't going to be a great actor, or even an actor at all, and that writing and letting others get on with the histrionics might be a much better idea. That's why we were sitting in RTÉ with a TV producer and his boxer bitch when we should have been in the library revising for finals. Trinity had brought us here, we had our first contract and, when I jumped to my feet to illustrate some point of comedy and the dog, thinking its master was under attack, leapt from its chair and bit me in the calf, it didn't matter at all.

Richard Fegen (TCD 1966–70; Ancient and Modern Literature) wrote four series for RTÉ TV and radio and became copy chief with Saatchi's in Dublin. He returned to TV in the UK and his work includes the sitcoms **Chance in a Million, The Labours of Erica, ffizz** and **The Brittas Empire** with Andrew Norriss. He wrote the children's series **Woof!** for nine years, winning a Daytime Emmy and British Comedy Award. He recently moved back to Ireland with his wife, Charmian, and is currently working in animation.

VERY HEAVEN

elgy gillespie

JUST AFTER I turned eighteen I went to Trinity College in Dublin, the place James Joyce once described as 'set heavily in the city's ignorance like a dull stone in a cumbrous ring', or something like that. Well, Joyce was jealous. It wasn't dull, never dull.

Arriving off the Holyhead boat, I smelled the fresh air of freedom. My Irish father had directed me to the Green Rooster or Bewley's for a fried breakfast and had pressed some Irish coins in my hand. But I was drawn straight to the dull stone in the cumbrous ring, an iron filing to a magnet.

What theatre! The entrance to Trinity was and is – ta-da! – a narrow archway into a corbelled dome over wooden cobbles leading from this stony vagina into a vast square of Palladian importance that would fit neatly into Bath or Cambridge. Garlanded with iron rails, the stones had turned iridescent mother-of-pearl in the rain.

Outside was duller and dirtier by far. The farmers were marching and horses were dragging coal and briquettes, scrap iron, and misery. Priests were unchallenged. The population was downtrodden. The archbishop made my cousins kiss his ring. Braying 'hell-air!' accents echoed round the Buttery bar from hyphenated blow-ins or exotic draft dodgers and Northern Prods. This was the late sixties, but it anticipated seventies props and lines.

For by the late sixties, Trinity was a stage set for an extravaganza. It was our very own playground and inside it, we Renaissance princes and princesses were busy giving birth to history and strutting our stuff, or so we thought. As Derek Mahon puts it in his wonderful poem 'To Eugene Lambe in Heaven', it was '… a time of drag and Pop Art, hair and clothes, Beardsley prints, floral design and rainbow hues of Quant and Biba, Shrimpton and Twiggy, lurid tights, gratuitous gesture, instant celebrity, insolent pose …'

We Freshers trooped past the giant Irish elk with bandaged knee into Dr Kennelly's first Theory of English Criticism in the Bear Pit, the Victorian holding-pen in the GMB. All sixty of us shuffled in: dozens of eager Mildreds and Johns and Keiths from Belfast Inst. and Academical in uncool college scarves, then blushing Sebastians, Simons and Julians from Downside and Ampleforth, the leftover colonials, and sprinklings of shy Orthodox Jewish Davids and Masheys in yarmulkes from Harold's Cross or Terenure; occasional exotic blow-ins like Dan Shine from the West Village and Northern Catholics like Jonathan Holland showed up eventually, looking a little shell-shocked. Then there were those first New Trinitarians, Catholics minus archiepiscopal approval, feeling awkward because they had or hadn't kissed Archbishop McQuaid's ring, and unlike Northerners they had no gonzo grants for sexy boots and some were rumpled from years of working on buses in Leeds or Bradford. But they were keen to rock august societies like the Hist that still wouldn't take women but soon would, thanks to Mary Robinson née Bourke.

Last of all, and always late, came the riotous ragbag of straggling, Julie Christie-ish girls in miniskirts with ironed-smooth Looby-Loo hair that was usually blonde, with big hoops of eye shadow under floppy purple hats and fuchsia boas, posh accents, and that irritatingly entitled smear of anarchy.

WE SHUFFLED into our tiered desks, steeply raked so that we could stare down on the young Brendan and his crumpled toe-rag of a gown. Then we stopped dead as Brendan declaimed, 'Ladies, gentlemen, it is our duty to re-apprehend the cliché!' We looked around: did he really say that? We strained to hear if anyone was going to ask anything but there was silence.

Did anyone not feel like an impostor back then? Of course we did. We were Fresher English, ergo sixty Hamlets covered with acne, and doing English because we had no idea what to be or not to be. The Beatles, Stones and soon Van the Man and Dylan ran on permanent sound loops inside our woozy heads, Janice too, courtesy of exotic and glamorous blow-ins from Stateside – Yul Brynner's son, Larry Adler's son, our Dan Shine. We knew we were the lucky few, all 4000 of us likely to pass. How we pitied those poor 40,000 bastards in Earlsfort Terrace who had to live at home and were unable to express themselves through their clothing and were obliged to wear – gasp! – anoraks, and had no drinking or smoking funds.

Okay, they had Denis Donoghue. But we had Kennelly and his youthful colleagues David Norris (still buttoned up) and Eiléan Ní Chuilleanáin and Eavan Boland and Harden Jay, chain-smoking in her miniskirt, and Morgan Walsh. We'd found the sympathetic mentors we craved, always ready to drink coffee with us or sink pints in McDaids or slump on the desk and snooze instead. What would we have to do to get thrown out? The only thing that might get you rusticated was staying inside the gates after ten if you were female, but plenty did and that changed by the seventies.

Our Northerners often got £400 a term from the welfare state, all fees paid! Our college doctor tried to prescribe the Pill whenever we went in with a sore throat or a broken toe or a case of blues. We had a college psychiatrist, an especially cute one. Not all our lecturers were young and fizzy and sexy, some were deeply depressed and on medication. Yet how endearing they were with their dishevelled and yellowing notes, their hungover mornings, their mumbled encouragements! We were fond of them, could still recite much of their lectures by heart, especially Kennelly's.

As a refugee from swinging London much troubled by cultural conflicts, I'd somehow scraped a tiny grant and wardrobe – Foale & Tuffin mattress-ticking miniskirt with matching lapelled jacket, tight Shetland mini-pull, scarlet PVC rain slicker, dusty pink corduroy trouser suit, feather-spitting boa, ankle-strap two-tone tap shoes from Anello & Davide (crippling size six and a half), Biba scarlet-and-gold-striped minidress, coffee-stained and stabbed by furious old ladies as I sped by, humming 'Lucy In The Sky' with skirts all the way to Alabamy. Tights were in but not yet in my size or to my taste.

A BOY from Hong Kong stuffed red roses into my bicycle spokes and handlebars. I fell in love. Next, just to complicate things I fell in love with a boy from Lismore at the Whisky A Go-Go, in the same Biba minidress. So I was eighteen and in love, as innocent as my clothes were not. I thought I was terribly ugly and stupid, of course, so a posture of bold defiance was the only defence. I was also very shortsighted so it didn't pan out well. But other than my great ugliness, what really troubled me were identity issues – half Irish, half English, half this, half that, half the other.

If it weren't for Caroline St John Brooks and Brendan Kennelly's mugs of coffee and chocolate-biscuit cake in the Botany Bay tearoom, and a couple of other mentors, I would never have survived those first few months. Together with Caroline I was sharing an attic at 11 Duke Street above the Knock Shrine Shop, much tormented by my demons.

'*Nil desperandum*' read the telegram my father sent that first exam day. Caroline was a rock of fortitude and common sense, and claimed I used to wake her up in the middle of the night to ask her if I was intelligent. We entertained half The Bailey nightly, giving mugs of coffee to all. One night the lighthouse-keepers from North Bull Wall dropped by and later I realized they saw the red bulb in our hall light and mistook it. As a result of mainlining Nescafé we couldn't sleep and couldn't wake either. So we downed more Gorillas – half-pint glasses of cider and stout – and more late-night coffees in hopes of not having to go down six flights to the toilet before noon next day.

We also played a game called Rollies. Essentially, it meant running out into Grafton Street in our Daisy Market nighties at 5 am and lying on the road till we heard a truck approach, then rolling away at the last second. Sometimes I dozed off. There was roof-high scaffolding outside McDaids that I recall us climbing. What can I say? I was falling in love again … so in love, to Dr Strangely Strange, the Incredible String Band or the Bonzo Dog Doo-Dah Band.

Suddenly – and I recall this moment exactly – one ecstatic Northern friend tossed away his uncool striped scarf and broke out his Grandpa's World War One greatcoat ('Torn from the body of a dead Prussian!' he bragged). Muff scouted a Lawrence Corner police jacket with epaulettes, then showed up in a bikini for a group photo. Caroline sported a section of pelmet in purple velour. Pal Angie Madigan ran up baby-doll gingham with matching knickers inspired by Basement Boutique; sister Sonny ran up Liberty print undies. Sonny and Angie could have opened their own boutiques!

So *Sgt. Pepper* had upped the ante and after *The White Album* we had to try even harder. I beat out those tired old summer-of-love Afghan coats and feather boas with an ivory minidress made from an altar cloth, another from a genuine post-office sack, and long white Victorian nighties.

Scouring the Iveagh and Daisy markets, I scored a balding pony-skin jacket with fox heads that were murder to sit on and that I squashed, giving them peculiarly foxy grins. To celebrate falling in love again I made a maxi Bonnie & Clyde skirt to wear underneath, together with a black beret and stormtrooper thigh-high maxi boots (Anello & Davide again). It was a lot tougher being a male student. No wonder the men we knew never changed their clothes – unless they made their own like Simon and Billy, gays ahead of their time.

Back in 1968 not all Trinity students wore crushed velvet flares, flower-strewn skinny shirts or granny glasses, or rolled their own joints. Only the Northerners had do-re-mi; the rest of us tried waitressing or child-minding or going to America in the summer. Even Northern lads often had other things to spend their grants upon, and promiscuously, in pubs like the College Inn and McDaids or another one at the back of the Rotunda where drinking lasted into the night and swallowed £400-a-term grants fast. Lacking any talent for fashion, they slept in grey pants and proletarian polyester.

And by this time I was headed for Lord Bertrand Russell's international student camp in Cuba's Pinar del Rìo where I planted coffee and hung out with what the French call the '68ers'. It's another story, but clothes were bourgeois so I went right off them. It wasn't hard because there weren't any, and after my return I tried to catch the excitement of French student protesters as Northern marches began to filter south towards us, as John Lennon sang 'Revolution' and the idealism of student protest spilled into the Buttery and up around the scholars upstairs over their jugs of Guinness.

So instead of clothes we now talked politics. Caffeinated fools that we were, we could just never stop talking. We'd already tried our first joint but it was before dope was everywhere, and all we could afford was Nescafé and Gorillas as usual. Dope changed many things forever; but not quite yet.

And it felt even wilder when Belfast and the North begin to erupt. To the strains of 'Blackbird' and 'Cypress Avenue' I was now editing *TCD Miscellany* with friends like John Mules and the McDonald brothers, Gerry and Nick. Incessantly, Van's *Astral Weeks* haunted the student body, thanks to Dan Shine's pioneer copy from Sam Goody's in the West Village. In the weeks up to Trinity Ball we ran a first interview with Bernadette Devlin, a true gift from a young Northerner, Des McCullough, and then an account of priestly child abuse in the children's own words by Jonathan Holland, and opposed the suppressing of another student mag carrying accounts of the events north of the border that triggered outpourings of angry Dining Hall rhetoric.

By late 1969 in the great tradition of Burke and Sheridan, student orators like Eugene Lambe and Ernie Bates were holding our student body spellbound on the Dining Hall steps. They invoked Ché. They brought back the experiences of Burntollet where Northern Protestants had broken up the orderly march for civil rights, comparing it to Sharpeville in South Africa and then to Selma in Alabama and the change that was sure to come. The struggle in the North was black fighting against white might in a way, too.

Again and again they went to the mountaintop and brought back Reverend King, comparing his struggle to that of the Northern minority, some of whom listened with us alongside the droves of Campbell, Inst. and Academical students. Ernie had enough charisma to sway a block of council flats. After a while we didn't know what was said; we were just riveted by their oratorical splendor. Some students even tried to scuffle up the cobblestones, using their penknives. A few southern Catholics like Mary Robinson were listening and arguing. Trinity was discovering diversity.

The Maoists were in ascendance and, yes, this was their day in the sun. Little Red Books twinkled around grey cobbles. Straggling demonstrations against arcane events like the Elizabethan Tea Party provoked more loud ridicule of the provost and Junior Dean's vain efforts to calm Front Square – and how surpassing strange that seems to me now as someone teaching immigrant survivors of the Cultural Revolution these days!

A fascinating confluence between the Maoists – some of them from very middle-class backgrounds, one the daughter of a millionaire captain of industry – arose with nascent nationalists under the civil rights banner, flourishing in unlikely fashion and resulting even in unlikely love affairs.

So we splashed Front Square with our high spirits, and left only when our J1 visas for summer work were threatened: all tremendous fodder for the college magazine. Even better, with UCD students I found myself a new cause in urban renewal, conservation and RAGE (Radical Action for Good Environment) and we tried to save the Marshalsea Barracks for a student housing project. Pictures being worth a thousand words, to illustrate my point I dressed in my best scarlet nightie and hung off a lamp post in Front Square wearing the words *Consummatum est* around my neck, in crude satirical parody of Jesus on the cross surrounded by my drag-wearing mag-layout assistants, then climbed onto Lecky's brass lap, waving a bottle.

Carried away, I then squandered a whole £100 on the 1970 May Week cover – four colours, with Bacchus puffing dope from a cornucopia. But it all ended in tears. 'You have killed a hundred-year-old tradition!' the secretary thundered through my sobs.

AS THE SEVENTIES broke, the discovery of dope was scenting the cobbles and protests had mellowed considerably. We were long past *Abbey Road*, and 'Let It Be' and 'My Sweet Lord' were the new hummables. The Beatles had retired. The Stones were on a loop. Clearly the Fractious Four were puffing their heads off in separate rooms and we were getting J1s and sneaking out of town for New York summer jobs, soon to be sadder if not wiser.

Nearly everything that can happen to two innocent rubes happened to Sonny and me and our contemporaries in America as we drudged through diners and steak houses around New York, hired and fired several times a week. And when I came back it was truly the seventies, we began to hear about women's lib and gay rights, but protest was shelved because it was time to study for finals, and it was that or time to drop out altogether.

What, you're surprised? In the words of Flann O'Brien, you're wondering if we ever opened a book at all? Well, thanks to our long-suffering and heroic teachers – Brendan Kennelly, David Norris, Eavan Boland, Eiléan Ní Chuilleanáin, Paula Simmons, Harden Rogers, Morgan Walsh; let me assure you – yes. Especially class swots Mashey Bernstein, John Heffernan, Paddy Lyons, Rene Kingston and Tamsin Braidwood. We gave it the odd college try.

Yes, thanks to them we loved Scottish border ballads, Henryson, and

Elizabethan sonnets. We read Wyatt and Sydney aloud in ecstasy, wallowed through Spenser and Shakespeare, and so on all the way up to Yeats's 'Crazy Jane' and 'The Circus Animals' Desertion' and Kavanagh's 'September', via picaresque James Clarence Mangan scraps and the slogworthy Victorian novels, Carleton and Maria Edgeworth, and back to all the Metaphysicals – our teachers indulging our unusual passions for Herbert and Marvell, and for Donne.

Thanks to Harden Rogers we embraced Restoration playwrights Congreve and Farquhar because of their sexy double entendres and Irish connections. Coleridge and Blake were favourites by a long mile because of the former's broken conceits and drug habits and the latter's popularity with Dr Strangely Strange and psychedelia.

Nowadays we would argue for a revised, more Irish canon, of course. But in the lines by that silly old sheep Wordsworth, we recognized truth from a soul brother from an adjoining island …

> Oh! pleasant exercise of hope and joy!
> For mighty were the auxiliars which then stood
> Upon our side, we who were strong in love!
> Bliss was it in that dawn to be alive
> But to be young was very heaven!
>
> 'French Revolution'

If I'm arrogant enough to say that we thought we were making history I'll be attacked again. But of course we did. We all thought we were making history. And it was very heaven.

If that's what making history was like, I have the feeling that any attempt to grasp the spirit of the seventies will have to pass through its music, its debris, its cultural touchstones, its victims as sad and illuminating as you have seen in any era – and also as difficult, because it doesn't want to be a clean-cut era at all, just an attempt to keep alive the noble, impossible promise of its day.

A couple of years ago I was strolling through Front Square towards the GMB to check on the giant elk's knee bandage, arm in arm with a close pal, and we talked about the mid seventies and how different they were from the late sixties to early seventies. He came four years after me and reaped greater diversity and more Irishness. He got a very different world, a world with less spondoolicks, more politics, and fewer opportunities.

He had to leave to find work, drop acid, fall into a bottomless hole of London squats … and listen to the Bee Gees. He still feels the pain. I just feel the love.

Elgy Gillespie (TCD 1966–73; English Literature) wrote for **The Irish Times** as a features writer until the mid eighties, before joining her brothers in Washington DC. After moving to San Francisco and editing the **San Francisco Review of Books,** she worked in IT for what eventually became Travelocity and edited the **Irish Herald** with Catherine Barry. She now teaches vocational ESL at City College San Francisco.

'RECALLING A PATCH OF THE PAST'
(Nabokov, SPEAK MEMORY, 1967)

nikki gordon bowe

MY FATHER WAS, I think, quite glad that my inability to grasp the spirit of Racine and Corneille, not to mention Euler's Circles and Xenophon, blocked my expected passage to Oxford. Trinity was equated in my parents' eyes as complicit in wild Oxford/Cambridge skiing trips, apart from the academic and athletic prowess of medical and classical forbears on my father's side. I was vague about Dublin, except for the annual spiced beef and turkeys sent from my great aunt's butcher in Blackrock, and some ex-Players luminaries, friends of an English neighbour, Roger Ordish. When I had failed to satisfactorily answer the only question on a Cambridge entrance paper, 'Will the sun rise tomorrow?', Trinity beckoned.

Admission to red-brick or cold northern UK universities was unappealing, and the vision of the chiselled features of the legendary Paul Wesley (friend of Joan Baez, whose copy of *The Catcher in the Rye* I still have) and other beguiling-looking flâneurs as I entered Front Gate, together with stories of a Trinity pack of hounds only recently curtailed, added to the attraction of a small, self-contained yet architecturally distinguished old campus in a largely unmodernized city. The ubiquitous friendliness and readiness to engage in fanciful conversation were other key attractions, despite the presence of stone not-very-hot water jars to warm my underclad body. (For Dublin then, unriven by cars and bad town planning, see Kieran Hickey's film *Faithful Departed* (1967), Bill Doyle's evocative photographs, or Evelyn Hofer's in V.S. Pritchett's *Dublin, A Portrait* (1967).)

Interviewed by a saturnine translator of Boccaccio so as to read Italian, entertained by a cousin of my father who lectured in philosophy – which he read under an umbrella in a bath in his front garden – and enchanted by the faded Edwardian interiors and eccentric courtesy of Jammet's, the Hibernian Hotel, a sumptuous array of pubs, and plush snugs in Bewley's, an exploratory visit augured well. I moved into digs in Raglan Road with Amanda MacAndrew, now a perceptive novelist, and Chloe Sayer, expert on Mexican craft traditions, where the clip-clop of horses' hooves announced the delivery of milk, and our hospitable landlady bellowed instructions to her needle-working husband. Houses all over the Georgian capital were full of often spacious flats in varying conditions of repair, long occupied by Trinity undergraduates, serviced by grocers' shops that stocked everything – from rarified Smyth's on the Green to the rumbustious Dolly's tiny all-night emporium in Baggot Street. During the comparatively short Trinity year, I relished the theatre that was Front Square, saved serious discussions for the Dining Hall, the Buttery and the now-defunct Coffee Bar, explored the decaying yet vibrant city on foot, drew my French and Italian lecturers (and anyone else I could capture) and realized that my heart was still with the art I had discovered and cherished in Italy. In the Art Society beside the Coffee Bar in Botany Bay (frequented by Roc Brynner and Jean-Luc Pittion in intense existential dialogue) I found Nick Robinson doing distinctively lively caricatures, Barra Boydell proclaiming on Dada and James Jocelyn sucking on a smokey pipe. I was impressed by the direction of Douglas Henderson (and later, Keith Hornby and Roland Jaquarello), the acting of Dinah Stabb and Gill Hanna (and later, Slim Lowry and Malachy Lawless) and the emergence of committed new talents among my contemporaries in Players (in its tiny cabaret-size quarters in Front Square), as well as by a perambulating Hayden Murphy, naked but for a fish, reciting poetry with Dom Moraes (minus the ever-radiant Brendan Kennelly).

There were those who performed as well offstage as on – such as Cyril Lynch who, after a heavy night's drinking, literally crashed through Switzer's shop window onto a bed he saw welcomely displayed, to the dismay of early-morning passers-by. My own performances were limited to dancing in discos (one of which, in D'Olier Street, I decorated with psychedelic murals) and dressing up for the many dances and parties, some stylish, some chaotic, others amazingly extravagant and exotic. The Iveagh and Daisy markets in the Liberties were regular repositories of so-called 'vintage' clothes, while small bespoke shops such as Bill Grant's, burgeoning boutiques and the stately Brown Thomas (before it was down-marketed and moved across Grafton Street to Switzer's former site) offered safer alternatives to the dizzying array available in London.

My regrettable tendency to become waylaid in conversation en route to lectures was marked by the inspiring Dr Owen Sheehy-Skeffington's presentation to me of an essay 'On Lateness', before I abandoned French for Italian in my final year. By then I had squeezed into a seedy flat in Upper Leeson Street with three friends, two of whom became fellow rowing companions on college eights – our team commemorated Jimi Hendrix in name ('Purple Haze') and dress (purple and mauve) – until we had to be rescued by the Gardaí team at Islandbridge when we got stuck on the weir. Such early morning forays enabled us to miss nine o'clock seminars, and repay our long-suffering coach with dressed crabs from Chatham Street for all the 'crabs' we'd caught.

In those days, unless you were a diligent, all-year undergraduate, the real book work had to be done in the summer if you were doing an honors degree, as exams were in September. For me, these were a trial, as I remember rarely putting pen to paper during the academic year. Italian seminars in Professor Tomacelli's rooms, where glasses of sherry lubricated the Barone's readings of sensuous passages from D'Annunzio's *Il Piacere* (the heroine's heaving bosom unleashing pearls onto the ivory keys of a resonating piano) often carried on into dinner at The Unicorn (then a hearty, family-run trattoria). The resolutely Italian accent of my namesake, Clotilda Bowe, even when speaking English, led to my mistaking the translated title (*The Betrothed*) of Manzoni's romantic historical novel, *I Promessi Sposi*, for 'The Beetroot'. She was mystified by my fascination with the harshly evocative novels of Giovanni Verga, which led me to Sicily after graduation on the first of three Italian government scholarships in Umbria during the summer vacations. In Sicily I would subsequently explore the folklore and subtle complexities of the lives of the fishing communities near Catania described by D.H. Lawrence and filmed by Luchino Visconti, while writing my first proper article on Catanese Baroque. In Urbino and Perugia, immersed in etching, lithography, woodcuts and languid, congenial company, the warm, sun-soaked honeyed stones of chapels nestling in vineyards competed with the cold granite of Dublin. The impassioned lectures on Michelangelo, Dante and Lorenzo di Medici by Corinna Lonergan (now Professor Emeritus of Italian) evoked the visual world of the Italian Renaissance I knew and loved.

Luckily, the redoubtable Miss Crookshank had been lured down to Trinity from the Ulster Museum in 1966 by Professor George Dawson, bent on engaging the university with contemporary art, and I was one of many from a wide range of disciplines who flocked to the brilliant and often witty lectures she organized as part of her new History of Art degree (still only General Studies at this stage). People squeezed into a stuffy underground bunker in Koralek's new Arts Building to listen, enraptured, to whatever she was expounding upon, regardless of what they were meant to be studying. Although I wasn't one of George Dawson's College Gallery team, through friends such as George Wynne Wilson, Julian Campbell and Bruce Lambert who were, I did help to mount exhibitions such as the eye-opening American Banners, Picasso and Peter Sedgley's Kinetic Art. Such shows, building on the exposure of the pioneering ROSC '67 and the exhibitions of contemporary Irish and international art mounted by David Hendricks at his immensely sympathetic Stephen's Green gallery were welcome beacons.

I remember the first time I met Jeremy Williams at a College Gallery talk organized in another subterranean bunker on Dublin Op-Architecture, during which I marked off Ogham-like strokes every time he said 'Um'. His eclectic knowledge and devotion to preservation and every aspect of the fabric of the city was shared by friends such as Elgy Gillespie, Phil McMaster, Brian Molloy and William and Philippa Garner, who became the creative custodians in palatial yet deserted Castletown House in Celbridge after it was rescued by Desmond and Mariga Guinness's Irish Georgian Society. William, a fellow co-founder of the Irish Victorian Society in the early seventies, was among those who modelled at the life classes a group of us started in the Art Society when it was relocated to the old Parade Ground warehouse in College Lane, parallel to Westland Row, in 1968.

Nineteen-sixty-eight marked a turning point personally and internationally: liberated Amsterdam offered new ideas of art, music and dance experience, students rioted in Paris, the Troubles erupted in Northern Ireland, and the NCAD lock-out and a shift to the 'science' end of Trinity led to joint TCD/NCAD life-drawing classes with the artists Brian Bourke and Michael Farrell, with friends as models. College Lane harboured Eugene Lambe's Anarchist library and macrobiotic foodstore, music workshop sessions with Jolyon Jackson and his group, Jazz Therapy, and practice sessions with Blues Assembly (James Morris, Chris Davison, Andrew Norriss and Mick O'Gorman), pottery classes with the two Michaels (Walsh-Kemmis and Braidwood), exhibitions of our own work, art classes for local inner-city children, soup kitchens, and the Experimental Film Society. Imported 'art' films by Kubelka, Brakhage, Snow, Harrington, Anger, Warhol, Hercules Bellville and so forth masqueraded as Bord Fáilte promos to avoid customs' censorship, culminating in a performance of Marc Boyle and Joan Hills's Sensual Laboratory's Son et Lumière for Bodily Fluids and Functions, where participants dropped down onto mattresses via a window of the Dixon Hall, rather than entering through the usual front door. New doors of perception were opened. Two terms in an open-house mews in Lad Lane with the Chinese New York artist Tien-Yi Ho led to new pubs (Toner's, Slattery's, McDaids) and friendships, such as Mary and Ivan Pawle of Dr Strangely Strange, among those who played at the 'Come Trip the Light Dythirambic' summer weekend twenty-first birthday celebration Elgy and I concocted for about 200 people around the stone quarry at Ballyknocken near Blessington.

My final year was spent in a Pembroke Road flat procured by great friends, Jane and Jerry Scott (married in their final year, whose flat above pounded with mind-blowing music imported after Jerry's eventful American cross-continental haulage adventures). This I shared with Jane Marriott, another Art Society and Christie Brown life model, where we gave black, green and purple dinner parties à la Huysmans and had to ward off brothel clients of the former tenants. At night, along with Anita Walshe, Angie Madigan and Scarfe-like Henry Bell, I drew illustrations for *TCD Miscellany* in the bowels of No. 6 under Elgy's eccentrically enlightened editorship, while the two Kathys (Gilfillan and de Hartog), John Rawlinson and Dan Shine were among those providing edgy copy. Other jobs included a painting for Peter O'Toole on his return to The Abbey Theatre as Vladimir in Beckett's *Waiting for Godot* ('Did he use the Gaelic knocker?') and a Findus Frozen Peas hoarding with Angie on the Four Corners of Hell crossroads beside St Patrick's Cathedral. Just before my last term, I met Paddy Bowe (an architect recently returned from Chicago) at a rather wild party at the Knight's Flat at Leixlip Castle, given by Jeremy and Richard Wood. This scotched my plans to permanently leave Ireland, as planned.

Lured back to Dublin by the elusive Beau Bowe, all I had was a BA Hons degree, myriad interests – related to art, film, music, mythologies and Symbolist literature – and a portfolio of lithographs made during another summer in Urbino (one of which I exhibited at the Irish Exhibition of Living Art in the Project Arts Centre in 1972). Rescued by Trinity friends, I drew portraits, bookplates and minutely detailed book illustrations, some of which I exhibited, restored painted furniture, painted pottery and murals (including a lion to frighten an interloping dean in Mayo), sold superior junk at the Dandelion Market, etched at the Graphic Studio in Upper Mount Street with John Kelly and the enchanting grandfather-like painter Gerald Dillon, danced, and became fascinated by Indian pahari miniature painting, even studying Sanskrit with fellow TCD life-drawing friend, Anthony O'Brien. This marked my initial excursion to the Early Printed Books Library in Trinity, then run by the intimidating Miss 'Paul' Pollard, where I also considered researching Italian Renaissance printed book illustrations.

Increasingly interested in research, I revelled in finding out and delivering information as a guide at ROSC '71, the (for Ireland) huge contemporary art exhibition that impressively took over the RDS, and got to know Anne Crookshank through her niece, Ros Hill, a fellow guide and close friend. Anne had encouraged me to embark on the Purser-Griffith diploma in art history, held alternately in Trinity and UCD, so that I commuted between lectures, seminars and the top floor of Castletown (approximately 200 stairs up and down), where my old friend, Susan Denne Bolton, and I were among a raggedy range of kindred souls living in faded Palladian splendor. Minded by Tiggy and

Skimper Ruthven, into whose kitchen wing Paddy and I subsequently moved, we each hid our assorted cats and dogs whenever pet-allergic Desmond Guinness arrived to collect the rent, and all featured in a haunting horror film made by Ted Thaddeus and Sally O'Sullivan, through our mutual friends, the recently married Roy and Aisling Foster. It was hard to focus on seminar papers when as yet unbuilt-up views from every window echoed the magical light and space of the place, and the walk down the majestic avenue of limes to the village bus served as a passage from one world to another.

By then I was hot on the trail of the early-twentieth-century Irish graphic and stained glass artist, Harry Clarke, after being stunned by a Clarke Studio window on a chance visit to Killarney Cathedral with my fairy godfather, Jeremy Williams. A visit to the virtually unchanged Clarke Studios in North Frederick Street confirmed my fascination with this major Symbolist exponent of the Irish Arts and Crafts movement. Conversations with Olivia Robertson at Huntington Castle in County Carlow, another beloved sanctuary, were among the many interviews and exploratory excursions I was to make over the next ten or so years, researching what turned out (due to Anne Crookshank's faith in my abilities) to be a PhD thesis. Back in Dublin, a group of us (including Jeanne Sheehy, doing pioneering research on the Irish Gothic and Celtic Revivals with a Leverhulme Fellowship in Trinity) co-founded the preservation-led Irish Victorian Society. Its manifold activities culminated in a seventieth-birthday garden party for our president, Seymour Leslie's old friend, the Poet Laureate John Betjeman, held at Clontra, the miraculously preserved Hungerford Pollen house belonging to the family of Trinity contemporary David Tomkin. At a contrasting twenty-first-birthday celebration at nearby Loughlinstown House, everyone wore blue and danced to Horslips.

Meanwhile I survived financially on secretarial work for £9 a week in an office, supposedly deciphering notes made on Carroll's cigarette packets by the then-Trinity architect, but instead making endless telephone calls, abetted by Persephone FitzGerald. Gaj's in Baggot Street became a regular meeting/eating place. More lucrative employment to fund my research led me to join old Trinity friends like Sue Bullock, Rosemary Rowley and Penny Clibborn, as well as Charlotte Bielenberg, teaching English to reluctant French oilmen at EuroLanguage in Upper Mount Street. When my research was, on the formal recommendation of Michael Wynne, deputy director of the National Gallery, registered for a doctorate (the third after Michael's and Julian Campbell's in the History of Art Department), I began working full-time in the National Library and Trinity Library and Manuscripts Room. Night classes at NCAD with Johnny Murphy showed me how to make stained glass so I could better understand my subject, and led to visiting lectures in the new History of Art, Design and Complementary Studies course set up there by John Turpin. Colleagues included Trinity contemporaries Jolyon Jackson and Shaun Davey. This eventually led to my establishing Design History as undergraduate and post-graduate degree courses in the college.

Invigilation at Trinity exams not only brought extra pocket money but introduced a welcome array of postgraduate students from every discipline. The arrival in the Manuscripts Library of most of the contents of the recently closed Clarke Studios led me to several years of intense study of this material, backed up by other private and public manuscript collections. Under the generous protectorship of its keeper, William (Billy) O'Sullivan, I beavered away in the light-filled eyrie above the Long Library he endowed with his scholarly interest, courtesy and unerring helpfulness.

Always immaculately dressed in the subtle tones of original Avoca tweeds, he and Anne Crookshank were my wise, encouraging anchors in Trinity. Anne's stern telephone call to George Dawson – 'Look here, George …' – insisting that I be involved with the Harry Clarke exhibition planned for the recently inaugurated Douglas Hyde Gallery resulted in my working closely with Sean McCrum on this landmark show in 1979. Its catalogue, produced in record time over sleepless nights, anticipated the three-volumed doctoral thesis I submitted to my alma mater in 1981.

Nicola Gordon Bowe (TCD 1966–70; French and Italian Hons) Associate Fellow, Faculty of Visual Culture, NCAD; Visiting Professor, Research Institute, School of Art & Design, University of Ulster; Research Fellow, University of Wales; Hon. Fellow, British Society of Master Glass Painters. Books include a Harry Clarke catalogue raisonné (1979); **A Gazetteer of Irish Stained Glass** (1988), with Michael Wynne and David Caron; **The Life and Work of Harry Clarke** (1989);

Art and the National Dream: The Search for Vernacular Expression in Turn-of-the-Century Design (1993), ed.; and **The Arts and Crafts Movements in Dublin and Edinburgh** (1998), with Elizabeth Cumming.

Nikki Gordon (left) with Jerry and Jane Scott in 1970.

TRINITY MADE ME

michael colgan

A SMALL BOY holding your father's big hand, you sweep the curve at the college front and stop at the main gate. It is your annual Christmas outing into town, and even though you live but three miles away, it is a special event. Looking through the arch you spot a man guarding the door in a strange uniform and what looks like a jockey's cap.

'Can we go in there, Dad?' you ask.

'No, son,' he says.

'Why not?'

'You have to be a student and a Protestant.' And with that, we move on up towards Grafton Street.

YEARS LATER at the public telephones in Cork city, returning from Irish College, I nervously phoned home to get my Leaving Cert. results. My father said, 'Well done, son, you can go wherever you want.' Without a moment's hesitation I declared, 'I want to go to Trinity.' He said, 'I thought you'd say that.'

And so in October 1968, I walked through Front Gate for the very first time. Although a Catholic and a Dubliner, I was entering a strange and exotic land. A secret garden teeming with exquisite creatures and beautiful, clever girls. In my first week, I spotted a student wearing a monocle, others wearing striped blazers and a chap with, of all things, a silver-topped cane. Worse, I didn't have the language. These masters of the universe were having difficulty with my accent. But never, never for a minute did I feel I had made the wrong decision.

Lest my confidence become irredeemably shattered, I needed the company of, shall we say, the less privileged and I needed money. I found it all upstairs over Front Gate in the perfectly named Junior Common Room. There the boys from Northern Ireland had set up camp and more invitingly, a scattering of gentle and dangerous poker schools. Every day our heroes were slowly and painstakingly dispensing of their generous college grants. I joined in.

In my first year this became my principal education. Different tables, different games. Seven Card Stud, Cincinnati, Southern Cross and the most terrifying of all, High-Low. A game in which I witnessed one unfortunate lose not only all of his term's grant, but his car. I decided to avoid High-Low. Nevertheless, by the end of my second term, I was earning a decent wage and had met my first college friend, the remarkable Eddie Shorts.

Eddie was the best poker player and the best snooker player in college. He was also the funniest man I had ever met. Years later, tiring of our wayward life, the daily round of cards, snooker and girls, I decided we should go to see a play. I dragged him to The Olympia Theatre and as we stood outside looking at the black-and-white photographs, Eddie said, 'I don't want to go in.' I said, 'Why not?' He said, 'I thought it was going to be in colour.'

My first encounter with Eddie was, funnily enough, at a game of cards. We were playing an ingenious form of poker called Screwy Louis and against the run of form he was losing and had left the table owing me ten shillings. He said he would get it to me that night and where would I be? I said I'd be dining at the Wimpy Restaurant on Burgh Quay. On reflection, the word 'dining' may have been a little strong, but Eddie arrived, duly paid his debt and joined the table.

We talked and talked and soon fell into a discussion of the Six-Day War. Eddie said he wasn't so keen on the Jewish race. I said, 'Funny that, I am.' Eddie said, 'Funny that, I'm Jewish.' I said, 'What's not funny is being secretly tested.' I turned away and he got up and left. Next day he apologized and we became the closest friends.

Soon after, with two philosophy students, we went on my first and only double date. I had warned Eddie not to play the 'unsophisticate' and that our best chance would be to go to an Eric Rohmer film, but Eddie, out of badness, got tickets for a Hammer horror movie at the Carlton. The film began with the caption '1839'. Eddie whispered to the girls, 'This is a very old film.' I thought it was funny, but as soon as we left the cinema, they disappeared.

Around that time and also in the Junior Common Room, I came across Paul McGuinness. He did not play cards, far too clever for that, but on that day was composing a letter to his mother – I think looking for money. I read the letter and thought it was a masterpiece. What struck me was the sheer ease with which a man of his age could use words like 'largesse' and 'mendacity', as if no other words would do. There was no doubt that he was going to be a force to be reckoned with.

And so it was in my first year I learned when to hold 'em, and when to fold 'em, became friends with a man funnier than Woody Allen, and in Paul McGuinness met someone I instantly admired and respected. I was learning the rudiments of psychology, reading the novels of Virginia Woolf, discovering a writer called Samuel Beckett and attending the inspiring lectures of Brendan Kennelly and David Norris. I was also falling in love.

On my first date with Flick Louden, I took her to the Gate to see Micheál Mac Liammóir in his one-man show *The Importance of Being Oscar*. It had a huge effect and as we left the auditorium, she asked, 'Would you like to work in the theatre?' 'Not in a million years,' I said, 'I'm going to be a psychologist.' She said, 'I'm sure you could do either' and I thought, this might be the woman for me.

We sat together at English lectures, under trees at College Park and even closer, in the 1937 Reading Room. We had every lunch side by side at the Buttery and so taken was I that I began to go to *her* lectures. Wherever she went, I went. When I think of it, heaven help the girl. It was my first time in love, hardly a sentence uttered without mention of her name. Eddie offered to get medical help. We went together to Trinity Ball and danced until dawn. The end of term pulled us apart, but oh the romance of it, we had a secret plan. We were going to meet up in London for the summer.

That memorable summer in London. The last of the sixties. When The Beatles walked over the zebra crossing and Neil Armstrong walked on the moon. I went to Hyde Park to see The Rolling Stones' free concert, where Mick wore a dress, and in a tribute to Brian Jones, read Shelley badly. It was all happening, man. We were learning new ways and new words – Chappaquiddick, Yoko Ono, Woodstock and Charles Manson. Our world was turning and we had turned nineteen.

Flick got a typing job through the ubiquitously advertised Alfred Marks Recruitment Agency, £18 a week. I, on the other hand, was working at a car radio factory in Neasden, for £11. 10s. But was I happy? Delirious. And then it all came crashing down. At the end of that fateful summer Flick prudently explained that we shouldn't go through the next three years so inextricably entwined. We needed to meet new people. Join some of the societies. I, of course, agreed, but immediately knew from her face that I had missed the point. Felicity, my true love's given name, was breaking it off.

Freshers' Week, my second year, I headed straight for the Junior Common Room. Not now my only haunt, far from it. As I strolled manfully across Front Square, I got nods of acknowledgment and even tentative waves from the occasional stripey blazer. But I needed the money. Sadly, my luck had turned, and the JCR held less appeal. In Front Square, all the college societies were actively drumming up new members and I was withering away dealing cards and losing money. Maybe Flick was right. Down to my last four bob, I left the table to get some air. I never came back.

Outside No. 4 was a blackboard enticing new members with free coffee and biscuits. I hadn't eaten all day. I went in. It could have been the Theological Society, but it turned out to be Players. Kathy Roberts was serving the coffee and she began asking about my interest in acting and theatre. Time to bluff, thought I, so I threw in the view that Beckett was the world's leading dramatist. 'Do you think?' she said, 'Oh, without question,' said I as she offered me another biscuit. My luck hadn't totally deserted me for, what seemed like only days later, he won the Nobel Prize for Literature.

She said there was a meeting the following Tuesday and asked would I like to become a member? Membership was five shillings. I had only four and they weren't certain as I'd left them at the card table. I said I'd come and pay on the night.

I went to the meeting and felt uncomfortable. I was well out of my depth. That's it, I thought, but a memory stuck of someone saying we should keep an eye on the Players' noticeboard for casting calls. Each day as I passed into college I would throw a glance, but in my heart it wasn't for me. I had other fish to fry.

Eddie and I were still telling lies to girls and I was spending more time devouring Beckett in the 1937 Reading Room. I remember laughing out loud on reading the first line of his novel, *Murphy* – 'The sun shone, having no alternative, on the nothing new.' But in that library there was another interest, a girl who never seemed to leave and was forever in the same spot. I think she read a novel a day. Always with her coat thrown over her shoulders and a strand of hair twisted in her finger. Her name was Emma Hogan.

I eventually got to know her and introduced her to Eddie. We had met our match – she was cleverer than both of us. She invited us to her penthouse apartment in Donnybrook where we drank tea and talked of English literature. 'Do you ever think,' she asked Eddie, 'of the gifts we might have received had Emily Brontë lived longer?'

'It had crossed my mind,' said Eddie. To which Emma replied, 'That would have been a short journey.'

A brilliant woman, but there were lots of them about. Rosemary McCreery, Dillie Keane, Merrily Harpur, and those mistresses of the acerbic and the surreal, the two Kathys – de Hartog and Gilfillan. I tried to date Kathy Gilfillan, but she was having none of it. Good thing too, we have never stopped being friends.

Trinity was a place of grey buildings and colourful people. My favourite was the Professor of Philosophy, A.A. Luce. He held, and I think he still does, the longest record for being a fellow, over fifty years and at the age of near ninety could be seen cycling through Front Square as though a boy. Once when going into the Rubrics I could hear him negotiate his bicycle down the stairs. We met on the first landing and I asked if I could help. 'Not at all, dear boy,' he said, 'it's at this stage I let gravity take care of the matter,' and he threw the bike down the remaining steps.

And then it happened. Blithely and innocently passing the Players' noticeboard, I spotted a cast list for the forthcoming production of *Andorra* by Max Frisch announcing that they needed two extras. I enthusiastically put my name down and sought out the director, Richard Fegen. We seemed to get on really well and soon after he contacted me. I didn't get the part.

These two unspeaking roles as Blackshirts had gone to John McBratney and none other than Paul McGuinness. How could Fegen not see that I would be the perfect Blackshirt? I contented myself with the line 'That's show business.' Days later, I chanced upon Fegen in Front Square who told me that McBratney had to pull out and that the part was mine. I'd made it.

What was required of McGuinness and me was to wear black shirts, hold a wooden rifle and twice cross front of stage looking fierce. A piece of cake. I have no doubt we were terrible. But the rewards have lasted a lifetime. Susan FitzGerald was playing Barblin, the female lead, Paolo Tullio the village idiot, James Morris had done the lighting and Chris de Burgh had composed the music. All would become friends, and in the case of Susan, more than a friend.

The play was a success – it ran for six nights. In the dressing rooms Tullio was the master of ceremonies. My first Renaissance man. He could do everything. He was the best actor in college, could play the guitar, was an excellent cook, spoke different languages and best of all, he had an Italian sports car. In his apartment, when I complimented him on an antique leather chair, he said, 'Thank you, I upholstered it.' – he wasn't lying. In the living room, mounted on oak, was the Tullio family crest. I was convinced it was authentic, until I noticed the motto, *Semper Erectus*. He had made it.

There was a lull in my career after *Andorra*. Clearly my performance as a Blackshirt hadn't struck a chord. The phone never rang. But being in Players then, as in my career now, was irresistible because of the company I could keep. Word had filtered through of an exciting production of *Hamlet* at UCD's Dramsoc. I went to see it and was utterly smitten by the performance of Jeananne Crowley as Ophelia. I was beginning to think like a producer – I wanted her for Players.

For some reason known only to himself, Mike Hoey gave me my first speaking part in his production of *The Tempest*. I was to play Stephano opposite Tullio as Trinculo. What an innocent I was. I'd no chance, but I was beginning to spot there was another job in theatre besides acting. Paul McGuinness was leading the charge as an exciting director. Our *Tempest* represented Trinity at the Universities' Drama Festival, but it was McGuinness who was the one to watch.

Things were hotting up. Not who you were, but who you knew. The stripey blazers were starting to recede. The Phil was watching the Hist and Players looked down on the Boat Club. The medics were not at the races and the engineers, well, they were engineers. We each felt our group was the best and I was clearly chuffed to be part of mine: Tullio, Gilfillan, Davison (Chris de Burgh), Roger Greene, McGuinness and the golden Johnny Harben. I was elected to the committee of Players as Hon. PRO and set about selling ads for our programmes. Susan FitzGerald was easily the most beautiful woman in college and fast becoming the best actress we had. She shone in *Look Back in Anger*, which was asked to transfer to the Eblana. It felt like an invitation to Broadway.

My last performance was as Schmidt in *The Fire Raisers*, again by Max Frisch. There must have been something in the water that kept drawing us to this minor Swiss playwright. I was playing opposite Roger Greene and remember knowing enough to know that I was truly awful. Roger was only marginally better. What was worse, I had to blacken my entire body every night. After my final performance, wearily trying to remove the vile make-up, I turned to Susan FitzGerald and said, 'That's it, I'll never act again.' She should have said, 'You've never acted before,' and the world should have heaved a sigh of relief.

I had learnt that the key to directing was casting so I asked Tullio to be in a one-man show I would direct called *Sammy*. Jeananne Crowley was brought in as my co-director. We took it to the Universities' Drama Festival in Galway and John Arden gave us the top prize. It was all Tullio. I was right, casting is key.

Players became my world. My tutor asked to see me. He gave me the worst piece of advice ever. He said, 'Now listen to me, you will never get a career in the theatre.' I nodded, looked contrite, but his words had no effect. Then I heard from Donald Taylor Black that Paul McGuinness was canvassing to be the next chairman of Players. The tradition was that the chair should go to the current secretary. At that time it was Horst Schnittger, and so I canvassed against McGuinness and for Horst.

At the election both men were nominated, but then, at the last minute, someone nominated me. The president of Players was a dapper, concise man called R.B.D. French. He sat on the stage and when it became clear that there were three nominations, he audibly muttered a word that I had never heard said before, nor have I heard since. He said, 'Strewth'.

White smoke. I waited anxiously to see who would be elected to my committee. Oh the joy: Susan FitzGerald as hon. sec., Roger Greene as theatre manager and Taylor Black and, I think, Derek Chapman also on board. Much work to be done. James Morris directed a sparkling review called *Mellow* and we went for broke with an ambitious production of the mystery plays by using three Guinness floats in Front Square. Jesus was crucified as the moon passed over the Campanile.

Tullio and I went about writing a panto. He would play the lead and I would direct. It was to be a Robin Hood special called *We've All Maid Marion*. It had a stellar line-up: Dillie Keane, later of 'Fascinating Aïda' played Marion; Tullio was Robin; McGuinness played Gopher; Roly Saul of Roly's Restaurant, the perfect Friar Tuck; Chris de Burgh was the Minstrel and Eddie Shorts was one of the Merry Men. We had Angela from the Buttery appear with a trolley, look at the audience, and say, 'Whoops, I'm in the wrong place.' It was a roaring success, but once more, the real talent was Tullio.

I got a phone call from The Abbey Theatre saying that the artistic director, Tomás Mac Anna, would like to speak to me. He said he'd like to rent our little theatre for a week. I drove a hard bargain, £75 I think. I put a sign up on the noticeboard calling on all committee members. No one turned up. I was up and down ladders, bought Mac Anna's cigarettes, found props, painted the stage and manned the box office.

At the end of that week he turned to me and asked, 'What are you going to do when you leave this Protestant establishment?'

'Become a psychologist,' I said.

'You will do nothing of the kind. You will join The Abbey. Ring me when you've got your exams.' Months later, when my results came out, I nervously rang The Abbey and spoke to Mac Anna's secretary.

'I'm sure he won't remember me', I mumbled, but she said, 'Hang on, I'm putting you through.'

'Did you pass your exams?' he said.

'I did.'

'Good' he said, 'you will start at ten o'clock on Monday.'

And so I did.

Michael Colgan (TCD 1968–72; General Studies) has been director of the Gate Theatre for the past twenty-eight years. In 2000 he received the honorary degree of LLD from Trinity. He was given the **Irish Times** Theatre Award for lifetime achievement in the arts in 2006 and, in 2007, was honoured with the title **Chevalier dans l'Ordre des Arts et des Lettres** by the French government. In 2010 he was awarded an OBE by Queen Elizabeth II for services to cultural relations between the UK and Ireland.

Michael Colgan and Flick Louden at Trinity Ball.

THE LONG WAY ROUND

fidelma macken

WHEN I PITCHED UP at Trinity at the end of the sixties, I was in a slightly different position to my classmates. I had been spending several years 'growing up' so to speak, by making my way around the world. For as long as I can remember I had an enormous curiosity about how other people lived.

I spent several years travelling around the world, delaying where I was happiest, such as South America and Asia. I remember getting out of Kabul quickly, where some rather terrifying men, probably early Taliban, took offence at my miniskirt – it was rather stupid of me to wear one – and Hong Kong, where a group of young prostitutes attacked me, mistaking me for a Westerner muscling in on their territory.

My early impression of students at college was that they fell into several different camps. There were, at that time, a large number of students from the North, for the most part Protestant students who had attended Portora, or Campbell College or wherever, and some of whom had even been to school in the South. They were probably at the comfortable end of the economic spectrum, although this was rarely noticeable, and in general were of the slightly naïve, gauche and protected variety.

There were a few others from a different end of the Northern spectrum, however, including a terrific fellow from the Sandy Row part of Belfast. I loved his earthy, cynical view of the world. Of course most of them, and also many who came from England, had the significant advantage of something called 'grants', an unknown benefit in Ireland at the time. It meant they frequently had a great deal more money than many of us from the South, who had to pay college fees and our own accommodation.

The English students at Trinity definitely fell into two or more subgroups. There were several students whose parents had emigrated to England during the forties and fifties when opportunities in Ireland, even for graduates with professions, were slim – their well-educated children often came to Trinity. And then there were students who were born and raised in Ireland but sent to English public schools, or whose Irish parents lived in places more far-flung, where employers paid for the children to be schooled in England. Many of these subgroups started out by mixing little with others, but this was probably no different, in retrospect, to the groups of Irish students who came from the same second-level school and who also stuck together like limpets, until they all found a better or more interesting niche for themselves. They eventually gravitated to kindred spirits at Players, or the Hist, or the Elizabethan Society, or to cricket, and so grew more rounded and cosmopolitan – at least in Trinity terms – over the years. The disparate nature of student backgrounds added a huge amount to the overall ambiance of college life.

Many, if not all, of this group of 'English' students arrived with one or two distinct characteristics. They all spoke with home counties or upper-class English accents. I have noticed over the years, however, those Irish students sent to English public schools and who stayed in Ireland or now live here have accents much modified from the early days at Trinity and closer to the local accent (I think of Shane Ross, David Went, Richard Nesbitt). Another thing I found curious was that many of them had double-barrelled names. Indeed, Trinity was replete with these, and not just among the students. The FitzGerald-Brownes, the Hosford Tanners, the Aliaga-Kellys and so on all made their respective accent marks. Many of these double-barrelled persons dressed very beautifully, in that most attractive, slightly languid Hugh Grant type of way. I'm not entirely convinced that it meant they were, in fact, any more exciting. But they sure as hell looked great, and attracted large numbers of the very beautiful young women floating around. Over the years in college, however, everyone melded into a mass of generically halfway mature graduates, including myself.

It was not just the students who were linguistically and sartorially memorable. There was the terrifying Professor Otway-Ruthven, who put the fear of the Lord into students. I think this was for a combination of reasons: she was not only an established academic but also a large lady. In her billowing gown she strode around college and her very physical presence was manifest. Not only did she have these traits, she also had that very impressive name: you might well be able to cope with most of the double-barrelled names, but her name was, unless you knew otherwise, pretty well unpronounceable, and made up of the most unusual combination of letters, no permutation of which came readily to my mind or ear.

Classes in the late 1960s were tiny: in my first year they were between twenty-four and twenty-eight. This meant that we knew everyone, and numbers were even smaller when some left as early as the first Christmas or shortly after it. There was a lovely fellow in my year, Mike Heelis, who came from the very north of England and thought he would like to study Law, but who quickly discovered he absolutely hated it; just hated it, so he left very early on, and I often look back and admire his courage to do so. We always pitied the science students who seemed to have endless practical trials to do, which required supervising late at night and regularly led to them having to leave parties early to check something hadn't died or exploded. Those of us in the arts end of things had a rather more relaxed time.

I wanted to go to the Bar so I signed up for Law, although if I were doing it again, I would opt to go via what is called the scenic route, that is, taking any other subject and then doing Law at graduate level. I think it allows young people to have a liberal arts or other background, before being immersed in what is a very focused degree. Of course nowadays training for the Bar is quite different, and much broader than when I was tackling it. But college life itself, so far as it concerned lectures and tutorials, was very structured in superficial ways, and really not at all in others. Wearing a gown was obligatory. So was attendance at lectures, and there was a roll call – just as in the most junior class in junior school. But no gown, no attendance. And I don't just mean no formal note in the attendance book. The lecturer would not even pretend to notice you existed. No questions permitted, and no answers given, if foolish enough to ask.

Our course, as with most degree courses, was four years, with rather easy terms of just three lots of seven weeks, or even eight, eight and five weeks, which made for long summer holidays – about which more later. There was absolutely no choice. You took four fixed subjects in each of the four years, and learnt nothing else. In many of the well-known universities elsewhere, even then, you could take the core legal subjects and then add on other law subjects of particular interest.

Another baffling thing about professors and lecturers in college, at least in the Law School, was the total rigour of some of them. There was one who was straight out of a Dickens novel. Tall, effete, very formal, he was always dressed in black from head to toe. Later – much later – I heard he had a wonderfully dry sense of humour, but that was utterly excised, either deliberately or innocently, when he stood before us. He lectured from a set of notes, from the 'off' at the end of roll call, to when he finished, which was at precisely five minutes to the hour. Not four, not six, but five. This had the result that his lectures could, and regularly did, finish mid sentence. Once, he had just referred to a very old case on an arcane topic, called [blank] v The O'Connor Don. None of us managed to transcribe the blank, so one brave student asked, 'How do you spell that, sir?' Cool as ice, he spelt out 'O C o n n o r', very slowly, then promptly closed his book and swept away. He must have known that no one had a clue what the blank was, but we later learned this was 'Iveagh', which he had pronounced in the traditional 'Iva'!

One benefit of my father's instance that I should be able to survive during my travels was that I could manage a passable shorthand. Since the lectures were delivered at breakneck speed, I soon learnt that if I took the notes this way, I could translate them word for word. So I did, typed them up and passed them over to anyone who wanted them.

A lecturer who stuck in my mind was a man called C. Bueno McKenna. He taught us tort and was then a very well-known and highly regarded senior counsel at the Bar, whose lectures always took place on Saturday mornings. When we arrived at 9 am, the very large blackboard – it took up the entire length of the wall at the top of the lecture hall – was always more than half full of the tidiest, neatest, and most precise lines of writing, which he interrupted, without comment, only to call the roll. He rarely, if ever, spoke to us. I have no idea what time he arrived at on a Saturday morning, but he must have been there at least forty minutes before us. Our job was to write as quickly as possible to catch up with him, and continue thus until the end of the 'lecture'. No sooner had he finished filling in the last blank patch at the right-hand side of the blackboard than he would wipe away what he had done at the start, and off he would go again. It was mind-bogglingly boring.

But it has to be said that when you read over these detailed notes, nothing was left out, and it was all so clearly presented that it was just like reading a textbook, though I don't know why we did not simply read one. Perhaps it was that at the time there was very little written material available as textbooks on the Irish law of tort, and in many respects our law had moved away from the English law, if only because of rights recognized by Irish courts arising from our constitution. I never met the man when I finally went to the Bar in 1979, and never exchanged one word with him during the entire time I was a student. I doubt if any other student did either.

Another lecturer who stands out is the late Kader Asmal, who taught us public international law. He had quite a reputation as a firebrand and for highlighting racial problems in his home country of South Africa, so he was well up to speed on world issues. He was one of the few lecturers who actually spoke to and discussed matters with us, although 'discuss' might not quite be the right word for what used to happen. He was so enthusiastic he would lose track of where he was quite readily, but we never minded because whatever topic he veered off on was always fascinating. It meant that the 'four essential principles' of whatever he had started on, and which we were supposed to note, never got beyond the first two, or occasionally, three. Someone would ask him something midstream and that was it. Gone forever. We didn't give a damn. It was far more interesting than whatever it was he was going to tell us, and ultimately it didn't really make any difference to results, except for those who were planning to do postgraduate work, I never came across anyone who was in the slightest bit interested in how well a student did in college.

We had eight hours of lectures a week and less frequent tutorials. Unlike other universities, our tutorials were also given by the professor or lecturer who delivered the lectures. Because tutorials consisted of very small numbers, from which a student simply could not escape, and took place in the rooms of the lecturer, they could be dreadfully awkward. We were for the most part a very reticent bunch, save for those of us too foolish or arrogant to avoid falling into a great deep hole, as I recall doing more than once. But on one occasion it was more awful than usual. Professor Heuston, a renowned legal scholar and author, was our guide and mentor in matters of jurisprudence, a subject whose value at that stage entirely escaped my pea-brain, although I subsequently become a fan. He had come straight from Oxford or Cambridge, I cannot recall at this remove, as the dean of the Law School. He was really a forbidding person for students. Intensely shy and gauche, he lived in a glebe in County Meath to which he invited groups of students for Sunday lunch. I was not among them.

Anyway, we had a tutorial in which we were discussing the question of the interpretation of some English statute. The question was whether, if a car chassis was being driven down the road at a speed way beyond the limit, was this 'driving a motor vehicle' for the purposes of the legislation. I piped up that of course it must be, at which confident statement he rose and said he would be back in a minute. He duly returned with a volume of the *All England Reports* in which there was a case that dealt with this very problem and had, for valid legal reasons, come to the polar opposite view. That was not so bad. What was awful was that he had been the presiding magistrate of the case. Although he was so shy that he would never look directly at me, it still took me a long time to pass him on the stairs without trying to disappear into the wall.

My life outside college changed in the January of my second year, when I got married. I was used to wearing long, flowing, flower-power maxi-dresses in college, and I would have got married in such an outfit. In fact (at my mother's insistence), I wore a beautiful, very fine wool crêpe dress in pale biscuit, by Balmain, but would not wear a veil, and so sported (to my mother's horror) a chocolate-brown hat. In those days Jurys still had their rather old-fashioned but stylish hotel at Dame Street so I organized the wedding breakfast there, and later went abroad on honeymoon.

Before that we had spent some time hunting for a house. My husband had lived in Dalkey all his life. He found a lovely mews house at the end of Sorrento Road, although it came with a much larger house on Sorrento Terrace in which lived an elderly lady with a right of residence for her life. This had the advantage that the large house, with which the mews was to be thrown in, was much cheaper than would otherwise be the case. And since she was elderly, she would surely die fairly soon. This was all in the days before Dalkey became awfully posh and no one could afford to live there any longer. Anyway, we thought we were home and dry, until the lady said she had had a better offer (of £500) from a barrister, and so we lost it and he got it. (The old lady, who was in her seventies at the time, lived until well into her nineties, so my barrister friend did not get to live in the house on Sorrento Terrace for another eighteen years or so.)

It was back to peering over walls for bits of sites, and we finally found one at the other end of Sorrento Road, where we built our small house and lived there for years. We had wonderful parties with lots of students who, not surprisingly, found it difficult to get back into town late at night, so we often had a house full of sleeping bodies. We later sold it and built another house, also in Dalkey. College life was therefore quite different for me, because I usually went home to meet my working husband. I cannot now remember how, since we had very little money, we managed to have a woman who came and cleaned and did the laundry and ironing.

I remember deciding to take one last and final pre-marriage trip. During my summers in college, I had always worked for a law firm in New York, usually making enough money to pay my fees and having something left over for pocket money. That September, knowing that I was going to get married the following January, I decided to come back from New York by boat, the SS *Rotterdam*. Well, it was a terrific six days and nights, and never once did I look at a note, despite the looming exams. There was a division between us in steerage and those in first class, who were truly well off; some even famous. A fellow passenger turned out to be a man named Winkelmann: to my horror, I discovered he was the treasurer of Trinity. I scuttled out of his company as quickly as I could and never again spoke to him on board. When I met him years later at a sailing regatta I admitted my past, but at the time I was far too terrified to do so.

My years in college certainly were rather different to the norm. They flew by. My treasured friends today, with few exceptions, include all those I made there. I suppose of all the things I am grateful for, and cherish, that is it. The rest of college was just the setting.

The Hon. Mrs Justice Macken (TCD 1968–72) undertook postgraduate studies at the London School of Economics (LLM 1973). In 2002 Trinity conferred on her a PhD (**honoris causa**). From 1979 she practised at the Irish Bar, taking silk in the mid nineties until appointed a judge of the High Court in 1998. In 1999 she became the first woman judge of the European Court of Justice in Luxembourg, serving until 2004. In 2005 she was appointed a judge of the Supreme Court of Ireland. She became the first Averil Deverell Lecturer in Law at Trinity, is chair of the Irish Centre for European Law, and a member of the Permanent Court of Arbitration in The Hague.

BIT PLAYER

roger greene

> 'I never really left Trinity.'
> Oliver St John Gogarty, *It Isn't This Time of Year at All* (1956)

IN THOSE DAYS you did what you were told. I had passed Matriculation at the age of seventeen but was deemed too young to start Trinity and was told to wait until the following year.

Parking Trinity for a year was a godsend. Horses had been a major part of growing up in Kildare and now I wanted to fulfil a childhood ambition to ride as an amateur jockey. For twelve months I rode three lots of racehorses every morning in Springfield House, the home of trainer 'Buster' Harty of that legendary Irish racing family. My days were filled with chilly eight-o'-clock starts on the gallops, banter with the stable lads and hard, physical work. I gained a level of fitness never attained before or since. There were racecourse rides here and there – Fairyhouse, Navan, Gowran Park, Naas, Baldoyle, Punchestown and Ballinrobe. I'd ridden them all and was determined to continue, Trinity or no Trinity.

When October 1968 arrived I didn't know how or if I'd fit in when I finally did 'go up' to Trinity. At that time Catholics were ostensibly obliged to request a dispensation from one Archbishop John Charles McQuaid, who clearly regarded Trinity an orgiastic den of evil Protestantism. Irish Catholicism was and is an anathema to me so I took a measured, responsible approach to McQuaid's edict. 'Bring it on bigot, fling me from your church!' Technically excommunicated, as I still am today, I have yet to burst into flames.

I was unsure about my four-year future in Trinity reading English, Philosophy and Economics. Tentatively I dipped my toe in Freshers' Week and found it to be a warmer experience than first feared. There were pints of Guinness to be had in the Buttery, O'Neills and The Old Stand, accompanied by an unexpected dose of liberation. During Freshers' Week, the strip from Front Gate to the cobbled square resembled an Elizabethan market place. You walked a gauntlet of colourful bunting, posters and other accoutrements as the undergraduate establishment screamed the benefits of joining the Fencing Club, the Historical Society, the Philosophical Society, the Cricket Club, the Rugby Club, the Boxing Club, the Boat Club and just about any other activity you wanted.

I've no idea why I joined the Philosophical Society, for apart from attending one or two events in my first month, my interest waned very quickly; but it did offer refuge, a comfortable chair and the newspapers. I'd also joined the Rugby Club – or Dublin University Football Club, to give it its correct title – but didn't play until my third year. Likewise the Cricket Club, though again it was a few years before I actually got around to playing.

Students in Trinity in the late sixties were predominantly English, Northern Irish, some Scots, and a few Americans. Native Irish students were thinner on the ground but we were increasing in number, heralding the transition of Trinity from a sort of outpost British university to an Irish one: for better or worse. Some said the Brits were in Trinity because they were too thick to get into Oxford or Cambridge and to a point that was true if not a tad unfair. For me Trinity evolved into a sort of Utopia. The eclectic mix of students provided a range of differing takes on life from backgrounds, which, on the face of it, seemed akin but were in fact very different.

For four years I'd been sheltered in a cauldron of English tradition and values known as the public school. This is not to denigrate the ethos, merely to point to its insularity against which liberation in Trinity rendered me a child in a sweet shop. Where to begin? How to direct myself? Where to focus? Much like removing blinkers from a horse, I wandered and sought purpose. It led inexorably to the fringes of hedonism. Maybe McQuaid was right after all.

They say that university friendships are for life. This is true to a point but should be predicated by the unwritten rule not to confuse acquaintanceships with friendships. My first meetings with lifelong friends in Trinity are hazy. I know I met Ken Donnelly, a medical student, in the first few weeks of October 1968 but where or when I've no idea other than I can be sure there was drink involved. Ken became the first Trinity UAU lightweight boxing champion since the early fifties. During his boxing career I attended some of his bouts and spectacular fare they were. A particular memory is a spat Ken had against an inmate of Arbour Hill. Before the fight we were sure Ken would be killed. How wrong we were. In under two minutes he'd floored his opponent and the fight was stopped. The flailing cowboy style of the Arbour Hill incumbent was outwitted and rubbished by the target precision and power of Ken's lightning jabs.

Over the years I played squash with Ken, after which he would inveigle me to spar with him in the boxing ring upstairs in the gym. I resisted most of these overtures but on a few occasions I succumbed, pointless though it was. I was rubbish and a coward. He said that all he required was a moving target. For a brief period I obliged as a sort of running punch bag. Until the inevitable happened. Whether it was the punch to my sternum or my head hitting the floor I know not, but I was rendered briefly unconscious and when I came round I couldn't breathe. I was told not to be ridiculous and to get up off the floor. He'd only given me a tap, apparently. Some tap. For a week I panted rather than breathed and walked with my upper body parallel to the ground.

The medics, as they were known in Trinity, were not generally given to integration with those of us reading arts, but there were exceptions. Medics had a unifying trait. They took drinking and flamboyant behaviour very seriously. Ken was one, as was Matt (not his real name to protect the guilty) who later went on to become master of the Rotunda Hospital. I have retained a snapshot of Matt to this day. On the morning of a rugby international and after a heavy session the night before, we gathered in the Lincoln Inn at roughly 11 am. No sign of Matt. After an hour or so we decided to make tracks to Lansdowne Road and let Matt fend for himself. Just as we'd reached this decision Matt appeared at the door in a condition that made Brendan Behan and Dylan Thomas look like teetotallers. He requested a glass of water for Alka Seltzer and a pint of

Smithwick's. No time for both, we decreed, so which was it to be? He opted for the Smithwick's. As he held the pint glass in one trembling hand he produced two Alka Seltzer in the other and popped them into the pint of ale. Jaws to the floor, we observed Matt's pint metamorphose into a pink, cascading fountain from which he proceeded to drink and shower involuntarily.

Theatre had been a passion of mine since the age of twelve when I was taken for the first time to a real theatre and not on the annual Gaiety panto-mime trip. From the moment the curtain went up on O'Casey's *The Plough and the Stars* in the Queen's Theatre on Pearse Street (the temporary home of The Abbey after it burnt down in 1951), I was captivated by all the magic and joy of live theatrical drama.

Once in Trinity I wanted to be part of Dublin University Players, which was to take over my life in college from midway through my first year in 1968–9 through to graduation and beyond. It became the major influence and absorbing force in my student life.

Joining Players was one thing, integration another. Payment of the annual sub did not necessarily lead to participation. You had to know someone – in keeping with the finest of theatrical traditions. It was early days and I knew no one in Players. Perusing the DU Players noticeboard in Front Gate I spotted a call for walk-ons for *Andorra* by Swiss playwright Max Frisch to be directed by Richard Fegen, a talented, unassuming and unique individual. I say unique as I have yet to meet another Eton-educated Offaly man.

I got a walk-on part and indeed a few lines. This was the beginning of a long association both as an actor, director and eventually a committee member with Players. I became glued to the place, along with others who started with me in *Andorra* and subsequently went on to work professionally in either theatre, the music industry, radio, television or film as I did. Paul McGuinness paraded the stage dressed as a soldier with a scary-looking gun, as did Michael Colgan. Paolo Tullio was the village idiot. I was the ultimate walk-on, a villager, aimless and self-conscious. Susan FitzGerald was the leading lady to Andrew Russell's leading man. Susan is now a successful professional actress. Andrew runs a publishing company.

Michael Colgan has been director of the Gate for many years and taken that theatre from its knees to prosperity and critical acclaim, due principally to his drive, determination and creativity, all three of which I witnessed on day one in rehearsals for *Andorra*. Richard Fegen had unwittingly acquired himself an assistant director when he cast Michael who, incidentally, had never before been on a stage. This did not deter him from expressing his opinion, as has nothing ever since.

Michael (or Mike, as he was in those days) and I struck up a close friendship, which we maintained throughout our four years in college and beyond. He became a man obsessed with theatre and like the rest of us devoted most of his energies and time to Players of which he later became chairman. He seemed destined for direction although he did act in two productions, *The Tempest*, and *The Fire Raisers* by Max Frisch, the latter directed by a mature student and professional actor, Wesley Murphy. In *The Fire Raisers*, Mike played Schmidt and I was Eisenring – the leads, or 'evil genii' as theatre critic Alec Reid daubed us in a laudatory review of the production in *The Irish Times*.

Amongst others in that production were Paddy Agnew, now Rome correspondent for *The Irish Times*, musician and part-time barrister Chris Meehan and solicitor Seymour Cresswell. One of the ASMs on *The Fire Raisers* was one Mary Broderick, a former Miss Fresher, with whom I became entangled until the end of my Trinity days, when she became my present wife.

In all I acted in six plays and two pantomimes. There were sprinklings of professionalism and cringe-inducing awfulness in equal measures in all six of the plays. Nonetheless all of them attracted near-capacity houses for each performance – though admittedly, Players' seating capacity was less than a hundred.

Of my two pantos, *We've All Maid Marion*, a liberal take on Robin Hood, was the main crowd puller. So popular was it that we had to increase performances to three a day: a matinée, the eight o'clock show and a late night. Each performance was packed to standing room. Amongst the 'gay' band were Paolo Tullio as Robin, Johnny Mulligan as Little John, Mike Braddell as Everard, Roly Saul as Friar Tuck and Paul McGuinness as Gopher with a bizarre French accent. Eddie Shorts danced frenziedly in the opening sequence as Alan-a-Dale, Louise (Dillie) Keane was Maid Marion, Chris Clarke was Will Scarlet and Seymour Cresswell the Soothsayer, which entailed walking the stage saying nothing but 'Sooth' throughout each performance. I played the Sheriff of Nottingham, or Notts County, as it appeared in the programme. Paolo Tullio and Michael Colgan were responsible for the wonderfully silly script and Mike directed.

Players' production of *The Tempest* was directed by Michael Hoey and assisted by Donald Taylor Black, who had arrived in Trinity in 1970, bringing with him an encyclopedic knowledge of contemporary UK theatre and an evident love of the medium. Donald and I have remained companions and colleagues ever since, working together for twenty-plus years on collaborative documentary film-making for the BBC, RTÉ, Channel 4 and other broadcasters. We are both now working in an academic capacity in the National Film School at the Dún Laoghaire Institute of Art, Design & Media.

Of course Players was not just about those on the stage. There were many who contributed equally vital roles such as set builder Tony 'Times' Sheridan, who brought sensible dimensions to theatrical production and kept any egos grounded; John Henderson on sound and stage management, Louise Lloyd Carson, Jane Marriott, James and Tim Morris, and the great lighting designer Rupert Murray who became Dublin theatre's first choice in lighting for thirty years until his dreadfully sad and premature death in 2006.

Players' standards were professional to a degree. But it wasn't all about the serious business of theatrical exactitude, there was fun to be had as well. In May of 1971 Mike Colgan and I had been invited by fellow Player Johnny Harben for a weekend in his family home in Oughterard, County Galway. Mike and I headed west in my Mini, with very little cash and a Northern Bank cheque book – a lethal combination. In those days a cheque book was as good as cash. We didn't quite make it for the weekend but did turn up the following Monday. Fun was had and drink was taken, as they say, but only by Johnny and me – back then Mike didn't drink, but this never prevented him from flowing with the mood as it declined to frivolity. By Friday, Johnny's mother, Iris, had had enough, and whereas we weren't told to go we took the hints, which had all the subtlety of a flying sledgehammer.

In sombre mood we headed for Dublin. Just as we pulled up at the traffic lights by Galway University Mike shrieked, 'Turn back!' I asked why, only to be told there were two girls hitchhiking but heading in the other direction. I turned the Mini around and the girls jumped in, explaining in Swedish accents that they wanted to go to Limerick for the night and on to Kerry thereafter.

Mike informed them, and indeed me, that as chance would have it this was precisely what we were doing and we'd take them the whole way. It seemed that there was a God after all. We had three glorious days and nights with Kayja and Strindberg from Uppsala, and the less said, the better.

You'll note that I have yet to mention academic affairs. In its way this reflects the prevailing attitude to study at that time. It was frowned upon to be too good at the books, so in the interests of street cred this dimension of my Trinity days took a back seat. There were exceptions, however. English lectures with Brendan Kennelly and David Norris were cherished then – and now, glancing back. Equally gratifying were John Gaskin and Peter Mew in Philosophy. I studied four weeks of every year just before exams. With the exception of my third year I had to repeat my Economics every September.

Although Players was my principal occupation in college I didn't allow it become my only involvement in Trinity life. In my Junior Sophister, or third year, I had been invited to join the committee of Trinity Week (the body that organized and arranged the celebratory events marking the end of the year each May). This involved most of the sports clubs and its highlight was the College Races, a rather grand affair in those days at which the president of Ireland was usually present. Male students dressed in full morning wear while the ladies wore elegant full-length dresses and hats – an almost Edwardian-style affair with Pimm's and champagne. How things have changed.

In my final year the members of the committee elected me secretary of Trinity Week, much to my surprise, as tradition had it that sporting prowess was the profile for secretaries of Trinity Week, not those from Players who were regarded as somewhat louche. Nonetheless, I became the chief, so to speak, and quite an honour it was. I drafted friends onto the committee to ensure support for this daunting task. Amongst them were Roly Saul, Rugby Club; Ken Donnelly, Boxing Club; Donald Taylor Black, Players and Football; and Aileen Galvin, Ladies' Committee. Paul Coulson was Trinity Ball secretary. I was never a great afternoon-tea imbiber but that Wednesday in May 1972 I had tea with the indefatigable Professor Trevor West and the then president of Ireland, Eamon de Valera.

In my final two years I rather belatedly began playing rugby and cricket, which I hadn't done since school. Whereas I had a few games for the third rugby team I later turned my allegiance to the taverners' rugby and cricket teams, known as the Ramblers. Mike Halliday, later to play cricket for Ireland, introduced me to the art of rambling. Our rugby teams consisted of six or seven first fifteen players with the balance of rather indifferent ability. I came into the latter category. Former Labour Party leader and tánaiste, Dick Spring, was one of the regulars as were Mick Fitzpatrick and Phil Orr. All three went on to play for Ireland so us lesser mortals were in very good company. On Sundays we toured the country playing teams in Kildare, Offaly, Cork, Kilkenny, Tipperary and Wexford amongst others. There was always a great welcome from these rural clubs who seemed to appreciate our making the journey from Dublin. After the match we were fed and well watered before making the return journey to Dublin at closing time. How we avoided death on the roads I'll never know.

On one occasion – one of my last games for Ramblers – we were in a little rural pub in County Kildare, after playing Naas. I was with some English members of our team when Dick Spring and Roly Saul sidled up and quietly told me to help get 'our lot' out of the pub. It seemed an odd thing to do so early in the evening but my protests were met with grim 'just do it' faces. I had no idea what was going on. In the car park we learned that the barman had said that while there were no active IRA members in the bar there were a good few committed sympathizers and that the English accents weren't going down too well. This had never before happened on a Ramblers tour. Why now?

It was Sunday, 30 January 1972.

Whilst we threw darts and lowered pints, the rest of the clientele watched the news of the Derry (or Bogside) massacre on television. We'd been totally oblivious to the murder of thirteen people, having not heard a radio or watched the television between our match and arriving in the pub. It was a defining moment in the first four years of the Northern Troubles. We had read, heard and watched media coverage of the Troubles from 1969 and beyond but until Bloody Sunday Trinity students seemed somewhat detached from the horrendous events in the North.

The sense of outrage escalated throughout the Republic over the next days, culminating in the march on the British embassy in Merrion Square on 2 February 1972. Reportedly the march attracted up to 30,000 furious protesters: ordinary working people and students from both TCD, UCD and further afield marched with the more aggressive cohort, which raised the level of demonstration to arson. By the time the group I was with arrived in Merrion Square, the embassy was blazing.

As dusk descended we stood and watched in silence.

Roger Greene (TCD 1968–72; General Studies) for twenty years produced independent documentaries for BBC, RTÉ, UTV and Channel 4, and directed live coverage of horse racing in the UK for the Racing Channel and BSkyB. He produced and directed **Derek Mahon: The Poetry Nonsense** (2009). For five years he presented **Media Matters** and **The Snug** for Newstalk 106. He is author of **Under the Spotlight** (2005), a book on Irish journalism. He lectures in media in IADT/the National Film School.

EARLY EXIT

paul m^cguinness

IN THE SUMMER of 1968, as we were doing the Leaving Cert. after six years at Clongowes Wood College, my friend Donnell Deeny told me that he had reluctantly decided to attend Queen's University Belfast to study Medicine. This was to oblige his father and to become the third-generation Doctor Deeny in Lurgan. Halfway through the summer I got a telegram to say, 'Changed my mind, going to do Law, see you at TCD in September.' I was delighted. I had been offered a place to do Philosophy and Psychology in the School of Mental and Moral Science, which was quite hard to get into. My Leaving Cert. gave me the minimum three honours in English, Latin and French, and at the age of seventeen, I scraped into Trinity College Dublin.

For the first weeks I was in digs in Drumcondra while Donnell was in Donnybrook. Quite quickly the fear of being overwhelmed by legions of cleverer people went away, as did the idea of using Trinity as a pit stop on the way to Oxford. Donnell entered the Hist and I got heavily involved with Players. He became the youngest-ever auditor of the Historical Society. I had a full maintenance grant from Dorset County Council, which should have made me quite prosperous and indeed it did for the first half of each term. I was terrible at managing my finances. Being in the centre of a great city with money in my pocket was exhilarating: I went to movies, theatre, Chinese restaurants, pubs, gigs, met girls, listened to records, and quickly switched from digs to flat life. I felt very sophisticated and bohemian.

I was a bad student. The Trinity Psychology Department, though prestigious, actually wasn't very good as well as being under a cloud following a scandal the previous year, when a professor had propositioned a woman student, promising her better marks if she slept with him. She got him to repeat the offer when she returned with a concealed tape recorder. She sold the story to a newspaper. He was suspended and she became a journalist. I have memories of bearded militant behaviourist lecturers and endless experiments with white rats, mazes and the Skinner Box. Psychology quickly lost its attraction whereas Philosophy became more interesting.

After a while I dropped out of Psychology and concentrated – relatively – on Philosophy, which required attendance at a small number of lectures and tutorials. Frankly, I did the absolute minimum. By now I was heavily involved in Players. To get on in Players you had to start by doing a bit of acting. I was not good at the acting, but I was marginally better than Michael Colgan. As Black Soldier No. 1 and Black Soldier No. 2 in *Andorra* by Max Frisch, we competed grimly to look fiercer.

My other great pals, Paolo Tullio and Andrew Russell, were much better actors. I recall they were also both very interested in girls. So was I, and was fortunate enough to meet the wonderful Kathy Gilfillan, the editor of this book. She was a beautiful Northerner who strode around Front Square in knee-high boots, hot pants and a maxi coat. I pursued her by showing her the peculiar cartoons that I drew for *TCD Miscellany* under the nom de plume 'Maxwell' (he of the silver hammer was the reference). She was quite serious about women's issues and produced a contraception guide for the Students' Representative Council. She was also elected student welfare officer.

By the time I got into third year, I was spending all my time between Players and *TCD Miscellany*. I did the minimum of academic work but managed to pass all my exams. I directed a couple of plays with some success. I also appeared in revues, including the legendary pantomime *We've All Maid Marion*. I thought it might be fun to be chairman of Players, a position elected by the members. I still have friends who were in that electorate: Chris de Burgh, Dillie Keane, Lucy O'Sullivan, Julia Kennedy, Michele Freyne and Susan FitzGerald. Players was a wonderful world of posing, dressing up and hoping to get into showbiz. There was no drama course in Trinity in those days but standards were high at both Players and Dramsoc in UCD. Jeananne Crowley succeeded in getting parts in both theatre groups – I think she managed to convince each university that she was attending it. To cut a long story short, I lost the election to Michael Colgan, who had even then grasped that there was another great job in show-business apart from acting, directing or writing: you could be in charge.

I also enjoyed the magazine. In those days the editor was 'Anonymous', in a Swiftean tradition intended to encourage fearless criticism of the college. Of course everyone knew who the current editor was. The rival *Trinity News* was printed free on the presses of *The Irish Times* through an ancient and wonderful indulgence. We *TCD Miscellany* types regarded ourselves as much hipper with our photolithography process, sticking the typeset words down with cow gum, drawing our own cartoons, selling a few ad pages.

The editorship was passed on from term to term amongst people who knew each other. Shane Ross passed it to me; I passed it to Donnell Deeny, who passed it to Jim Hamilton, who passed it to Tom Haran, who passed it to Don Knox. It was great fun to work extremely hard for a term and produce six or seven weekly issues of a magazine. There was traditionally no supervision of the content, though the magazine received a small grant from the Societies and Publications committee. Each term the style of the magazine would change depending on the interests and proclivities of the new editor.

My issues as editor, 'Spring Term 1971', featured regular columns such as 'Frank Bannister Apologizes', which teased a pompous boy, and 'New Ways with Old Holborn', which slyly and deftly instructed readers how to roll a joint, make a cabbage chillum and so on, complete with wonderful illustrations by Merrily Harpur. I encouraged satire, smut and humour. Paolo Tullio and Chris de Burgh (*né* Davison) obliged under a jointly owned moniker, 'Denis Oddfinger'. We had sports, chess, reviews and gossip columns. I thought it was very funny. The gossip column was by 'Man of Straw', the name a challenge to would-be litigants. The agony aunt advice column, 'Dear Father Brendan ...' was written by my future wife. (The real Father Brendan Heffernan was Trinity's first Catholic chaplain, who later married us.) A regular subject of our attention was Professor George Dawson, who we described as 'well-known art lover, wit and geneticist', which lent him a sinister air. He loved it. We made fun of the venerable R.B. McDowell, who also had a sense of humour and didn't mind being caricatured.

The Irish poet Brendan Kennelly was a popular, convivial and gregarious lecturer in the English Department. In those far-off days, a more relaxed attitude was taken to fraternization between staff and undergraduates. Kennelly was also the Junior Dean responsible for student discipline. He lived noisily in rooms off Front Square beside the ones I shared with Deeny, and entertained a lot. He also had accommodation in the English Department, plus another office as Junior Dean. I ran an article in *TCD Miscellany* pointing out that all this space occupied was rather a lot for one diminutive Kerryman, particularly at a time when there was a severe shortage of housing for students. I quickly heard that Kennelly was furious. In another issue, I ran an amusing piece, unsigned, about a power struggle within the Choral Society. In it, the writer referred to another woman chorister 'using the c-word'.

This really set Kennelly off. Ignoring the tradition of editorial anonymity he fined me personally the enormous sum of £50 for the – hitherto unknown – disciplinary offence of libel, for publishing the Choral Society piece. I appealed the fine to the Disciplinary Committee. My 'barrister' or 'Mackenzie Man' was Shane Ross. He represented me so ably that the committee found for me, and informed Kennelly that he had no power to impose such a fine. What happened next was that the board of Trinity College informed the Disciplinary Committee that they were only a subcommittee of the board, and that the fine stood. At that point, I paid the £50 with a TCD Miscellany Ltd cheque, and liquidated the company.

This was towards the end of my third year. Around this time, I was informed that the Junior Dean had refused me academic credit. What this meant was that he had decided that I had not attended sufficient lectures to be allowed to sit my third-year exams. This was a bit of a blow: though I had indeed attended very few lectures, I was confident that I would have passed my exams. I left Trinity. My Dorset County Council student grant was withdrawn, and I spent a year in London saving the money to repeat my third year. When I returned to Dublin in 1972 to do that repeat year, most of my friends had moved on, and I found I wasn't very interested in college. Then I was offered a job as the location manager on John Boorman's movie *Zardoz* being filmed at Ardmore Studios with Sean Connery and Charlotte Rampling. (Coincidentally, years later, I am one of the owners of Ardmore.) I took the job and embarked on a career as a freelance film production manager and assistant director. I cast a few of my Trinity pals as extras in *Zardoz* – Dillie Keane, Andrew Russell, Mandy Walker, Lucy O'Sullivan, Julia Kennedy to name a few. It was a great summer and though I fully intended to sit my exams in September, by the time the date came round, I was working on another movie. Though I promised my parents I would go back to finish the degree one day, I never did. Years later, UCD gave me an honorary doctorate in recognition of my small role in setting up their Film Studies programme. At the conferring ceremony, I said to my mother, 'Mother, this degree will have to do.'

What did happen, as I worked on dozens of television commercials and the occasional feature film through the seventies, was that I became interested in the music business. Donnell Deeny's elder brother Michael was bored with his job as an accountant in Kennedy's Bakery, and had started Orpheus Mobile Discotheques, which meant I became an occasional DJ, playing records and supplying go-go dancers to parties and hotels around Ireland. This enjoyable activity developed into us becoming concert promoters, and under the banners 'Trackless Transit' and 'Headland' we put on some hippy concerts in the Mansion House and the RDS, with international acts such as Alan Price, Georgie Fame and Donovan. One of the local Irish acts down the bill was Horslips, and Michael became their manager.

In the seventies, as Horslips signed international record deals and toured around Europe and the US, I watched from close quarters and absorbed a great deal. I started looking for a band of my own to manage. After a false start with Spud, a folk-rock group that included my Trinity friend Don Knox on fiddle, I was introduced to U2 in 1978 by another Trinity friend, the late, great Bill Graham, the *Hot Press* writer. The rest, as they say, is history.

Looking back, I have happy memories of Trinity. It seems incredible that in 1968 we were still subject to 'the ban', under which Catholics were forbidden by Archbishop John Charles McQuaid to attend Trinity. That was also the last year of unrestricted intake of students from the UK. The resulting polyglot atmosphere was extraordinarily tolerant, and the relationship between Trinity and the city was affectionate. It's hard to believe that in those days, by seven o'clock at night, the streets of the city centre were deserted and foggy. You could seek out your pals quite reliably, because you would know whether they were *habitués* of The Bailey, McDaids, The Old Stand or O'Neills. There were a few cafes such as the Wimpy Bar on Wicklow Street, Puffins on Grafton Street and The Green Rooster on O'Connell Street. I was extremely fortunate that my pal Paolo Tullio's family owned those three. It wasn't the only reason we were friends, but it was an excellent start.

In retrospect, I suppose I should be grateful to Kennelly for preventing me from doing my third-year exams. I've never spoken to the man, but once or twice I've seen him across a room. He looks away if I catch his eye. I often walk through Trinity nowadays, and every time I do I feel younger for a few minutes.

Paul McGuinness (right) directing Paolo Tullio (left) and John Streather in **Malcolm** by Edward Albee.

Paul McGuinness (TCD 1968–72; Philosophy and Psychology) left college to work for film director John Boorman on **Zardoz**. He was assistant director in film and a TV-commercials director until 1978, when he took on the management of U2, having cut his managerial teeth on folk-rock band Spud. He also manages P.J. Harvey. His company, Principle Management, is based in Dublin and New York. He was an Arts Council member, 1989–2000, is Honorary Doctor of Law UCD, founding partner of TV3 in Ireland and an owner-director of Ardmore Film Studios. His consortium runs Phantom FM in Dublin. He is married to Kathy Gilfillan (TCD 1968–72). They have two children and live in County Wicklow.

DON'T MARRY A PROTESTANT

eugene murray

MY TIME in Trinity in the early seventies provided me with the most valuable of possessions – close loving friendships. Having spent five years in a boys-only Jesuit boarding school I entered Trinity, in spite of the bishop's ban, and with a warning from my normally liberal mother not to marry a Protestant. I first met my wife Avril Burgess – yes, a Protestant who was studying English literature – at a party in a swimming pool.

When I arrived at Trinity, an innocent, in the autumn of 1968, I was greeted by hordes of students manning Freshers' Week stands. The principal enticement to join college sports clubs and societies comprised of promises of lots of free drink and so involved a few weeks of regular hangover-induced missed lectures. I never understood why the college authorities didn't insist in having a week of lectures before Freshers' Week – it might have saved a few lost souls.

Having settled in to my course in Business Studies, I wore the college scarf proudly around town. The white afghan coat came later. There were many student style gurus – the most colourful was Ephraim Santiago, the most debonair Derek Moran and Ted Smyth. I stuck with the brigade wearing duffle coats in winter and hippy cheesecloth in summer.

Being a Catholic culchie from Limerick, I befriended fellow students of my own type. Billy Hawney arrived in Dublin for the very first time from Tralee, having hitched a lift in a Denny's delivery truck. Living in flats on a diet of beans on toast and takeaway fish and chips was relieved by the kindness of one Dublin family who took me under its wing: my fellow student Frank Kelly, from Churchtown, who gave me a 'carrier' on the crossbar of his bike home for Sunday lunch with his family. This became a regular and sustaining ritual. To this day Billy, Frank and the other boys from De La Salle College Churchtown are my best friends.

I became politicized fairly quickly. My eldest brother John had been president of the Union of Students in Ireland. Much to the annoyance of senior university managers, John had secured negotiating rights to USI for the first time with a Minister for Education (Donagh O'Malley) and managed to avert a proposed significant increase in university fees. USI was then aligned to the Soviet-backed International Union of Students and *Trinity News*. John had gone briefly missing in Mongolia while attending an international student conference. In those days, mobile phones did not exist and telephone contact in East Asia was well nigh impossible.

Liberal inspiration also came from musicians such as The Rolling Stones, the edgier funky folk music of Fairport Convention and the rejuvenation of Irish traditional music by Planxty and Christy Moore. Films such as *Midnight Cowboy*, *Deliverance* and the promised, delightful revelation of the mysteries of sex in the *Sweet Sins of Sexy Susan* – I was, I must confess, a total innocent in this field of endeavour. Like many students at the time I dabbled with marijuana and had a one-off introduction to what was known then as 'dropping' (tripping) on LSD, a very dangerous adventure.

I PLAYED an active part in college social life: poker in the Junior Common Room and snooker at the top of the GMB. In summer it was frisbee in College Park. Not for me the committees of college societies, although I was records secretary of the Business Society for a short period. After a rugby injury, I played Gaelic football for Trinity Roots in the Dublin Junior league, a raggle-taggle bunch of Sunday boozehounds organized by Joe Revington, a former Students' Representative Council president. A number of prominent guest inter-county players studied in Trinity: on one occasion Dick Spring, by then a rugby international, defied the GAA ban by making an anonymous appearance on the Roots team.

I first met the charismatic Paul Tansey playing poker. He was president of the SRC and a brilliant economist with a great sense of humour, and recruited me to student politics. My first involvement was through helping Paul produce the SRC paper, *Liaison*. In those days there were two other college newspapers, *TCD Miscellany* and *Trinity News*, which was professionally printed. *Liaison* and *TCD Miscellany* were put together with ribbon typewriters, Letraset, scissors and glue and then photographed for printing. Shane Ross edited *TCD Miscellany* in 1971 and was described by the next editor as follows: 'His prevailing vice is not gambling, gin or the ladies, but idleness. His editorials dealt solely with bureaucrats, whom he greatly disliked.' I succeeded Paul as president of the SRC in 1971.

Some time before I took up office the ban on Catholics attending Trinity had been lifted and the genial Father Brendan Heffernan appointed the first Catholic chaplain; he was preparing to say the first Mass in the newly consecrated Exam Hall. Father Brendan was anxious to get a prominent Catholic student to read the lesson. The problem was that we had all moved beyond the church by that stage. Paul Tansey, Donnell Deeny (the auditor of the Hist) and Paul McGuinness stuck to their principles and turned down the invitation. I was well down the list but agreed to do it, given that it was the beatitudes from the Sermon on the Mount – the principles of Christian pacifism – well, that was my excuse as a radical student!

My time as SRC president was initially preoccupied with attending sleepy board meetings and trying to get some policy changes such as liberating female students from the confines of the boarding-school type residences at Trinity Hall in Dartry. Sexism and sexual discrimination were rife. In the late sixties meals at Commons and membership of the Hist debating society were confined to male students, with the Hist only admitting women in the early seventies. Mary Harney became the first female auditor in 1976. The Elizabethan Society was the female-only debating society most famous for its summer garden party of bonnets, strawberries and cream in College Park. There was also a 'Miss Fresher' selected during Freshers' Week. Things changed rapidly in the seventies and I remember that during the contraceptives debates – illegal at the time – Kathy Gilfillan, the SRC welfare officer, controversially published the first guide to birth control for students in an Irish university.

We also convinced college to allow General Studies students to take repeat exams in the autumn – they previously had to wait a whole year. We failed to change the rule that prevented moderatorship (honors degree) students from repeating final exams. I had one very good friend, an excellent student who left without a degree because of a collapse in confidence in the days leading to his finals. There was no continuous assessment in the seventies.

Professor McConnell was provost but the real power resided with the college secretary, George Giltrap and the college treasurer, Franz Winkelmann. The academic fellows on the board were mostly conservative with the exception of George Dawson. My favourite was the elder professor of philosophy, Francis La Touche Godfrey, who was generally ignored by the provost. On one occasion the provost was trying to remember a procedural precedent and patronizingly said to Francis, 'You must know what the previous board did!' and he replied, 'I do, but I won't tell you!' Or so it was said.

The SRC vice-president with whom I shared rooms was the genial and clever Tommy Hamilton, a brother of James Hamilton, probably the best orator never to become auditor of the Hist. Tommy died very young while working overseas after college. He was a great organizer and we ran campaigns against the high food prices in Trinity: a cup of coffee cost twice as much as it did in UCD. Tommy organized an alternative lunch service with one menu item – normally a curry with rice – in the GMB building. Joe Revington, the former SRC president, was the chief cook. These activities greatly annoyed the catering manager, Betty Pickering, but not as much as the times at meetings when she was, predictably, called Petty Bickering.

While president of the SRC I became embroiled in a public war of words with the chairman of the Central Societies Committee (CSC), the Reverend Peter Hiscock, over the failure to properly regulate the financial affairs of college societies. The CSC dispersed the student capitation fee to college societies, and while controlled by the larger societies, which received the bulk of the funding, many societies were just fronts for subsidized drinking dens.

There was also an undercurrent of reactionary Catholic nationalists – in other words, Provos – within college. The Laurentian Society was a society for Catholics attending Trinity and the Cumann Gaelach promoted the Irish language. In common with many of the smaller societies they held events at which drink was available free or very cheaply. While the leadership of these societies was genuinely committed to their ideals, they attracted a small, unpleasantly aggressive nationalist Republican element.

Having settled into academic life quite easily I did just enough to get by until final year when a bit of effort, cramming and a honed exam technique was required to secure the honors degree. Economics, Accounting and Business Studies were not very challenging as such subjects did not exist in the Leaving Cert. at the time: furthermore, these school subjects are more much advanced today than what we learnt in college forty years ago. But we had very good lecturers in Basil Chubb, Louden Ryan, John Bristow, Paddy Lyons, Dermot McAleese, Antoin Murphy, Geoffrey McKechnie and others. My one strong memory of college exams was the ritual of a good friend, Bob Mullally, who had a nervous distaste for exam time – he waited for the Campanile bell to toll on the hour at 9 am, signalling the start of an exam. He then vomited into the toilet and, having completed his ritual, quickly made his way to the exam hall to start his exam five minutes late.

I had a confrontation with a lecturer in Labour Law who was visiting from the US. His only recommended reading was a US State Department bible on the evils of organized labour. He insisted that I stop interrupting his lectures with challenges to his version of US labour history. I complained to the dean of the school who politely reminded me that we had all shades of political opinion among the teaching staff and the previous student to visit his office was complaining about the views expressed by a more liberal academic.

At the time Trinity had lost its two most radical academics in the human-rights champion Owen Sheehy-Skeffington and Máirtín Ó Cadhain, whose politics were a mix of nationalism, social radicalism and anti-clericalism. The most prominent new radical to join the teaching staff was the late Kader Asmal, who founded the Irish Anti-Apartheid Movement with his wife Louise.

Influenced by Asmal, who lectured me in Company Law, I joined the United Nations Student Association (UNSA). UNSA co-ordinated Trinity's protests against the Springboks' rugby tour in 1970. My friend Frank and I came off a motorbike on our way to protest at the team's hotel in Bray – our bloody faces gave the journalists a false impression of so-called police brutality. One of our most vigorous campaigns was to organize a Free Greece Week to protest against the fascist Greek Junta. In UNSA, friendships with Val Roche (who also ran a food co-op in college), Milo Rockett, Ken O'Brien and others led to my joining the Resources Study Group. We published two well-researched pamphlets outlining the rip-off of Ireland's mineral and gas resources by US multinationals. These led to the setting up of a national pressure group, the Resources Protection Campaign, whose most prominent activist was Eamon Gilmore, then a student in Galway.

Anti-American sentiment was rife because of the Vietnam War and the killing of students in Kent State University in May 1970 by the Ohio National Guard. The students were protesting against the Richard Nixon-inspired American invasion of Cambodia. There was huge international outrage and in Trinity the Internationalists, a Maoist group led by David Vipond, had a field day. I gravitated towards the left and following the shootings in Derry on Bloody Sunday in January 1972, became a bit of a Republican socialist. My friend Frank, a pacifist to the core, surprised me by joining in with a group petrol bombing of the UK-owned Macy's furniture store on our way to witness the burning of the British embassy.

I had rooms in college for two years, one a sabbatical while I was president of the SRC. I shared rooms for a year with Eamon Mallie, a teetotaler, renowned ladies' man and later a prominent broadcaster in Northern Ireland. Other presidents of the SRC in the seventies who went on to become well-known broadcasters include Joe Duffy, Mark Little and Aine Lawlor and her husband, 2fm producer Ian Wilson, who was also a very innovative entertainments officer.

I loved the campus – Front Gate and the Porter's Lodge, the Junior Common Room, the cobbled Front Square, the old basement Buttery, Botany Bay where I roomed, the Fellows' Garden (now occupied by modern buildings), the lunchtime oratory on the Dining Hall steps, the Rubrics and the pavilion in College Park. I once spent two weeks on campus without venturing into the outside world! My only architectural dislike was the catering extension, which even today stands out as a total misfit of a building.

Keeping discipline on campus, especially after the pubs closed, was the responsibility of the deans. The Senior Dean, Professor George Dawson, did little of the donkeywork carried out by the two Junior Deans who patrolled college and tried to keep order. This was particularly difficult on evenings when groups returned from the 'Stations of the Cross' – a pub crawl of fourteen pubs on either side of Grafton Street. The lovable Dr Roy Brown succeeded Brendan Kennelly as Junior Dean and became instantly unlovable as he struggled to contain the high jinks of late-night revellers.

To this day, forty years later (a grandfather and still married to that lovely young English Literature student I met in Trinity), I enjoy entering through the back gate and walking through College Park to meet the cobbled Front Square and relive all those memories of people and events that forged my values and created everlasting friendships.

Eugene Murray (TCD 1968–73; Business Studies) obtained a Master's degree in Economics. He was president of the Students' Representative Council in 1971. On leaving Trinity he became a radio and television producer with RTÉ, a member of its executive board, head of Television Current Affairs, editor of **Today Tonight**, director of Digital Media and director of Business Planning. He is now chief executive of the Irish Hospice Foundation.

EVERYTHING WAS DIFFERENT

robert o'farrell

I WAS IN Trinity from 1968 to 1972 and, to be frank, I find that I am a little hazy as to what took place in what year – and in what decade. And when, for that matter, can we say that the seventies actually began in Ireland – 31 January 1969? It was certainly the sixties when I arrived. Trinity had had its own little riot the summer before, so there was still a whiff of tear gas in the air, mingling with a hint of counterculture from across the Atlantic (together with the feeling of an economy running on empty).

At some stage in my Fresher year I went on my first 'demo' when I joined a well-heeled crew protesting the planned demolition of Georgian houses in Hume Street. Later on I joined another group of revolting students marching against cuts in higher education – or was it the Trinity/UCD merger? I can't remember and I suspect I didn't know then. 'London, Paris, Rome, Berlin,' opined a duo of my fellow *enragés*, 'We shall fight and we shall win!' Then the same two class warriors nearly lynched a confused-looking *Evening Press* delivery boy whose Lambretta had skidded into the mob.

The demonstration I really remember, though, was one that took place on 2 February 1972, three days after Bloody Sunday. We watched from rooms as that huge mass of people, some sombre, some angry, surged up Westmoreland Street, around the front of college (where a huge black banner simply bore the number 'thirteen') and towards the British embassy in Merrion Square. The actual burning of the embassy, which some of us went to watch, was almost a good-humoured affair, although things got nasty later on, when King Mob ran out of control. For people with an English accent, being around in Dublin was a little uncomfortable. Quite soon afterwards the Boat Club travelled north to compete in Derry Head, and that was tricky, too. Interesting times, indeed – perhaps that was when the seventies really started in Ireland.

I had grown up in an Irish household in suburban Surrey and, although I had holidayed in Ireland every year of my life, I had never been to Dublin before I arrived in the city on the Monday of Freshers' Week. Like my contemporary, Donnell Deeny, I can remember the excitement of coming through Front Gate for the first time. (I like to think that it never ceased to thrill, although I also find myself retrospectively attributing a romantic aura to that ghastly London–Holyhead–Dublin journey.) Was not Front Square, to paraphrase Napoleon, 'Dublin's drawing room'? Our manners may not have always been becoming of a drawing room, but what magnificent setting it provided for our student shenanigans – here we cavorted and paraded, showed off our finery and flirted, listened to actors, Internationalists and evangelicals, fled Junior Deans or just hung out. And, although Trinity was a sort of enclave – a walled and gated community, crammed with wonderful buildings and spaces – it was still a public thoroughfare, a short cut from Merrion Square to the Bank of Ireland. You just couldn't keep the city out.

Nor did we want to. Our social life was based on Dublin's pubs and people's flats far more than on the Buttery and rooms. As a Boat Club man I drank in O'Neills on Suffolk Street; there were other pubs for other occasions, but O'Neills was the default watering hole. It was a rather staid city centre pub with wonderful 1950s (or was it 1930s?) décor, where we were expected to behave ourselves. You could sit at a table and ring a bell to summon a barman, who would bring, as well as pints, cream crackers and cheese, served with a jar of mustard. If you were known, Mr Salmon, the manager, would cash a cheque for you, or even treat you to a pint at Christmas. He did ban me once, though.

I lived out in Clontarf during my first term, in digs run by the spinster sisters Brennan (seriously untouched by the sixties). In the morning I enjoyed the view across the bay to the Dublin mountains as the bus passed through

Fairview. I also enjoyed looking at the neat behind of fellow Clontarf resident and later femme fatale, Mary-Ellen Synon, following her as she sashayed north from Abbey Street. Clontarf was limiting though, and the bright lights beckoned, so I took up residence at the St Andrew Hotel, just across the road from The Old Stand. Yes, I lived in a hotel, along with quite a few others students (John Payne, I recall, and Jeremy Kimber). It was what you called a 'commercial hotel', extinct in Ireland now, I imagine, along with high tea. As well as students there were old ladies in permanent residence (very J.G. Farrell) and commercial travellers passing through. I think we paid £3 a week for our bed and breakfast.

After the hotel, I was in a flat on Stephen's Green, where the view from the back was of the Iveagh House gardens, and then the mountains. So my journey to college consisted of an uplifting saunter across the Green and down along Grafton Street. Various friends had flats around (rather than in) Fitzwilliam and Merrion Squares, or on Mount Street, or by the canal or in the finer parts of Ballsbridge. They were more often attics and basements than *piano nobile*, but, still, how lucky we were to be able to live like that! In my final year, as Boat Club captain, I was in Rubrics, in 23.01. Upstairs, denim-clad Professor Webb plied young men with sherry, while many ladies came and went from the rooms of rugby star Dick Spring, later leader of the Labour Party.

My fellow students were certainly a mix in terms of ethnicity. I was aware that around me there were Dutchmen, Nigerians, Americans and at least one Iranian. Most people, though, fell into four basic categories: Northerners (mainly Protestant, some of them quite mad), Dublin Protestant bourgeoisie, the English and the West Brits.

Ah, the West Brits – now there was a tribe untouched by the sixties. They came as quite a shock to a young lad from Surrey. I had met them before, sailing off West Cork, but I never experienced them on their home ground, and never in uniform. The men wore clunky brogues, cavalry twill or corduroy trousers, blazers and soft brown trilby hats. What the women wore below the neck I cannot remember, but their heads were covered with silk scarves, fastened on the chin with huge knots (rather like moderate Muslim women today). They were, by and large, handsome and healthy, despite the fact that many of them lived in Georgian houses with leaky roofs. I was rather terrified of them at first, but grew to know and love many of them later on.

The English came in all shapes and sizes. Among them were the so-called Oxbridge rejects, including me. However, I had come from a very middle-class/ minor-public-school background, and had never met an Old Etonian before, nor the products of any number of schools considered superior to my own. To a Fresher from England, school background appeared to matter quite a lot; later on it didn't because I had sort of 'gone upper-middle' myself (though I never referred to my parents as 'daddy' and 'mummy').

By the time I arrived, Trinity was already cutting down on the English intake, but the real change in the composition of the student body came with the ending, in 1970, of 'the ban' – the decree that forbade Catholics in the Archdiocese of Dublin from attending Trinity. Symbolic of this were the arrival of Father Brendan Heffernan as first Catholic Chaplain, and the celebration of Sunday Mass in the Exam Hall. I remember one day on the riverbank getting a funny look from our sometime coach John Gaskin when I told him that the crew I was coaching were all Catholics and Irish speakers.

There was also the question of gender. I knew about girls, of course, and had even had girlfriends, but I had only brothers at home, and had attended a boys' boarding school, so there was a lot of ignorance. In addition, we were far less aware in those days about girls maturing earlier than us boys, so I was not well prepared for the experience of being around smart, savvy lady sophisticates. Even my female fellow Freshers, now in Trinity Hall, swarmed around Front Square in scary wildebeest-like herds. One got the hang of it eventually, but it might have been better if I had attended that Freshers' Week lecture, 'Male and Female made Him they'.

I joined the Boat Club in Freshers' Week, and rowed for three out of my four years. Having rowed at school, I went straight into the Senior VIII under Captain Desmond Hill (in whose company I still delight at Henley). Although we had won an event before Christmas, I was dropped from the crew after Easter, and I subsequently never really achieved much distinction on the Liffey; I was strong and diligent but, to be frank, no great stylist. I could thrash with the best of them, however, and, being adept at publicly singing the sort of bawdy songs the Boat Club liked to sing, I was made choirmaster, the first Fresher to achieve such a 'distinction'. Thrashing was a big part of life in the Boat Club; that we were better known for it than for winning silverware highlights the fact that we were finding glory on the river (above all, at Henley) harder and harder to achieve. We were hit by the loss of ready-made English oarsmen (better ones than me, that is), by growing academic pressures as exams were moved from September back to May, and by the fact that our Islandbridge rivals – Garda and UCD – produced a succession of very fast crews in my time.

I enjoyed my rowing, though. I liked the challenging athleticism, the company, the travelling to compete in distant parts of Ireland where no other Trinity teams were seen, and where we were still regarded with some respect. Every year we ran a big, two-day regatta at Islandbridge, an amazing achievement for a bunch of students. Crews from England sometimes came over, mainly for action ashore. Tom Freeman was the master of revels; after the Regatta Ball we would retire to his rooms whence a furtive squad would eventually be sent to 'lurk' a barrel from the Buttery bar. How on earth did we keep it up?

In my final year I was made captain. There were still some talented oarsmen in college, but most of them declined to row. Instead we concentrated on producing junior and novice crews. We had some success and disappointments, and our share of good and bad luck. Looking back, I feel the fact that everyone seemed to have enjoyed their rowing – and thrashing – that year was an achievement in itself. None of us at the time, though, could imagine that Trinity would win again at Henley only five years later.

One aspect of Boat Club life that I disliked was the expectation that we would provide a reactionary rent-a-mob every now and again. Once it was something to do with DUCAC (Dublin University Central Athletic Club) and a Springboks tour, while another occasion concerned keeping women out of the Hist. Even worse was the time when, during my year as captain, I was approached by Jane Williams who asked if we would be prepared to let women row. I could see that she was quite serious and highly competent, and my heart shouted 'yes', but I said 'no' because it would have been another damn thing to worry about. I like to think that I have made up for this since, supporting the admission of women when I was captain at a big club in London, and later becoming a keen advocate of women priests and bishops in the Church of England.

Combining the Boat Club with Players, as I did, was unusual, but it made good sense, since I was probably better at acting than rowing (although that is not saying a lot). My Cliff in *Look Back in Anger* (opposite Susan FitzGerald) achieved some good reviews (amazingly, my Welsh accent did not mutate into stage Pakistani). Ditto my Caliban; we toured that production of *The Tempest* (with Michael Colgan, Paolo Tullio and Danny Reardon et al.) down to Cork, to the amazement of my aunts and cousins.

Players was an impressive organization in those days. There was massive talent and I can still remember outstanding productions of *The Glass Menagerie* (with Sorcha Cusack), *The Alchemist,* and *The Importance of Being Earnest,* all staged in that tiny, intimate theatre in the corner of Front Square. I also remember *The Malcontent* at Castletown House and the cycle of medieval mystery plays staged with a huge cast in Front Square, on lorry trailers provided by the Guinness brewery.

Some of the most memorable Players moments were the free Sunday night shows. I was once recruited to go among a troupe of 'modern dancers', flagellating them – mine not to reason why. Another memory was of leaping on stage as Caliban on the black-tie opening night of *The Tempest,* to see Merrily Harpur and Margaret Hickey sitting in the front row, not more than three feet away, with glasses of wine in their hands, their sparkling eyes focused just on me. Later on in the run, I broke wind backstage and the whole house heard it.

Players was very much an English concern, I recall. We Freshers were addressed by the tall, suave Stephen Remington – later director of Sadler's Wells – who finished by saying, 'If you are interested, Petronella will take your names.' Petronella! I'd never met one before, and Players had two! I am very glad that I did Players as well as row; it kept me from developing a Boat Club lager mentality that was easy to slip into. I considerably widened my circle of friends, drank Bloody Marys in The Old Stand, did all manner of new stuff and got my picture on the front page of *The Irish Times,* eating strawberries with Henrietta Mahaffy at the Elizabethan Society garden party.

All that rowing and acting – not to mention *flâneur*ing in Front Square – did not leave much time for academic work. I have to confess that I was a pretty hopeless undergraduate. Lacking a mathematical mind, I wasn't really suited to study Economics. Lectures were optional, and I went to very few. I did enjoy Louis Cullen for Economic History, though; likewise Frank Keating and Ronald Hill for French and Soviet Government (I later taught all three subjects, using my Trinity notes). The Economics Department, under the wonderfully laconic Professor Ryan, was quite go-ahead at the time, giving us frequent tests and eight weeks of lectures. But the tutoring was rubbish; at no stage was I hauled up and ask to explain my slavish underachievement. Overall, I lacked the maturity to develop any real sense of respect for scholarship. I kept my head down in seminars and had no interest in cultivating the company of brilliant scholars such as Andrew Somerville and Patrick Kinsella, both in my year. I remember, as a Fresher (and fresh from success at A levels), looking at a final-year General Studies History paper in Tom Freeman's rooms. Noticing a question on Napoleon, I declared, 'I could do that.' Said wise Tom, 'Ah, but you won't be able to do it by the time you've done four years in Trinity.' Alas, he was right.

I got through end-of-year exams by a sudden burst of very hard work, which rather spoilt Trinity Week for me. My finals, though, were in September, mine being the last year of this strange custom. I was really up against it. It was not a question of revision – I was doing a lot of stuff from scratch, and I was haunted by a real fear of failure. I moved into Front Square rooms at the beginning of August and somehow rekindled the blitz spirit of my A levels. Plans and patterns of work were drawn up and strictly adhered to, topics mastered and ticked off. Morale was maintained with simple pleasures – a pint in O'Neills, or an afternoon trip to the mountains. I think I took up smoking. In many ways, that eight-week 'extra term' through to the end of the exams was my best time in Trinity. My 2:2 placed me right in the middle of my year, more or less the right place. I have reflected since that I might have done if I'd had the maturity to work a lot harder from day one. But would a better 2:2, or even a 2:1, have made much difference to my life and career? Is it not possible that all those hours put in on the river, on stage, in O'Neills and in Front Square might not have made me a better teacher and, who knows, a better class of human being altogether?

Robert O'Farrell (TCD 1968–72; Economics and Politics) taught economics, politics and rowing in a variety of schools and ran a small antiquarian book business. He now lives in Somerset and recently directed a production of Chekhov's **Three Sisters**, sang bass in Mendelssohn's **Elijah**, and did the Glastonbury festival. He doesn't do Twitter.

Robert O'Farrell and Susan FitzGerald in **Look Back in Anger**.

UNFINISHED BUSINESS

susan slott

> 'Decide that you like college life. In your dorm you meet
> many nice people. Some are smarter than you. And some,
> you notice, are dumber than you. You will continue, unfor-
> tunately, to view the world in exactly these terms for the
> rest of your life.'
>
> Lorrie Moore, *How to Become a Writer*, 1985

I HAD WANTED to study in Paris, had wanted to enroll in the *Cours de Langue et Civilization Française* at the Sorbonne and immerse myself in French culture. Actually, what I really wanted to immerse my seventeen-year-old self in was a bohemian life in an atelier shared with a handsome, Gauloise-smoking artist. Oh God, was there also a beret and a matelot shirt involved?

After some gentle intervention by my mother and my teachers at Alexandra College, I was persuaded to at least postpone my Gallic fantasy and apply to Trinity instead. I had arrived at Alex from America via Switzerland, where I spent a year studying at the École Internationale in Geneva. It served as a kind of halfway house between the sunny yet woefully inadequate California public-school system and the dark, austere but educationally superior halls of Alexandra. All this was on the heels of the death of my father after a long illness. The effect of these transitions was monumental, but after oh, thirty or forty years, I was just fine.

Once the decision to apply to Trinity was made – did I have any say? I forget – I spent a year trekking from Earlsfort Terrace, where Alexandra was then housed, to Haddington Road, where I took intensive Latin grinds. My tutor was a centenarian with a worrying penchant for schoolgirls but he got me through my Leaving Cert. with honours and I was accepted into Trinity. I enrolled in English, French and Philosophy, otherwise known as General Studies. I think I felt slightly inferior to those doing the more specialized honors degrees, which makes me sad now, sad that I didn't appreciate the privilege of third-level education.

My memory of the early days is hazy. I do recall thinking that Freshers' Week was like a Middle-Eastern bazaar, but with Old Etonians hawking their wares around Front Square, beseeching the uninitiated to join this club or that, extolling the virtues of societies with mysterious names: the Phil, the Eliz, the Hist. They were like carnival glad-handers, shameless as used-car salesmen, but it was all colourful and heady stuff. I joined the Elizabethan Society for no other reasons than that I liked the name and my aunt had been a member. They had a lovely, big, quiet room where, it being the late sixties, I would go occasionally to meditate. Transcendentally. Well, twice. I'm sure there was a greater purpose to the Eliz, but I never explored what exactly it was.

I found my true home that week, though, when I joined Players, the Dramatic Society, and the little theatre in No. 4 became the cradle in which, for better or worse, I spent my time in college. Walking into the theatre for the first time, with its sawdusty smell and shabby walls, the names of students long gone roughly chiselled into the black flats, I swear it had a beating heart. I must have seen a notice for auditions on the Players' board, a wood-framed glass cabinet inside Regent House that displayed news of all theatrical goings on: readings, cast lists, love letters. In those days Trinity did not yet have a Department of Drama. That wasn't established until the mid eighties, so the only way to learn was to dive in head first. God knows where I found the courage to put my name down to audition for a part in J.P. Donleavy's *Fairytales of New York*. I knew no one and was in the process of figuring out how to camouflage my dread of almost everything. But I read for Sebastian Greene and surprised myself by getting the part. Donnell Deeny was in the cast, a fellow Fresher, and also Dan Shine, an American and a Jew, and therefore safe and familiar to me. I immediately developed a crush on him, though I doubt he ever knew. That happened a lot.

It was after *Fairytales of New York* that I met the two Pauls, Paolo Tullio and Paul McGuinness. Paul cast me in a play (the name of which escapes me now) opposite Paolo. It was, I believe, his directorial debut. He was very good, but I was having difficulty with the part and I have an abiding memory of him during rehearsals, imploring me to be sexy. 'Susie, could you be sexy? Please … could you be sexier?' And I was mortified and swallowed a contact lens – which were like gold in those days – and forgot all my lines. I wonder did I put him off a career as a director, I wonder did I ruin his life? I spent a lot of time with Paolo Tullio, I don't know quite what we did, it wasn't anything romantic, but he is very much part of my Trinity memories. I see him in my mind's eye, a sleek little Italian whippet with beautifully tailored clothes, a magnificent vocabulary, and a great love of the good things in life.

There were some wonderfully ambitious productions in Players. I suppose there is a freedom in university drama from commercial constraints and some-times we could really let rip. There was a spectacular, one-night-only enact-ment of the medieval mystery plays in which I played the Devil and which we performed on huge wooden carts in Front Square lit by flaming torches. There was very serious stuff, of course. I remember doing a harrowing reading of Peter Weiss's *The Investigation*, directed by Patrick Boyd-Maunsell, dealing with the atrocities of Auschwitz, and it took me ages to recover. But mostly I was involved in comedy, and mostly it was written by Richard Fegen, Andy Norriss and James Morris. They wrote such wonderful revues, all smart and funny and innovative, with great music by a certain Chris de Burgh (known to us then as Chris Davison), Jerry de Bromhead, Adrian Brunton and Shaun Davey. *Nuts in May*, *Just Add Water*, *Baroque Bottom* and *Mellow*, to mention a few. We brought *Baroque Bottom* down to the Wexford Opera Festival one year for a late-night run at White's Hotel. The stellar cast, made up of gorgeous Sorcha Cusack (with whom everyone was in love), Richard, Andy, James, all under the kind and ever-patient eye of B.A. Maxwell, rented a foul-smelling cottage in Kylemore Quay. We woke every morning under sheets sodden from condensation and at night no one came to see the show, so both bodies and spirits were dampened. It was a great introduction to the glamour of showbiz.

And there were pantos, a tradition only vaguely familiar to me then. I remember a beautifully cast *Treasure Island* with the larger-than-life Johnny McCormick as Long John Silver, little Cockney Dave Burke as his sidekick, the Parrot, and I think the multi-talented Cathy Roberts was there, too. Occasionally, Richard would ask some of us down to his family home in Offaly to rehearse whatever show we were doing. Once, a few of us were invited to the Westmeath Hunt Ball. It was delightful. The hunters were all lovely, jolly people who drank G&Ts and told funny stories. And never once did my young mind make the connection between what actually went on during a hunt and this witty cocktail banter. Not once. And I'm a vegetarian, for Christ's sake.

My uncle, who is ninety and a Trinity graduate, told me that in his day almost everyone, staff and student alike, was English. I came in at the tail end of this long era and I'm so grateful I had a chance to experience that almost Oxbridge-like atmosphere. I became close to many English students studying here on government grants, and even though initially they seemed intimidating, possessing a sophistication and polish beyond their years, really, adulthood was new to us all. It is extraordinary to think that it was only in 1970 that Trinity's doors were opened to Irish Catholics. Sadly, even today, I know Dubliners who have never set foot inside the gates, and who would find the idea of a stroll through this city centre oasis far too daunting.

I went to the Trinity Ball one summer night. It was touching to see everyone wafting across a moonlit Front Square in flowing gowns and dinner jackets instead of the scruffy sheepskin coats and wedge heels that were de rigueur at the time. How there were not more injuries sustained by trying to negotiate cobblestones in those towering shoes, never mind Isadora Duncan-like tragedies from the long scarves we all wore, I do not know. But everyone scrubbed up well and Trinity looked beautiful. We stayed out all night and went to an early-opening pub, but truth be told I think I was a little disappointed by the whole experience and happy to go home.

I was living in a tiny top-floor flat in Kildare Street above an old Dublin establishment with the Runyonesque name of Jules the Barber. I shared this with my mother and briefly, my younger sister as well, before she became a child bride at seventeen and one of the few young mothers to enter Trinity in the early seventies. It was a joy to be just a hop and a skip from college, the next-best thing to having 'rooms', which were not available to female students anyway. We paid the princely sum of £12 a week, lived there for a year, and then moved out to my mother's cottage in Glencullen. The sublime to the ridiculous, or the other way around? I'm not sure.

I remember getting a lift (curiously, considering the distance from Trinity to Kildare Street) late one night with Chris Davison. He was dropping Andy Russell, the beautiful Susan FitzGerald, Paolo Tullio and myself to our respective homes. Out of the blue he decided that we would drive to the de Burgh family castle in Wexford. Susan wisely insisted in getting out of the car, but the rest of us carried on. Paolo was in the back on a different sort of trip altogether. Andy, always good-humorously decadent, probably had the comfort of a hip flask and I spent the whole time fretting about how worried my mother would be if I didn't come home. We arrived in the middle of the night, were greeted warmly and hospitably by Chris's family, and shown to our (separate) rooms. The next morning after breakfast we drove home again. Sex, drugs, rock and roll? Not.

I suppose everyone had their own patch in Trinity, their own private, well-worn path and in my case it was Kildare Street to theatre to Buttery to lecture halls. Ah, lectures, how incidental they became in my university career! And yet I had the best of teachers, wonderful poets like Eiléan Ní Chuilleanáin and Brendan Kennelly. What was I thinking? What *was* I thinking? I struggled with philosophy, or rather, I struggled with logic. This was not what I had signed up for. The Wax Argument, perhaps, but P vel Q? N ~ R? What nightmare world was this? I took grinds in the Buttery from a fellow student, and passed, but I heard later that he had failed. I felt terrible. I hope I didn't ruin his life, too.

Most students in Players whizzed industriously about with so much talent and enthusiasm and energy, all the while, in the background, studying for their degrees. I, on the other hand, succumbed to the lure of the Buttery. It was my gateway bar and I began to seriously neglect my studies. In those days I took flight the way others took drugs and at the end of my second year I left Trinity. I told no one on the staff I was going; I simply and surprisingly escaped into a short-lived marriage.

I did go back to do a couple of Players' productions, which was probably not allowed. One of them, *Black Comedy*, directed by the gifted Deirdre Keir, won an award at the All Ireland University Drama Festival in Cork. And I did two summer seasons with a small rep company, Metamorphix, which hired the theatre during the three- or four-month summer break. I never returned as a student.

Last year I attended a play in the sparkling, well-equipped theatre that serves the university now. I had not crossed Front Square for a very, very long time and as I did I experienced, fleetingly, the most delicious frisson of optimism and anticipation and I wondered: what will I do when I grow up?

Susan Slott (TCD 1968–70) has been working in Dublin on stage, television and radio for over thirty-five years. She is married and has two adult sons, both of whom are musicians. She still hopes to study in Paris one day.

A COUNTRY PROD IN PURSUIT OF A NEW IRELAND

ted smyth

I CAME UP to Trinity in 1968 without a clear idea of my own Irishness. I did not realize that many others, including Trinity itself, were searching for a new identity amidst profound change and dissatisfaction with the state of Irish politics. I was unhappy with the old models on offer: the detached Protestant Irish model with a shadow of original guilt hanging over the past, or the exaggerated Catholic nationalist model of the Patrick Pearse school that had been mythologized during the fiftieth anniversary of the Rising two years earlier.

Trinity was a startling liberation for me. I had no idea that behind that cold Palladian front there could be such an abundance of choice, identity, hope, imagination, debate and friendship. In my four years from 1968 to 1972 I was never bored for a minute. There was too much going on and we had the freedom and security to explore beyond our comfort levels. Trinity was an incubator for the changes that were challenging the religious, social and political verities of Ireland. This was not the 'Protestant garrison' that was the subject of sneers, nor the affected Trinity of J.P. Donleavy's *The Ginger Man*, frolicking among the 'Oirish'. This was a Trinity that itself was seeking a new role as it helped to create a New Ireland. Some challenged authority in the company of hundreds of other students (and professors like the late Kader

Asmal, Mary Bourke Robinson and David Thornley) who were fed up with the denial of fundamental rights, whether in South Africa, Northern Ireland or, at home in the Republic, to women and the poor. The Catholic Church's ban on the faithful attending Trinity was based on a fear they might become Protestant, but by 1970, when the ban was lifted, the greater fear in Trinity and UCD was that the faithful would think for themselves. A popular ditty at the time satirized the ban: 'Your young men may loot, pillage and rape, and even have carnal knowledge, but however depraved, their souls will be saved, if they don't go to Trinity College.'

Yes, Trinity was becoming 'Irish' as we moved through the seventies but it was melding into a different sort of Ireland, a questioning, non-sectarian, inclusive and confident Ireland. In 1970, George Dawson, Professor of Genetics, predicted that by 1975 Catholics would comprise 60 per cent of the student body at Trinity, compared to 40 per cent at the time and concluded that the university would become 'increasingly representative of the Catholic tradition'. Professor Dawson has been proved wrong as young Irish men and women embraced a broader, more secular identity over the following decades. In 2008, my nephew Tim Smyth, the then auditor of the Hist, invited me to chair the Honorary Members' debate and Trinity seemed even more dedicated to the liberal pursuit of knowledge.

IF TRINITY WAS was an incubator of change, the Hist was a Petri dish where the issues of the day were fiercely debated. In my first weeks I was drawn to the successor to Edmund Burke's Debating Club where I learned as much about politics as in class. Notable exceptions were lectures by Moody, McDowell, Aidan Clarke, Jim Lydon and David Thornley. The latter was elected to the Dáil as a Labour member and he invited politicians to joust with us in seminars, including Cathal Goulding, chief of staff of the Official IRA. I once asked Thornley how he reconciled his Marxist and Catholic loyalties. With a broad smile, he said, 'Smyth, you're a bastard.'

I was elected to the Hist committee for the Bicentenary session of 1970. I remember being disappointed by the dullness of Senator Kennedy's rather academic address (and puzzled by his ill-fitting formal trousers that were above his ankles) when he opened the week of Bicentenary celebrations in March.

That night, Teddy displayed little of the fire and hope that Bobby had stirred up in the 1968 presidential campaign before his assassination. And the next night Gene McCarthy's speech to the Hist equally failed to capture the excitement of his presidential campaign when his surprisingly high anti-war vote in New Hampshire had convinced LBJ not to seek a second term. We seemed to be witnessing the death of American liberalism, with the left unable to understand how their divisions had handed the election to Nixon and emboldened the forces of reaction and war.

By contrast, in Ireland and Trinity, the seventies offered new hope and, finally at the end of that first week of Hist events in March 1970 we heard something different and exciting. It was termed the 'Irish Debate' on the subject 'That Emmet's epitaph be now written'. I had not heard John Hume speak before in person and his speech that night was fresh and visionary. He spent the next forty years consistently preaching the same message of non-violent politics to bring peace and justice to Northern Ireland. He never wavered when many others were 'sneakin' regarders' of violence or when British policies were so inept as to increase support for the Republican and Loyalist death squads. Hume also was instrumental in convincing Irish-American leaders like Ted Kennedy, Speaker Tip O'Neill, Pat Moynihan and Hugh Carey (the Four Horsemen) to lean on the British to adopt a policy of equality between the two allegiances in the North. Many historians sneer at the 'great person' school of history but John Hume stands out in my mind since that time as the person who did more than anyone else to bring peace to Northern Ireland.

In 1972 I was halfway through my final year at Trinity when we heard on the radio that British paratroopers had opened fire on unarmed marchers in Derry. I was auditor of the Hist and we adjourned our meeting the following Wednesday, 2 February, 'as a mark of respect to the thirteen people killed in Derry on Bloody Sunday'.

We were furious and helpless with rage, all the more so those of us who were non-violent constitutionalists. Whether it was internment in 1971 or Bloody Sunday in 1972, it seemed the British could never get it right. That Wednesday night I joined a protest march on the British embassy in Merrion Square. It was misty and dark as we stood outside the embassy when we heard glass breaking and saw flames shoot out of the windows. The burning of the

British embassy seemed to me at the time like a natural symbolic reaction; the staff had emptied the building, the Gardaí stood aside and no lives were threatened. However, such acts also contributed to the murderous cycle of retaliation that followed.

In addition to the North, the other compelling issue that impinged on our Trinity bubble was whether Ireland should join the European Community. At Hist debates since de Gaulle's veto of British entry in 1963, the mood had swung for and against membership. In the summer of 1971 I was hitchhiking around Italy with fellow history student Hugh Frazer, on our way to link up with Jenny Graham, a beautiful and charming student from London. I bored them both regarding what line I would take on membership of the EC at my inaugural address in October. I seem to recall that Hugh saw some merit in EC policies that countered social inequality and he later went on to become head of Combat Poverty in Ireland (and to marry the bright Hist committee member, Hilary Simms). In the end I decided that the loss of our sovereignty was too big a risk to take and that our interests would be ignored by the big powers. Instead of being subject to one large power Ireland would be at the mercy of three and capital would flow to the centre and away from the peripheries.

The Hist was eclectic and lively in the early seventies, debating both serious and not so serious issues. There were votes in favour of legalizing abortion, a secular constitution, and liberating women and votes against Stormont, the use of political violence, the release of Lt Calley (responsible for the My Lai massacre) and the proposed Arts Block. Happily, the motion that 'Sex kills romance' was also defeated (I invited Peter Sellers, but he declined, regretting the fact that he could not come 'to dirty up dear dirty Dublin'). The motion that 'Mad dogs are preferable to Englishmen' was carried, largely with the support of visiting teams from the Glasgow Union and Edinburgh Spec.

Most Irish people are now familiar with Shane Ross, who has earned a deserved reputation as the scourge of greed and ineptitude. At the Hist he was an iconoclastic and witty debater who also seemed in search of his Irish identity, having been sent to an English public school. Richard Clarke, who preceded me as record secretary, became a respected Church of Ireland bishop in the new non-sectarian Ireland. Ernie Bates was a dangerously charming advocate for the school of violent Republicanism. Donnell Deeny preceded me as auditor and, to no one's surprise, is a judge of the Northern Ireland High Court. Director of Public Prosecutions Jim Hamilton and I faced off for election to auditor. During my tenure he sportingly remained fully involved as the leader of the 'loyal' opposition and nearly impeached me one night, until by 4 am exhaustion had set in and some additional allies had been roused from bed. My treasurer, Donal Donovan, appropriately became a financial advisor to the IMF. He had an unfortunate habit of bursting into my rooms on Front Square to wake me mid morning to deal with some crisis or other. Declan Kiberd, who succeeded me as auditor, was a brilliant and impish debater who is a celebrated Professor of English at UCD and columnist in *The Irish Times*. Donal Curtin seemed perpetually amused at life and became a senior economic advisor to the New Zealand government. James Connolly, the Censor, was a strong debater and became auditor two years later, Two years later, Mary Harney became the first female auditor, displaying a political gift that subsequently enabled her to become tánaiste.

Lectures were stimulating although we were dreadfully underworked compared to the suffering of engineers and doctors. I under-appreciated the joys of Jim Lydon's exam questions such as, 'How important was the so-called Geraldine supremacy as a fact in Irish political life in the fifteenth century?' Or Professor Otway-Ruthven's 'Discuss the character of the French monarchy under Philip the Fair'. The Ott, who had been finally recognized in 1968 as the first woman fellow in Trinity, threw me out of one of her classes for not wearing a gown – 'Mr Smyth, you are academically *neuude*' – but I got my revenge by organizing the Otway-Ruthven Bloomer Football contest. She showed real class by presenting the voluminous knickers I had bought at Clery's to the winning team.

We students were now agitating for more say in our affairs and one result was that John Healy (later president of Atlantic Philanthropies) and I became the first student representatives on the History School committee. In a February 1970 memo we argued reasonably that Latin should not be an admission requirement to the School of History and that British history should not alone be part of the core in the first two years, but should be broadened to include all European history. We also argued that the final exams should begin before the end of September, which at the time resulted in grades not being known until the middle of October! This archaic custom meant that two years of exams were crunched into five days with two three-hour exams every day. It buggered up the summer holidays and gave one a false sense of comfort during the school year. I still have nightmares of, one week before the final exam, opening a folder on a class I had taken in my Junior Sophister year (Eighteenth-Century Economic History?) and finding nothing in it.

I made enduring friendships in History classes, including the centered and world-wise Jonathan Bailey who, with the gregarious and hilarious law student, Joanna Kennedy, became the organizers of our History/Law social group. Mrs Sheila Harbison was our class mother and the actual mother of the state pathologist at that time, John Harbison. Recently widowed, she had decided to get a degree and she kept many of us sane as we battled with our demons. Clodagh O'Brien spoke beautiful French and took her focus on social justice to Brussels where she works on African development. We had weekend outings to Wicklow and, being fairly penniless, were grateful for the hospitality on Sunday evenings provided by Jonathan's parents or by Justin McCarthy's mother. Justin had grown up in Beirut when his father was one of the first Irish army officers assigned to UN peacekeeping duties.

We were none of us wealthy and evenings in Slatts were limited by the cost of a pint. It was much more affordable to get drunk on cheap wine or sherry at club gatherings or in rooms. My white-tie outfit for the Hist cost £5 at the Council for the Blind on Dawson Street, where the racks of tailcoats were a monument to the passing of the Anglo-Irish. Cars were an asset in socializing and my parents had bequeathed me an imported London taxi that could accommodate quite a few. Trouble was it had a faulty starter and on frosty mornings I would give passers-by the choice of turning the key or spraying ether into the gasket to fire the engine. There were the horsey balls and the Trinity balls but these were the exception. More socializing was done in the cave of the Buttery or on the soup runs where we searched for homeless people who had not found shelter from the wet night. Every year I took part in the Belfast–Dublin Walk and finally completed it in 1971 with the help of loyal friends who took turns to keep me company on the road. I walked the 104 miles in thirty-two hours non-stop, a testimony to doggedness if nothing else. Many of us sang in the Choral Society, loving the *B Minor Mass* and *Oratorio* under the direction of Dr Groocock, who urged us in his thick German accent to have what sounded like sexual rehearsals. My room-mate in Front Square was Dermot Agnew, a Northerner and a very talented musician and organist, now based in London.

There were really no drugs in our group but a reasonable amount – though never enough – of sex. It wasn't flaunted as people discretely paired off, quite a few later doing the decent thing and getting married, Tony Aston to fellow law student Jenny Thomas, Arthur Moran to Amanda McVittie, Patsy Read to James McCarthy-Morrogh and Sally Figgis to Colin Keane.

The juiciest sex scandal relating to our time occurred twenty-five years later in London. Rupert Pennant Rea, who was a year ahead of me in History, became editor of the *Economist* and then deputy governor of the Bank of England, the heir presumptive to Eddie George. Unfortunately for him, he hooked up with another former student from Trinity, Mary Ellen Synon. The relationship subsequently cooled on his side and scorned, Mary Ellen took the steamy story to the tabloids, giving birth to the memorable headline, 'The Bonk of England'.

Like most students I was assigned to digs for the first two years. I was lucky to live with Miss (not Ms in those days) Helen Fleming in 117 Leinster Road. A fellow lodger, Richard Pine, wrote later in an *Irish Times* obituary that it was probably the only digs where the lodgers conspired against the landlady and insisted on putting up the rent. Miss Fleming had a heart of gold. She was devoted to her ancient auntie and her four students who doubled up in the front two rooms of a Victorian-style villa. She insisted on mixing two English and two Irish students and would grill us on why we didn't have a social life if we came home before midnight. On dreary Sundays when we felt homesick but were also sick of home, she brightened us up with pancakes laced with whiskey. Because of Miss Fleming's generous habit of buying us fabulous food and drink when she had money, we had to work out a staggered system of paying the rent so that there would be some funds for meals at the end of the month. Her first generation of students included my cousin-in-law, Homan Potterton, former curator of the National Gallery, who has written an excellent book on growing up Protestant in rural Ireland.

We organized protests against the proposed Arts Block in Trinity on the grounds that nobody should tamper with the unique and extraordinary beauty of Trinity College. By the grace of patronage from Grattan's Parliament, we enjoyed one of the most beautiful and spectacular eighteenth-century campuses in the world. Even on depressing, rainy days I never ceased to be comforted by this oasis within the city centre, with the broad expanse of Front Square highlighted by Charles Lanyon's campanile and flanked by Chambers' Examination Hall and Chapel. The campus is only forty-two acres, and constantly adding buildings for the worthwhile goal of accommodating more students destroys a unique college, when more imaginative and forward-looking planners would have established a second college elsewhere in the city.

In 1972 I invited Professor Heuston of the Law School to speak at a debate opposing the Arts Building. He declined, writing that the 'promoters of the building have adopted the motto "never explain or apologize" and I don't believe there is the slightest chance of them changing their mind'. In 1965, thirteen houses in Lower Fitzwilliam Street had been demolished, despoiling one of the most magnificent Georgian streets in the world, and replaced with a Soviet-era design by Sam Stephenson for the ESB. Many of our local protests tried to prevent a recurrence of this vandalism, especially the later Hume Street destruction.

In my final year at Trinity I applied to become a third secretary in the Irish Diplomatic Service. I was the first member of my family to join the Irish government service but it seemed like a natural extension of the journey I had begun in the sixties, identifying with and participating in the shaping of our nation, rather than standing on the sidelines. I was encouraged to apply by Freddie Boland, Trinity's chancellor, who had a prominent diplomatic career and who had broken his gavel as president of the United Nations General Assembly, trying to bring Khrushchev to order. A number of my fellow history students were also recruited to the Irish Diplomatic Service, including Brian Nason, Eugene Hutchinson, Paul Murray and Isolde Moylan. This was a time when scores of English recruiters came to Trinity, so I applied to Lloyds bank and Ford, mostly, I must admit, to get free trips to London.

As I look back nearly forty years later I realize that my sense of identity has broadened considerably, as has that of those Trinity friends who continued to live in Ireland. I had the privilege of fifteen exciting years in Irish diplomacy and then took leave of absence in 1988 to live in the United States, which my wife, Mary Breasted, had missed since we left New York in 1981. I was also curious to see what life was like outside the cloisters of diplomacy and to explore the business sector that is meant to generate the jobs and taxes necessary for general prosperity. I was asked by one business leader if I wanted to serve God or Mammon. It seemed like a false choice since the overriding purpose of business should be to benefit society. (Interestingly, the work culture did not differ that much in practice; when asked the difference between the private and public sector, one diplomat friend joked, 'In the private sector it's dog eat dog, but here it's just the opposite.')

While I hold Irish and American passports, I feel at heart a citizen of the world, as well as Ireland, the United States and Europe. We have all become more interdependent than ever in the face of globalization, the diffusion of power, terrorism and climate change. The most important challenge of our time is to tackle the obscenity of growing inequality. We must create a new economic model that gives men and women the dignity of earning a decent living and which protects us from reckless boom bust cycles. And as Ireland struggles through another crisis of confidence, we can take heart from Heaney's 'The Cure at Troy':

> History says, don't hope
> On this side of the grave.
> But then, once in a lifetime
> The longed-for tidal wave
> Of justice can rise up,
> And hope and history rhyme.

Ted Smyth (TCD 1968–72; History and Political Science) worked as a diplomat on the Irish peace process, was chief administrative officer of the Heinz Company and is today executive vice-president of McGraw-Hill in New York. He is a trustee of the Ireland Funds, Glucksman Ireland House and the Clinton Institute in UCD.

PLAYING THE FOOL

paolo tullio

IT WAS NEW to me in more ways than one. I'd arrived in Trinity fresh-faced
from an English public school with improbably high expectations of what I
was going to find there. I was sure that after the cloistered life of boarding
school, in university I'd find young minds of high intellect, of questing curiosity and a level of sophistication that I had not yet experienced. I know, I
know, it was perhaps more than a little optimistic. Still, Trinity was in Dublin,
and after the bucolic backdrop of rural Somerset, there was the excitement of
urban life, the other prong of novelty for me.

The Trinity of those years – the cuspal years that covered the end of the
sixties and the start of the seventies – was a mix of Northern Irish students on
a beneficent grant, public-school boys like me who had failed to gain entry to
Oxbridge, a smattering of Church of Ireland students and a very small band
of Catholics. This lack of Catholic representation was due to the diktat of
John Charles McQuaid, Archbishop of Dublin, who had decreed that Catholics going without his express permission would be excommunicated. Since I
had already been excommunicated – you should know that the simple act of
reading a Protestant bible results in an automatic excommunication – I really
didn't give a toss what the old dinosaur thought.

Like all newcomers to any institution I wanted to be noticed. I affected a rather thin goatee beard and Carnaby Street clothes – Mr Fish shirts and kipper ties, knee-length boots, and, in particular, a rather fine gold brocade cape with a high black velvet collar and a walking cane. Thus attired I did manage to look different from those students in jeans and T-shirts, as well as looking like a proper prick.

I'd come to Trinity to study Legal Science, mostly to please papa, who was himself a doctor of jurisprudence. The student lawyers were an interesting bunch and I found myself drawn to a young man from Lurgan called Donnell Deeny, who was gifted with a fiercely bright intellect. After a few weeks he said, 'I think you might like to meet a friend of mine, Paul McGuinness.' It seems that they'd been best friends all through their years at Clongowes.

The meeting was arranged and sure enough Paul and I got on like a house on fire. Paul was more iconoclastic than Donnell, more inclined to risky behaviour, and so this inclination of his, coupled with mine, ensured that our first year was spent behaving very badly. Remember that this was the era when many things arrived simultaneously – the contraceptive pill, great music and drugs – and combined with youth and a sense of immortality, that was a heady mixture.

Very early on I met another ex-public-school boy called Richard Fegen, who got me involved with Trinity Players by asking me to take part in a review he had written called *Nuts in May*. I'd been involved with dramatics ever since prep school, but having a proper theatre to play with was a real thrill. And that began my love affair with Trinity Players.

Although my attire was odd enough, I wasn't the only one who dressed egregiously. There was a student I'd noticed as he strode across Front Square; he had a russet moustache and he always wore a sports jacket with white trousers and a flat cap. No jeans and T-shirt for him, either. I finally got to meet him during a production of *Andorra* where I'd been typecast as the village idiot and he was playing the third pike-bearer. His name was Michael Colgan, a Dublin Catholic and therefore a fellow excommunicant. I liked him enormously – he had a ready wit and a kind of street smart, something unknown to those of us who had grown up in the sheltered communities of boarding schools.

Trinity Players became my home. I spent much more time in No. 4 than I ever did anywhere else – like in tutorials, in the library or in lectures. It was in Trinity Players that I made my friends. There was Chris Davison, another public-school boy who had the extraordinary talent of writing really tuneful melodies, which he'd sing while accompanying himself on his guitar. There were nights at parties when Michael Colgan was inclined to say to Chris, 'Just Beatles tonight, Chris, none of your makey-uppy stuff.' There was Chris Meehan, amazing on the piano, Dillie Keane, another pianist and a terrific comedienne. Like a carousel, we'd combine for a new show, disband, then regroup in a new combination for another new show.

My first year went by in this whirlwind of plays, reviews and pantomimes and then it was time for the end-of-year exams. It was abundantly clear to me that I hadn't done remotely enough study of all things legal to pass the first-year exams, so I took Paul McGuinness's advice. 'Do the course that I'm doing. It's called Mental and Moral, there are only four lectures a week, and they're all in the afternoon. That would suit you.' And it did; I enjoyed it far more than learning about the law. It also gave me more time to enjoy Trinity Players.

Mental and Moral was divided into two – philosophy and psychology – hence its name. It was in the psychology classes that I met Bernard Griffin, intense, highly intelligent, and like me, keen to explore the wonders of psychedelia. And oh, did we explore. We began to wonder after a while if there was a drug out there anywhere that we didn't like. Illicit substances and whole days spent in Trinity Players were great fun, but not particularly good for the academic side of Trinity. Having missed too many lectures, tutorials and term essays, I found myself downgraded to General Studies, which meant I could still continue with philosophy and psychology, but now I added English to complete the three necessary subjects for this most gentle of degrees. I was lucky, I had Brendan Kennelly and David Norris to inspire me to a greater love of language.

Together with Paul McGuinness and Chris Davison, I began to take an interest in Trinity's student publications – TCD *Miscellany* and *Trinity News*. I loved writing articles under assumed noms de plume, like the Greek Mikokis Sturdi, or Ivor Biggan, or Hugh Jarce. Meanwhile Paul devoted himself to the Health Page while Chris wrote under the improbable alias of Denis Oddfinger. Eventually Paul became the editor of TCD *Miscellany*, which gave him great scope for his biting wit. Unfortunately it ended badly when Brendan Kennelly, in his position of dean of discipline, decided to end Paul's academic career in his last year over something he had published. I can't remember what it was, only that it was relatively harmless. You could argue that possibly this was the catalyst that began Paul's stellar career in the music business, but Kennelly's act still rankles with Paul to this day and I suspect that peace will not prevail between them.

I suppose it was inevitable that two big personalities were going to clash, and eventually they did, when both Paul and Michael ran for the position of chairman of Trinity Players. In Paul's mind, and mine too, the result was a foregone conclusion. Paul had directed a number of highly acclaimed plays, whereas Michael had not. It was a profound shock to us both that when the results of the ballot were counted, Michael had won. It was perhaps the first time that we learned of his skills in manipulation, the same skills that have made him the international impresario he is today. He had cleverly sold himself to the voters not as a talent, but as a skilful manager. Although this caused a period of no-speaky between Michael and Paul, eventually they reconciled and are, even today, still firm friends.

It was through Michael that I met Eddie Shorts, who I remember had impressed me with his dancing skills. I loved Eddie; he was quick-witted and funny and made a perfect sparring partner for Michael. After Paul had been forced to leave Trinity, I spent more and more time with Michael. We began to write pantomimes together, with such wonderful titles as *We've All Maid Marion*, which was a camp 'men in tights' years before the idea occurred to Mel Brooks. Naturally all the gang was in it: Dillie Keane as Maid Marion, Roly Saul as Friar Tuck, Chris Davison (later to become Chris de Burgh) as a wandering minstrel, Roger Greene as the wicked sheriff, Eddie Shorts as Alan-a-Dale, Paul McGuinness as the Frenchman, and myself as the campest Robin ever. Michael also directed it. I was looking at the script recently and it's full of all-time great comedy lines, like, 'Where's Robin?'

'Out riding.'

'Horseback?'

'No, not yet.'

Or the eponymous 'Who's Maid Marion?'

'We've all made Marion.'

Timeless, immortal comedy.

I think it was after the run of this particular panto that Michael and I were discussing high art. 'Have you noticed,' I ventured, 'that when we put on a comedy there are queues waiting to get in, but if we do a piece of Brecht you can end up playing to a house of four?' I often wonder if this early experience has coloured his choices for the Gate.

My collaboration with Michael continued, with him directing me in a play called *Sammy*, a one-hander, which we took to the IUDA festival in Galway. I remember that we got up the noses of all the other competing universities because we Trinity Players were staying in the Great Southern Hotel, while they were all staying in B&Bs in the outskirts. Actually we revelled in this lack of fairness and anyway, we walked away with the trophy, adding victory to our perceived patrician snobbishness.

During my second year my parents had left Dublin to return to Italy and I found myself with a fine flat in Herbert Street, just across Merrion Square from Back Gate. This nearness to my place of study didn't prevent me from driving to College Green every day. God be with the days when you could park there unmolested. I had a handsome white Italian sports car, designed by Bertone, which I felt needed to be seen. The Italian number plate also had the advantage of making parking fines unenforceable.

Between the car, the flash flat and more money each week than I could spend, sent monthly by my kind papa, I had a better standard of living then than I have had ever since. Unlike my poorer peers of the time who have now amassed great fortunes, I seem to have travelled in the opposite direction, going from a gilded youth to a parsimonious middle age. This too has given those Trinity years a golden hue – years of youth, disposable income, fun and parties.

Whether it's the effect of too many illicit substances or simply advancing years I'm unsure, but the fact is my memories of those happy days are sparse. When old Trinity friends start sentences with, 'Do you remember the time when …', inevitably my answer is, 'No, not really.' Somehow some of the best years of my life seem to have faded from my memory, which I hope excuses the exiguity of this memoir.

But the greatest gift I got from the Trinity years was the friendships that I made then, friendships that I continue to treasure and that thankfully are still there to be enjoyed. It was a golden time for all of us and it gave us a sense of

invulnerability, a useful sensation to have in a world of uncertainties. To paraphrase Viv Stanshall of The Bonzo Dog, if I had those years to spend again, I
would waste them in exactly the same way I wasted them the first time around.

Paolo Tullio went to TCD in 1968 to study Legal Science. This proved to be
a mistake, so he changed to Mental and Moral – philosophy and psychology.
After spending a year in Trinity Players instead of in study, he was asked to leave
Mental and Moral and do a General Studies degree, which he completed. He
writes for the **Irish Independent**, does a weekly radio slot with Sean Moncrieff
and has been in nine series of the TV show **The Restaurant**. He has published
four books and has appeared in a few movies.

A SENTIMENTAL EDUCATION

antony farrell

TIME IN TRINITY was determined by space. Those elliptical boundary walls
and railings encompassing squares and crescents, rectangles and rhomboids,
horizontally determined, vertically expressed. Beyond, the babble of voices, the
rumble of rubber on tarmac; above, the melancholy long screech of wheeling
seagulls. It presented a grey spectrum in contrast to the glorious technicolour
of the previous month's Isle of Wight festival with Alvin Lee, Roger Daltry, Joni
Mitchell, Jimi Hendrix, Leonard Cohen et al. We were birds of passage all of us,
69ers marooned in the seventies, hungry for love.

It began with the journey east from Westmeath, trunks strapped to a car,
down the Old Cabra Road – destination 13 Palmerston Road, Rathmines. A
group of us lodged with Mrs Becker, a Cork tea-merchant's widow of formidable mien, who cooked for her 'boys' each morning, fag in one hand, frying
pan in the other. We were a callow crew: myself; Charles Naper, my stepbrother;
Jonathan Shackleton and Peter Newell – all fresh from English public schools,
Harrow, Stowe and Wellington, by way of those preparatory Irish dormitories
Headfort and Castle Park.

The 128 bus took us from Palmerston Road into college. Its conductor was
a fellow autodidact eager to share his reading. Mrs Becker's sons had left their
black Penguin Classics within reach of our candlewick beadspreads – all the

European masters, Chekhov, Tolstoy and Turgenev; Balzac, Flaubert, Fournier, Sartre and Stendhal, a lodestar. Marquez I found tortuous, Borges a joy. The dialogues of Plato and interstices of Lucretius became roads to freedom.

I elected to study Economics, a new discipline, a compound of maths and sociology that was neither science nor humanity. (I'd been a whizz at the subject at school and mistakenly believed it might be a path to an unknown career.) I endured and looked around, enlivened by government advisor Basil Chubb but lowered by the scald of Northerners who surrounded me, bent on commerce, scorning clubs and other frivolities. They were fulfilling parental expectations in the degree factory that was Trinity, eschewing girls and culture but not drink, afforded by British grants (though they were but subjects of the UK). I switched to History after a year, my path to English blocked by Brendan Kennelly.

Fifteen months later, in February 1972, after Bloody Sunday, we citizens of the Republic were to learn something of our past on the streets as we fire-bombed the British embassy (the first time since the Boxer Rebellion in China). Only Shackleton was with me that day (Newell had opted out after year one, while Naper stayed on in Machu Picchu). It was our 9/11, and what conse-quences it had, politicizing if not radicalizing a generation. There was a march in London – where a future pop impresario showed initiative at the head of the protest by delivering fourteen empty coffins to Whitehall – with scaffolding poles strewn under Metropolitan Police horses and tear gas thrown into the House of Commons. It was the deepening of a tribal clash in the north-east that was to last another thirty years.

MY SECOND-YEAR FACULTY teachers brought personality to the table, feeding and informing us as they could. David Thornley was colourful and thuggish-looking, his florid countenance a shade deeper than his MG; he purportedly packed heat in class, a small Luger beneath one armpit, a rumoured flask of gin beneath the other. His subject was the late modern – 1916 and all that. He had poliltical ambition and was a brief star in the ascendant. J.G. Simms was my 'moral tutor', brother of the Protestant Archbishop of Dublin, mild of manner and wearily disengaged from life. He taught Jacobite history and brought his class on an annual visit to the site of the Battle of the Boyne, where we tram-pled the rich fields of that unlovely valley in search of monuments, conjuring enactments and finding solace in Slane's Conyngham Arms. Theodore Moody held impassive seances in No. 42 New Square where we pondered other aspects of seventeenth-century Ireland. His passion was for Beethoven, on whose noble bust his own head was said to be modelled. His Quakerdom was manifest in astringent rules for punctuation and capitalization passed down to the History School – a copy-editor at heart, he imposed order on the unruly. An invitation to his home to quaff sherry with his charming wife was a welcome rite of passage. Aidan Clarke, a 1640s specialist, was a gentle bear of a man, all pipe and eyebrows. He imparted erudition with a twinkle, scattering the seeds of learning in impeccable Hiberno-English. His colleague Louis Cullen dwelt in the eighteenth century with little concession to his listeners, speaking without pause or paragraphing in a rapid, toneless monologue, incoming waves of fact and interpretation challenging the surfers to stay upright.

Our sentimental education took varying turns, fuelled in part by alcohol, in part by narcotics, set against a soundtrack that helped define our unravelling experiences. Music unleashed in the late sixties and developed through the early seventies became the sounding brass of our emergent sensibilities.

An early experience, sealed in the memory, occurred during my first autumn at college after a drunken club function behind Kennedys of Westland Row. As I sat slumped, a young lady bestraddled my head, releasing an involuntary golden shower. I recall its warmth as it coursed down behind my ears, neither of us giving a damn as we made our bleary way home.

So many Trinity characters performed offstage. One was Gary Villiers-Stuart, whose mother brought the Baha'i faith to the Republic. He seemed on a permanent high, his smile radiant, his occasional pronouncements vatic. He drifted across Front Square, females in his wake, and presided over secularized ashram meetings where we would hunker down and talk of Kant's universalizing consciousness. Elton John's 'Rocket Man' pulsed in the breeze. Encountering Gary one summer's evening in the departure lounge at Dublin Airport, barefoot and beatific in a flowing white cotton shift, he was for all the world like our Saviour come back to earth.

Another presence was Becky Peterson, usually accompanied by her friend Jane Stephenson, Miss Fresher of 1971. Becky's hair fell in dark ringlets, framing a face fashioned by Botticelli. Her voice was soft and low. She carried the allure of the Americas (her father was a diplomat in Equador) in her long embroidered skirts, with sequinned tops setting off perfect clavicles. My friend Jamie Wolsey brought her down to my twenty-first in Westmeath, where she charmed my mother, and the birds in the trees. When we shared a bed at last in her Ballsbridge flat, so innocent were our yearnings that nothing actually occurred. I was to lose my virginity months later on a spring visit to Paris, to a girl with whom I'd corresponded over six years, as *Abbey Road* played itself out on her portable gramophone: 'And, in the end, the love you make, is equal to the love .... you take.' This event gave me a lifelong fealty to all things French.

The writer who came to define Trinity to my generation was 'Mike' J.P. Donleavy, who had became a neighbour in Westmeath. His son Philip was a friend at college, while his wife Mary Wilson supplied copy for *The Onion Eaters* and developed a fine seat on the hunting field in pursuit of the fox and assorted Guinnesses. Visits to his house, Levington Park, on Lough Owel outside Mullingar, were marked by meetings with occasional fellow visitors such as Clive Donner and Malcolm McDowell (star of *If....* and *A Clockwork Orange*), beating a much-worn path in an attempt to secure movie rights to *The Ginger Man*. Mike's second novel, *The Beastly Beatitudes of Balthazar B*, corresponded more to our Trinity experiences in the bouts of loneliness and isolation it described, and the poetry of deprivation borne by its eponymous hero.

After a dinner at Levington Park on a black winter's evening, I drove back to Dublin with an English writer who'd been anxious to meet the great man. In a line of traffic between Kilcock and Maynooth a figure loomed out of the dark onto that snub-nosed bonnet, crashing through the windscreen and spattering us with his blood. He had been trying to make his way home along the pathless road. The wake in Maynooth two days later for the eighteen-year-old jockey was a lesson in humility, with his family welcoming me and closing the circle of our humanity. Afterwards I sat immured for twenty-four hours in rooms in No. 32, overlooking Botany Bay, unable to speak. Then a paper on which I'd scribbled some nostrums lifted from the wall where it was pinned, signalling, 'I forgive you, be at ease.' It may have been an updraft from the gas hissing in the grate, but it answered a call.

Charlie Naper and I spent weekends in Monkstown with a group of Trinity extra-muralists called Healy. There were four sisters, Una (newly returned from

California), Emer, Moya and Orla. Their father, Seamus, was a distinguised Abbey actor, their brother, Seamus Óg, a producer in RTÉ. The living was easy, the dope pervasive, the post-Woodstock music never stopped. Big Tom, Una's occasional consort, was a printer who ran a lighting-and-sound outfit called Trackless Transit. He provided decks and ceiling-height amps in that bungalow bliss. Dan Casey, a two-tour Vietnam vet from Texas, spent his time sharpening knives and propounding Keyseyean certitudes. Patrick McGivern, a bearded New York short-story writer, made up the gang. Sustenance came from home-cooked lentils and breads, and a continuous loop of Hendrix, Captain Beefheart, Yes, the Grateful Dead, CSNY, and Dr Strangely Strange. Heaven was in our heads, and the doors of perception were opening wide.

We made occasional forays to the Dandelion Market off Baggot Street in town, where Una ran a clothes stall selling Afghan coats and Indian cottons, and to the country and lakes of the midlands. There Big Tom provided sounds for my twenty-first, and the Healy sisters added an air of bacchanalia. R.B. McDowell was an honoured guest – he nimbly danced the night away, apostrophizing the rising dawn as he advanced backwards up the staircase from the main hall before disappearing out of view.

An institution that harnessed the zeitgeist was Captain America's, a Grafton Street burger house opened in December 1971 by my pal Tom Haran, Johnny McCormack and Mark Kavanagh. Jim Fitzpatrick provided the wall cartoons; Chris Davison, the first live act, sang 'American Pie' in exchange for a glass of red, a hamburger and £2; the chef sprinkled grass on the salads; half the waitresses were recruited from Trinity, and a no-bra policy was unarticulated but understood. Hedonism had arrived in Dublin: 'I'm on the Pill and it's all right.' The music was essential, the food incidental.

Pat Egan, all big hair and snake hips, sold vinyl from The Sound Cellar at the other end of the street, in a basement next to the Berni Inn, where the bolder among us tried to lure coy but willing young Spanish virgins sent by their parents to complete their education in a Catholic city, little suspecting it harboured a nest of sex-starved Protestants across the way. There in troglodytic gloom lay the defining sonic treasures of the age: *Sticky Fingers, Bridge Over Troubled Water, Harvest, Moondance, Tupelo Honey, Holland, New Morning, Who's Next, Tapestry, The Aynsley Dunbar Retaliation, Me and Bobby McGee.*

I boxed for a year, joining the elite if ragged brotherhood that was Trinity's Boxing Club. It was yet to attain its glory days under the Christle brothers later in the decade. Fred Teidt, our cabbage-eared coach, was a dear man who had been famously deprived of an Olympic gold in a split decision back in Melbourne in 1956: he ended his days, God help him, as Michael Smurfit's muscle. The training was rigorous, and Fred schooled me to take the Irish university flyweight title in Belfast against a Galway farmer's son I gave weight to; he was ahead on points in the third until he stove in my gumshield. I lost my cool and some front teeth but came back to win, and hung up my gloves with an undefeated record dating back to my captaincy at Harrow and a bareknuckle apprenticeship at Headfort.

As with most students, life in Trinity was to follow two trajectories, the voyage in and the voyage out. Literature powered the first, with books as vehicles of understanding. Dublin provisioners included Webbs on the quays and upstairs in Greene's of Clare Street (where one of the Pembreys kindly saved me from myself in asking me to return some slim volume I'd stuffed down my trousers), downstairs in Fred Hanna's, the Eblana Bookshop at the top of Grafton Street, and Parsons across the canal. The second journey was enabled by planes and trains, courtesy of USIT, Trinity our point of departure, our gilded containment vessel, somewhere to come home to; hence the affection in which it is consistently held in these pages.

Summers were spent in a broadening of horizons. I took the hippy trail east, joining a Norwegian girl in Copenhagen en route. We'd met the previous year on a hostel rooftop in Pireaus, where I'd finished imbibing *Ulysses* begun on my father's yacht, *Gay Gander.* (It was a book that more than any other interpreted my own culture to me; I was proud to become its first Irish publisher in 1997.) We flew to Istanbul then bussed to Tehran, taking a night train across the sands of eastern Persia, as it was then, to Herat and on by coach to Kandahar, the hottest city on earth, and Kabul. In Peshawar, Gudrun and I parted company, mutually relieved of our (non)sexual obligations, and I travelled on solo to Delhi and north to Kathmandu.

The journey was a Lucullan sensefest: the monkey temples, the chai and hashish, the intense poverty, the tender tolerance of our host nations. I'd shed my western gear for a dhoti and a broad-brimmed camel-skin hat made by a stallholder in Kabul, which gave me shelter from the sun and shade for my reading: *Magister Ludi*, Yogananda's autobiography, *Island*. Several chillums on, I returned in a painted VW van picked up in Afghanistan and travelled back with Mitch and Max, a Philadelphian couple. The trip was funded by their assignment of embroidered karakul coats, haggled for in the hills above the Khyber Pass and destined for resale in Amsterdam. I joined my father and *Gay Gander* at Bodrum for a brief respite, and spent the remains of the summer in Westmeath, reading and recovering from jaundice.

In 1972 I flew west to New York with Arthur Shackleton for another exploratory summer. That experience, among the welcoming and mixed tribe of lapsed Asiatics, Hispanics, Africans and Europeans, who called themselves American, was no less educational. We worked upstate in Albany as busboys in a Jewish resturant, where the black Baptist family who ran the kitchen were not allowed beyond the swing doors. (The first evening one of them asked me to get them a coffee. Black or white? I enquired. Just plain coffee, he replied, eyeballing me gently.) We attended Mitch and Max's Jewish wedding in Philly with a Caribbean conga band playing funk in a backyard lot of that divided city. We drank beers on our ride across the Midwest while our raddled driver picked up bar girls to satisfy his thirst; we slept under a freeway bridge in Las Vegas, a surreal starship springing from the Mojave Desert; hitching out of Huxley's LA, I took the wheel of a red Mustang automatic up Highway 1 via Miller's Big Sur, arriving at Brautigan's Bay Area in San Francisco as the car owner slept off his all-nighter run from the Mexican border. We stayed on campus in Berkeley, TCD's younger sister, testing out new theories of vision with a professor who took us to hear presidential candidate George McGovern speak at a Labor Day rally outside the city.

Reading salted the road before us: *The Electric Kool-Aid Acid Test*, *One Flew Over the Cuckoo's Nest* and *Sometimes a Great Notion*, *The Armies of the Night*, *Life Against Death*, Stewart Brand's *The Whole Earth Catalog*, the poetry of Robinson Jeffers. Hauling north via Seattle to Vancouver, we enjoyed that city's famed hospitality (free bed nights for visitors) and rode in a painted van back east across the Rockies by way of Montreal and Boston. An inebriate Indian picked up somewhere outside Winnipeg seemed to symbolize a forgotten and despised people, strangers in their own land.

A sidebar on my later days in Trinity lay between the pages of *TCD Miscellany*, an occasional monthly edited by Ken Bruen, a charismatic Galway tearaway in a long leather coat, a fierce lover of women and narcotics, friend to the legendary Phil Lynott, and now Ireland's most successful crime writer. I penned miscellanea under the name Homunculus, a Shandean nod, while my friend David Cole furnished delightful cover art (see over) in the comic-book tradition. At weekends we would hawk our sheaves of newsprint like mendicant missionaries along the windy esplanades of UCD.

BACK AT COLLEGE, late one evening, I pushed a Mini Minor bought with hard-earned US dollars across Front Square towards the curfewed Front Gate, in need of a jump start. Two figures in dinner jackets emerged from the sodium penumbra, lurching across the cobbles: David Norris and Brendan Kennelly. Norris was all concern and lent a willing shoulder. The Kerryman informed me that I 'couldn't drive a spider off a dung heap'.

After exams, the world drew us into its maw, and we took flight from Dublin again. Most of us went to London or farther afield, for there was no work to be had in Ireland. In Portugal I had met Emma Stacey, who crewed for my father. Her father, Tom, ran a publishing company in Covent Garden's Henrietta Street. That winter of 1974 I packed books as his ex-army warehouse staff fecked Christmas titles out to the local pub across the way in exchange for beers. Tom went bankrupt six months later and I helped him rapidly shift stock to his house in Kensington Church Street one Sunday.

The adventure had begun.

Antony Farrell (TCD 1969–73; History and Political Philosophy) worked in London publishing until 1980, returning to Westmeath to found The Lilliput Press in 1984. He moved to Dublin in 1989 and published the first Irish edition of Joyce's **Ulysses** in 1997. He is also a director of Houyhnhnm Press, a sister imprint, which in 2010 published the first revised edition of **Finnegans Wake**. He has two children, Bridget and Seán, and one grandson, Fintan.

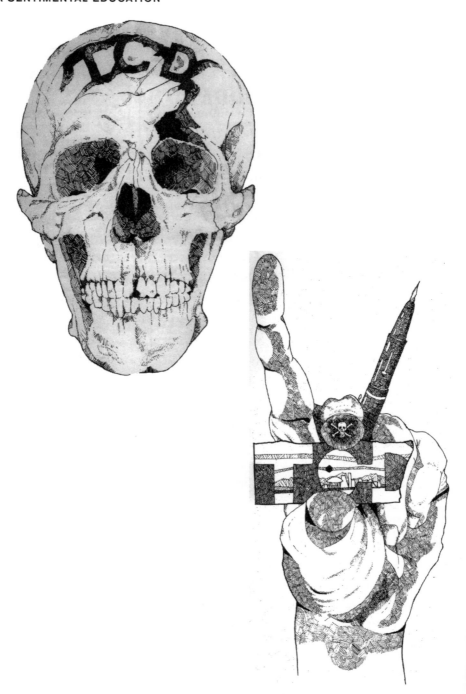

David Cole's cover art from **TCD Miscellany** in the 1970s.

PLANT A TREE (UNDER WHOSE SHADE YOU WILL NOT SIT)

kingsley aikins

TRINITY in the seventies – Trinity in the anythings. What is it about the place that seeps into you, nestles in, hunkers down and, like a benevolent computer virus, never leaves? It becomes part of what you are and who you are. All-consuming at the time, it fades quickly as more immediate challenges invade, the velocity of career takes over and the invite of the unknown replaces the comfort of the familiar, and the job tides whisk us away to places and people far from the cobbles and the Commons. And yet, and yet, something about the place never leaves you.

Trinity in the seventies was internet-less, Google-less, iPod-less and BlackBerry-less and yet we seemed well connected. Communication was more face to face than Facebook, and someone wanting to be your friend desired to spend more time with you as a person than know you through some surrogate gadget. Thankfully, revelry (or ranting as it was called then) never got recorded to show up on screens in perpetuity – it lived on, suitably embellished, in memory, never losing anything in the telling. In an era where social media didn't exist we were all the more social. Honed in the Junior Common Room, the GMB snooker room and the Buttery, we learned to con; connect and confuse.

Were those days better, happier and more stress-free than now? Probably not. Northern Ireland was at its worst and the Dublin bombings brought the horror of it close to home and pieces of shrapnel onto the College Park cricket crease. Stroppy Northerners from both sides left their quarrels at home but there were undercurrents. The massive gender imbalance was just plain unfair and contrasts sharply with contemporary college life in Trinity and all colleges. I met an old college crony the other day and we were reminiscing about Trinity days and I clichéd, 'Those were great undergrad days – sex and drugs and rock and roll,' and he replied drily, 'I remember the drugs and rock and roll …' Testosterone got sidetracked into sport, the Buttery and the Lincoln. Pints were endless as was capacity though money was tight and everybody was, as J.P. Donleavy memorably put it in the *Beastly Beatitudes*, 'hanging on the rim of a round'.

Northern Prods, Southern micks, English chaps and the odd colonial collided and colluded to build a unique *esprit de corps*, a Hibernian mish-mash where class and caste got relegated and everybody had to stand on their own two feet. Confidence grew as the years flew. I probably didn't realize that friends made then would remain with me for life and despite their scattering across the world the Trinity diaspora would become a global network of afflu-ence and influence. We all succumb to stereotypes and none more so than Trinity medical students, surely the wildest and most irresponsible of all the student body. I still dread the day when I come out of a coma or anaesthetic to see one of my old Trinity Med. friends leering down at me. If nothing else they had stamina and seemed to do more in a week than most of the rest of us did in a term.

Trinity's talent was to be transformative. On leaving we all felt very different animals than when we arrived as raw rookies. Rooms were the icing on the cake – a genuinely unique living experience. Waking up on Sunday mornings in the sleepy, hungover centre of a European capital was sobering in the real meaning of the word. Sunday morning rugby training was brutal and meant to be, and for the true rugger aficionado there was the Lincoln Ramblers – a scratch collection of rugby odds and sods looking for an afternoon to forget and an evening to remember. The Ramblers would set off to rural rugby outposts such as Athy, Tullamore and Carlow. Corinthian and cavalier, the

Lincoln Ramblers espoused a 'Barbarians' approach – bumblebee scrums and lifting in the lineout (then illegal) brought the game to new heights. Sheep were shooed off pitches, touch and try lines were rough approximations and referees were open to bribes and intimidation. Showers weren't cold – they just didn't exist and the *après-ski* bluff and banter were epic – earthy wholesome stuff, the soul of the game. Rumbling Roly Saul was the moral compass and creative cricketers Halliday and Harte the Elvis and Costello. Serious it wasn't and PC it wasn't and yet the memories are as vivid as 'real' games against the likes of Cork Con. and Garryowen who so relished giving a warm Munster welcome to 'them fancy lads, them undergrads'. In the overall schema of things results didn't matter that much and, by and large, we all subscribed to the maxim 'When the great scorer in the sky comes to mark against your name, he marks not that you won or lost but how you played the game.' Values lived on longer than results – a metaphor for life, perhaps.

Slipping into Trinity in the early seventies from a somewhat cloistered school and family environment was truly a shock to the system. I'm sure that in those days, Trinity appeared to be a bastion of liberalism, slightly Anglo, and not part of contemporary, mainstream Irish life. Challenging orthodoxy and displaying a feisty independence from the rigidities of the day it attracted a student body who, for the most part, wanted to query and question. Messrs Vipond and Revington did so in a demonstrative way, the rest of us less so, but we were all on a journey: flotsam and jetsam on the Trinity river where we experienced something we never really had before – choice. Not just academically, but in terms of courses, friends and activities. The latter defined many of us and determined our friendships. A number of us migrated towards the Rugby Club, conscious that we were part of a club with a great pedigree – the second-oldest rugby club in the world and the oldest university rugby club with an awesome history of national and international players. To play regularly with truly world-class players such as John Robbie and Phil Orr and national greats like Dick Spring and David Sutton was a privilege but the real joy was the sense of belonging, the sheer pride in wearing the jersey and playing on a superb rugby pitch in the centre of a great capital city. It doesn't get any better than that.

Despite how rose-tinted the spectacles may be, for that long-ago era a brief look at the seventies' photos did confirm one brutal harsh reality: in all the

400-plus years of Trinity's illustrious history there can be few other decades of worse dress and hair sense. Both were truly abominable and we really did look like a bunch of psychedelic clowns. How could we possibly have considered ourselves in the slightest bit stylish or attractive is beyond this writer. It was visually gruesome and an assault on the senses. Did I really wear royal-blue flared bell-bottom hipsters with a two-inch white belt, cheesecloth shirt, white shoes (to go with the belt, of course) and an old German army coat? Topped off with a Jimi Hendrix mane it was guaranteed to strike fear in all and sundry and repel the opposite sex, which it did most successfully. Who did we think we were? At the time we thought we were kinda special – the world was our lobster and Trinity was a neat four years to prepare for us for the decades of success to follow. For a brief period we were masters of our small universe, lulled into thinking it would always be that easy and that we would spend lots of similar times with people we really liked, without regard to anything except who they were as individuals. Perhaps Trinity had the last laugh, giving us a false sense of the inevitability of success, our educational finishing school setting us up for the glories ahead. That the reality turned out to be so different, that successes were often outnumbered by failures, that life was not a cakewalk and was full of struggles and battles, was not on the Trinity hymn sheet. Or perhaps Trinity gave us some 'ammo' to help us all cope, a base to lean on, the lessons of empathy and emotional intelligence providing us with the interpersonal tools and the linguistic dexterity to see us through. Having worked in a number of countries, many with Trinity graduates on full throttle, I was always amazed at the networking capacity of the Irish and how many doors it opens, how many deals it facilitates and how much good it has done.

Hindsight, as they say, is twenty-twenty and I know I never really appreciated during my time in Trinity how great the institution was and how privileged I was to be part of it. Being one of four siblings who went to Trinity in different periods we all felt we were lucky to have gotten in and out before it all went downhill. I suspect the same is true today. In a brutally competitive global educational market, Trinity has done us all proud with superb rankings, though it will be a battle to retain them.

However, the harsh realities of running and funding the institution make sobering reading and the future, in a country struggling to finance core educational needs, is clearly uncertain. How one badly needs more Chuck Feeneys (and some homegrown ones) – an extraordinary man who has invested, philanthropically, over one billion dollars in Irish universities. It would be wonderful to see Trinity as a truly independent university ranked in the top twenty-five in the world – a world-class institution that could look to over 400 years of achievement, confident that the best is yet to come. Those of us who have been there and benefitted so much from it have a responsibility and an opportunity to ensure Trinity has a viable future as a top-notch college.

What has made the US university system the greatest is simple – private philanthropic support. Harvard is the gold standard in this regard. Today, despite the stock market shenanigans over the last couple of years, it has an endowment of over twenty-five billion dollars. This allows the university to admit its high-achieving students on a needs-blind basis – all are picked on merit alone and scholarships awarded to the financially needy. No student will not go to Harvard for lack of money. Harvard attracts the brightest and the best not just from the US but from around the world. It was an outstanding university in 1660 and still is today, thanks to its passionate and committed alumni who believe in supporting it. This private support is very much the American way (*à la* the recent billionaire pledges of Buffett, Gates etc.) but we must import it here and introduce dramatic tax changes that will make giving to education more attractive. Ireland has been smart at using tax as a creative incentive, particularly to attract US companies here, and there are literally trillions of dollars tied up in Dublin. We need to unlock and harness this resource to benefit the university sector.

The title of these essays, *Trinity Tales*, suggests the recounting of hitherto untold, salacious events and, perhaps, breaking the unwritten *omerta* that surrounds their disclosure. Fortunately, the statute of limitations probably applies to the protagonists who are now mostly pillars of society and, possibly, bastions of power and privilege. They would not want their children getting a whiff of what the old man – or woman – got up to during their student high-jinks days.

The Australian writer Patrick White wrote, 'I forgot what I was taught – I only remember what I have learnt.' Perhaps this is what the Trinity experience managed to straddle. The totality of the experience – and this included the summer jobs and all the extracurricular activities – meant that the sum of the parts was more than the whole. Everybody got out what they put into it, and more. There were those who purely engaged to the minimum with their courses and had a life outside of college. That seemed to be such a waste.

Trinity polished us rough diamonds and helped us shine in the real world. For that we all owe a debt of gratitude and perhaps in helping the college we can all respond to the call to be good ancestors, to make an impact the results of which we will never see, as in the words of the proverb – plant a tree under whose shade you will not sit.

Kingsley Aikins (TCD 1970–4; Economics and Politics) worked in London and then Australia where he represented the IDA and the Irish Trade Board. He moved to the US in 1993 and was CEO of The Worldwide Ireland Funds until 2009. Now based in Dublin, he is a member of the Institutes of Marketing, Export and Linguists. He represented Trinity College, the Irish Universities, Vichy (France) and Leinster at rugby. In 2008 he was awarded a CBE for services to British–Irish relations. He is married to Claire, and has three children, Grattan, Darcy and Devin.

BEFORE REAL LIFE BEGAN

dillie keane

WHEN I THINK now of my student days, almost forty years since the day I hauled my glaringly new suitcase up the stairs at Trinity Hall, it is with a mixture of emotions, the overriding one being melancholy. Not for my lost youth: I was a skittish creature, hysterical from years of incarceration in a convent and an even more rigidly Catholic home, neurotically plunging into anything that looked even vaguely louche. I prefer the person I have become with age, and age suits me. No, my sadness is entirely because so many of my memories are peopled by ghosts who should be here to write their own entries.

Amanda Walker. I met her on my first day of Freshers' Week. We were both in Trinity Hall, and there was a ghastly drinks party the first evening where terrified newbies glugged cheap sherry and introduced themselves to each other. We clutched at anyone we thought might be vaguely friendly. I had already met my room-mate, about whom I remember very little except that she seemed pleasant enough but a relentless goody-goody. I'd known enough goody-goodies at school, and all I wanted was unlimited sex, drink and theatre, not necessarily in that order. Not necessarily in any order, actually. What I most desired was unholy disorder.

The room seemed to be full of nice girls from the country called Breda and Bridie and Brenda who bored me on sight. Then I was introduced to a pugnacious girl with brown hair, a slightly prominent, pointed chin, a snub nose, and the most beautiful eyes I'd ever seen: enormous, deep brown pools (think of Reese Witherspoon).

'You're from England?' she said, in a light, melodious English accent.

'Yes. Where are you from?'

'Scotland,' she replied. 'My father's a GP in Prestwick.' I replied that my father was a GP in Portsmouth.

'Brothers and sisters?'

'Yes,' I replied, 'two sisters and a brother.'

'Same as me,' she said. 'I'm the youngest.'

'Me too.'

'What order are they in?'

'Well, first two sisters, then my brother, then me.'

'Same as me,' she said. 'My brother was at Trinity, but he's left now.'

'My brother left Trinity a year ago. You went to boarding school?'

'Yep,' she said. 'Convent.'

'Me too,' I said. 'What order?'

'Holy Child. Harrogate.'

'Sacred Heart. Woldingham.'

'I was expelled.'

'So was I.'

Of course, with so much in common, we disliked one another immediately, and thus became the greatest of friends, inseparable and warring. We understood each other with a horrible precision, like reunited twins. We fell in love with the same men, drank the same stupid quantities of beer, went to the same parties, and hung around with the same crowds. Mostly, we just cried and cried with laughter. I never met anyone who made me howl like she did.

We lasted one term at Trinity Hall before we were asked to leave, and Amanda (who was much more efficient than me) set about finding us digs. We moved into a house in Havelock Square with Alison O'Donoghue, her husband Neil and their three children, Sovay, Emma and Philip. Alison was only twenty-four, English, and had also been at Trinity. The house was small enough with the five of them, but money was tight and they rented out their front room to the two of us.

Alison, still one of my greatest friends to this day, became adept at lying to our worried mothers who would ring up with great regularity wanting to know (a) where we were and (b) whether we'd been to Mass. Actually, I was still going to Mass then, mainly because we had a very charismatic priest called Father Heffernan who was the first Catholic chaplain at the University in nearly 400 years. Father Heffernan was clever enough to recognize my vanity and propensity to show off, and got me to attend regularly by asking me to read the Epistles and inviting me for sherry afterwards. The post-Mass drinks became a regular feature of my life.

I ENDED my first year on several high notes, which I remember with great fondness. I fell in love for the first time. Stephen Navin was in fourth year so it was considered a great coup, especially as he had apparently resisted vast legions of girls who'd hurled themselves at him. Towards the end of the Summer Term, Stephen announced he was going on the hundred-mile walk, an annual endurance test. Normally, the walk was from Belfast to Dublin, but the Troubles were in full spate and this time the walk was starting from Waterford. Amanda and I decided to join in, and set off the evening before the event to hitch to Waterford. Foolishly, we left home far too late in the afternoon and finally got to the Naas Road at about 7 pm. It didn't occur to us that it was a bit late for hitching a hundred miles, so we stuck our thumbs out and after several short hops, finally arrived in New Ross just after 11 pm.

Being incompetent young idiots, we'd done nothing about arranging any kind of lodgings – we'd set off with toothbrushes, a clean pair of knickers each and a bucketload of hope; that was all. However, we realized that we weren't likely to get any farther that night, so walked into the centre of town to what was the only hotel. A small bedraggled crowd of people was standing outside, so we excuse-me'd our way to the front and knocked on the door. A fella in shirtsleeves opened the door a crack, and an appalling cover version of 'Candy Man' wafted through the door.

'We'd like to book a room,' said one of us in our crisp English.

'No chance,' said he, 'eyz're not gettin' in that way.'

'We don't want to go to the dance. We just want a room.'

'No!' he shouted. 'Be off wit' ye!'

Inside, a room full of revellers was giving it welly to 'Tie A Yellow Ribbon'.

We remonstrated, we waved fivers at him, all to no avail. And so, while New Ross throbbed to ABBA, we trudged off through the dark streets to walk onwards to Waterford. A mere twelve miles, but not appealing after midnight, and we had no idea where we would stay when we got there. As we trailed hopelessly through a particularly dark street, Amanda produced the last of our chocolate and I got out our only form of light, which was a long white candle. We lit the candle, and laughed at how useless it was. Suddenly, a voice from behind whispered, 'If ye value yer life, lads, run! Follow me!' You don't get time to think at moments like that. We took to our heels and ran like the clappers, up and down dark streets, our mystery saviour urging us on, and the sound of other feet running some way behind us. Finally, we made it over the bridge, and onto the open road to Waterford.

Our knight in shining armour was a gypsy-looking chancer called Pedro, half Spanish and half Irish, with an earring, fairly *outré* in those days. He told us that we'd been spotted waving our fivers outside the hotel and were very lucky not to have been attacked, robbed, and left for dead somewhere.

'Lads,' he said, ignoring the fairness of our sex, 'New Ross is rough, I'm tellin' ye.'

'Yeah, we're not staying, we're thumbing a ride to Waterford.'

'Don't t'umb, lads! Oh God, lads, don't t'umb!'

We were stuck. He wouldn't let us thumb to Waterford, although in fairness there were no cars going by. Nor would he let us go back into New Ross to get a taxi, because desperadoes were waiting there to mug and murder us. His only solution was to walk with us to Waterford and then he'd walk back to catch the boat out in the morning.

We were reluctant to set off on the dark road with a strange young man, so we sat on a wall in what passed for New Ross suburbia under the only streetlight and exchanged life stories. He told us his mother had had an affair with a Spanish sailor, and certainly he looked very Mediterranean. Looking back, he seems like a character straight out of a Brecht/Weill song. Suddenly, he stopped talking. 'Ssshh!' he whispered. 'Voices!' Sure enough, very faintly we could hear a small crowd in the distance.

'Hide, lads, hide!'

We were over that suburban garden wall before you could say knife, into the rose bushes where we lay quivering. The crowd drew nearer. They seemed to be singing. Suddenly, Amanda leapt back over the wall. 'It's okay! They're singing "Onward Christian Soldiers"! Murderers don't sing hymns!' It was none other than Joanna Kennedy and a couple of other TCD students. We fell on their necks like Ben Gunn seeing human beings for the first time in years. They were planning to join the walk and had been equally foolish with their travel plans and found themselves stranded in New Ross. (Joanna and I had been incarcerated together at not just one, but two Sacred Heart Convents in England.)

The adventure ended quickly. Pedro melted away into the dark. We commandeered a taxi driving by, and ended up sleeping on someone's floor in Waterford. The next day we were too knackered to do much – I walked about twenty miles, Amanda managed about thirty. I spent the rest of the walk travelling with the organizers and bathing the painful and bleeding feet of the surviving walkers, particularly Stephen Navin's. He was the first to walk into TCD to huge cheers, and the next night he kissed me for the first time. Oh, young love. It's still as clear in my mind as if it had happened yesterday.

A few days after that, I was voted Miss Elegance at the College Races. Eamon de Valera was the guest of honour, and I was chosen to serve tea to him. There was a frightfully grand tea in the clubhouse overlooking the sports field at the back of Trinity, and if you were 'in' you got invited. The men wore morning suits and the girls were long dresses and hats, just like a wedding. Of course, my heart was later crushed when Stephen, who had just completed fourth year, went off to his new life in London without a backward glance. That's first love for you.

I could, I suppose, be telling you of my triumphs on the stage with Players – and there were some of those. I always had good timing and no shame at all, vital qualities in comedy. I appeared as the eponymous heroine in *We've All Maid Marion*, the funniest pantomime in the history of the world, written by Michael Colgan and Paolo Tullio – and the only time I've ever played the title role. I wore a dress made of different bits of green and beige silk, badly stitched, torn and patched, but wonderfully buxom and perfect for a maid living in a medieval forest. It gave me an air of wanton dishevelment, as though I'd just been rogered senseless in the bushes by most of the Merry Men.

During the run of the panto, I was invited to the Colours Ball by Ben Underwood, who was *none other than the Captain of the Trinity Team*, which was (a) an astonishing honour and (b) what most girls could only dream of in those days. I was incredibly excited. I had bought the most ravishing, sexy, backless yellow crêpe evening dress with an enormous gold rose at the neck, and hung it in the dressing room to change into after the performance.

Ben arrived to watch the show and take me to the ball straight afterwards. As soon as the curtain came down, he grabbed me and said we were going straight to the ball. 'But I've got to change!' I cried, 'I can't go in my stage frock!' No chance. I discovered that you can't wrestle with a rugby captain, and before I knew it I was in a car heading for the dance. At the end of the evening, he took me back to his place, because apart from leaving my gorgeous dress hanging, unworn, in the dressing room, I'd also left my handbag, my money, my coat, and my house keys, such was the haste with which Ben had whisked me from the theatre. His flat seemed very palatial – the whole top floor of a big house in south Dublin. 'Don't worry,' he said, as we curled up together, 'I'll get you back home in the morning.'

ABOUT MIDDAY we got up, and showered, and I put my smelly old stage frock back on, now reeking of cigarettes and beer in addition to Sherwood Forest floor. Then he took me down to a large kitchen and horror of horrors, he introduced me to his mother. This was Ben's home. I mean *home*, where his parents lived. A lovely, affluent home where he had the top floor to himself. Remember, this was in the day when nice young men didn't bring floozies back to Mummy and Daddy's house to stay in their own bedroom, and if the floozy in question did so, then *she* certainly wasn't a nice girl either.

Picture the scene. Ben Underwood, handsome captain of the Trinity Rugby Team, a young man from a decent middle-class Irish background, with a bright and golden future, brings home an English trollop in a filthy, ragged dress with her tits falling out, last night's stage make-up cleaned up with tap water as best as could be managed, no hairbrush, no nothing. I laugh now when I picture how I must have looked to that proud mother, and she was as polite as she could manage, but oh my God, I was mortified. I was so mortified that when I next met Ben, I ignored him. So if you ever read this, Ben, sorry I behaved like a prune but I was just too embarrassed to even speak to you.

Back to Amanda. We decided life was too bloody hectic together, so in second year we went to live with other people. Patty Norton – an old school chum – and I rented a huge, first-floor flat on Palmerston Road, above a sweet little old lady who was only too delighted to overcharge us for her shabby, arctic, rickety old cesspit. And the sweetness only lasted till we moved in, whereupon we contrived to make each other's lives absolute hell. It turned out she was a Dublin Protestant of visible morals, and took black affront if our blinds weren't pulled to the exact six inches below the top of the window. She banged on our door with a broom if we had male visitors after 7 pm. And when we had our first elegant dinner party, she called the Gardaí to tell them we were running an illegal house and have us arrested. They left, amused and mystified, telling her firmly not to waste police time. We retaliated by jumping up and down on the ceiling. So she called the guards again, and we told them we were members of the TCD Morris Dancing society, and had been rehearsing. The rozzers were less amused this time, and told her they'd prosecute if she bothered them again.

I lurched through my Music degree, scraping by. My professor was Brian Boydell, a dry, humourless academic who'd been a scientist before he turned to music full-time. He had blown his hair off in an experiment. One remaining tuft leapt pointedly from his oddly patched pate, and with his remodelled, Spock-like ears, he resembled an ascetic gnome. He didn't think much of me.

At the end of second year, I managed to find myself being elected to some kind of position in the Boat Club – I think I was the chairman of the Ladies' Committee, which basically meant I had to organize the tea on the day of the Boat Club races. In addition to making the tea, we'd entered as a team in the Maiden Fours. Patty Norton, Louise Lloyd-Carson, Amanda and I. You never saw such a useless foursome. Patty caught a crab, fell backwards onto Amanda and knocked her off her seat, the seat came off the runner and Amanda threw it into the water. Louise and I were still rowing home an hour later.

In third year, Amanda and I shared a beautiful little mews cottage at the back of Ely Place with a law student called Chris Arnold. We were terribly contented as a threesome and it was really my first experience of making a home. Being so central, we had a constant stream of people dropping in, so life was one long mad party. We took to drinking in Toner's in the evening, but if we wanted a lunchtime pint, we'd put our coats on over our pyjamas and dressing-gowns, and overcome our hangovers in the quietly anonymous corners of O'Donoghue's. Under cover of darkness, we'd slip off to the Gallagher building site and relieve them of a plank or two, which Chris would saw into pieces for the fire.

We gave a grand cocktail party after the English–Irish match. It was spring, and we decided our courtyard was a little bare, so we went down to Amanda's grandmother's house in Dundrum (now Roly Saul's restaurant) and picked hundreds of daffodils, and stuck them in our empty flower beds at the mews. Everyone thought we were wonderful gardeners.

I don't know if our experience was unusual or whether it was the norm, but it seemed that there was little divide between town and gown in Dublin. Many of our friends weren't students: Maureen Gallagher, for instance, warmed herself at our hearth, which blazed with wood stolen from her family's building site, and married our good friend Roly Saul. Chris Meehan, rather older than us, played stonking piano, introduced me to good music and inspired me more than anyone else I ever met.

And then there was Don Nelligan, the actor. Nelly was witty, quick and great fun, and very much part of the scene. I was mad about him. (My gaydar wasn't fully developed then.) He took me out for dinner and I assumed he fancied me, especially when he asked if he could stay the night at the mews. I brought him home after dinner, where the other two were finishing a game of Scrabble. I have to explain the layout of the mews. It was one large sitting room-cum-kitchen downstairs, with an open-plan staircase along the long wall at the back. Upstairs, there were two bedrooms and a bathroom. Chris soon excused himself, said goodnight, and walked up the stairs to bed. Amanda and I sat chatting to Nelly for a while, during which I slipped upstairs and asked Chris if he wouldn't mind sleeping in my bed that night. Dear old Chris, he got out of his bed and went next door. I went back downstairs, and at about 1 am, Amanda excused herself and went upstairs to bed.

'Is it really ok for me to stay the night?' asked Nelly.

'Oh, absolutely!' I said, and showed him upstairs into Chris's room – and at that moment it dawned on me that I'd read the situation absolutely wrong and there was no way Nelly and I would be getting into bed together. Far from being embarrassed, I thought it was terribly funny, and went into my bedroom where the two beds were now occupied by Chris and Amanda who were giggling quietly at me. There was nothing for it but to share Amanda's bed. 'Dillie?' Nelly was calling.

I got up and put my head round the other bedroom door. 'Yes?'

'Is it really ok for me to stay here?'

'Yes, it's fine,' I said airily.

'But where's Chris?'

'Oh, he's gone out.'

'At this hour?'

'Oh yes.' I had to ride this one out. 'He has a girlfriend who's a waitress in Phibsborough. She's on late shift.' I heard a muffled wail of laughter from Amanda.

'But I saw him go upstairs a while ago.'

'Oh, he leaves by the window.' Another wail escaped the pillow next door.

'What?'

'Yes, he always climbs out the window. He has a very advanced sense of adventure.'

'Oh,' said Nelly, defeated. 'G'night then.'

'Night night,' I said. 'Sleep well.'

Back in my bedroom, both beds were rocking as the two of them wept with laughter. Chris, who had an incredibly high-pitched and infectious giggle, was trying not to make any noise as he wasn't supposed to be there, while Amanda and I were giggling helplessly and uncontrollably. It's always difficult trying to describe an event that three people found utterly hilarious, but it was the funniest night of my life. We laughed until dawn. And when we got up, after snatching a couple of hours sleep, we found Nelly downstairs making himself a coffee.

'Morning,' we said breezily.

'Morning,' he said rather guardedly. 'What was all that giggling about last night?'

'P.G. Wodehouse,' said Amanda, insouciantly. 'Killing, absolutely killing.'

At that moment, Chris walked down the open plan staircase, smiling broadly. 'Morning!' he said. Nelly looked at him in blank astonishment. 'I'm off to my lecture.' And as he left the house, he murmured, 'Ah, Phibsborough, Phibsborough, site of my passion.'

I still laugh at that story. But it's tinged with a terrible sadness, because all three of them are dead. Nelly died of an overdose, discovered by Roly Saul. Amanda drowned off the coast of Spain aged thirty-four. And Chris died of cancer in his late thirties, leaving behind his broken-hearted wife and daughters. So young. Far too young.

At the end of my third year, I became very ill. I was playing Madame Arcati in *Blithe Spirit* in Players, and it was a revelation to me to play a part so ideally suited. My parents came over to see it, and noticed that I was scarcely able to get up out of the chair. Dad, a GP, had a look at my knee, which I could hardly bend for a huge, bright-red and agonizingly painful swelling. Down my shins more lesions were beginning to appear. He immediately diagnosed me with erythema nodosum, an odd secondary disease that is frequently sparked by a streptococcal infection. That evening, I was lying in a hospital bed in the Adelaide with a cage over my legs to protect them from the bedding – suddenly, anything touching my legs was unbearable agony and the swellings were increasing and merging into one huge lesion.

I remained in hospital for three weeks, and missed my Part II exams. I wouldn't have passed them anyhow, I hadn't done enough work and I hated the degree. My decisions were made easier by the fact that part of my exam was to conduct a full orchestra, and Professor Boydell refused to convene the orchestra again for a resit. So I would have had to repeat the year, making it a five-year degree. The thought was appalling, so I left the university without a degree, and eventually got into LAMDA where I truly began my adult life.

I often regret the delay in starting my career so old – I was twenty-six by the time I left drama school, too old to play real juve parts. That was definitely a mistake. But I made some wonderful friends, in particular Amanda Walker. I had sixteen and a half years of her friendship: we alternately tormented and entertained one another, but no matter how badly we rowed, we always became the best of friends again. I was her bridesmaid, and godmother to her beautiful daughter Jessica. At the time of her death, our friendship had settled, and I'm so glad I was able to tell her I loved her.

I still miss her. It's like having an emotional limp, a feeling that one will never be quite whole again. I discovered that real grief lasts forever.

Dillie Keane (TCD 1971–4; Music) was born and brought up in Portsmouth, Hampshire, and left college via the Adelaide Hospital sans degree. She went on to study acting at LAMDA, 1975–8, and had started a respectable acting career when she was hijacked by the success of Fascinating Aïda (begun as a bit of fun between jobs). She has enjoyed a maverick career since then – acting, journalism, radio – garnering nominations in New York, London and Germany. She received an Honorary Doctorate of Letters from the University of Portsmouth, her proudest moment. She has finally given in to the forces of darkness that chain her to Fascinating Aïda (the Voldemort of the cabaret world), and swears she will not try to kill it off again.

'Miss Elegance' winner 1972 Louise (Dillie) Keane, Roger Greene and Paul Coulson (left) at the Trinity College Races, 1972.

LOOK BACK IN LAUGHTER

lucy o'sullivan

DUBLIN, 1970. I knocked. The door swung open. Aspidistra land. Dark oak staircase. Church-cold. Deathly quiet, except the tick-tocking torpor of a grandfather clock. Silent servant shuffling back down the passage. I entered the girls' sitting room. Three huddled round an open fire: one, ruddy faced and wiry haired from the North, another, nun-like, from down the country, and this third one, with an English accent, staring at me prettily now, with cool eyes and a determined tilt to her chin. I listened and smiled at them all and then at Cool Eyes again in her long, heavy brown coat.

'I suppose your father's a bloody general?' I jibed, trying it on.

'How did you guess?' she fired back, not missing a beat.

That look. That no-nonsense approach. Lifelong friends and mutual godparents. Thank you TCD accommodation for playing gooseberry.

But our digs were a clash of cultures. I, for one, was not about to start eating supper at six. And then there's only so much stuffed marrow and other culinary delights you can tip down the loo. Or that many late-night romantic phone calls you can cope with while the ancient, night-capped landlady is lying next to you listening, because the only phone is in her bedroom. By her bed.

Liz Glover (for yes, it was she) and I moved out of Mrs Grove White's sharpish to Rathmines and a gentle, doddery, non-cooking landlady with a squash-ball-sized hole in her forehead. And where my tennis racket's strings bust from the damp and where the great, late, Matt Gormley visited us at the dead of night by climbing onto the roof of the house and clinging upside down from the guttering, like some deranged gargoyle, to appear, corkscrew-curled and manic-faced against the first-floor window; I am in fits of laughter again as I type.

Trinity had been a bit of a toss-up for me. Firstly, I was turned down because, precociously, I had taken some extra UK exams a year early and was told that I now had too many 'sittings' for a place. I wrote back immediately pointing out their absurd logic and, trying it on again, threatened to throw myself off the nearby Clifton suspension bridge unless they changed their minds. Fortunately, I received an offer by return. Secondly, when I left school, my recurring fantasy was to join the UK's National Youth Theatre. So, on going to TCD I vowed somehow to satisfy that Thespian calling – mission was accomplished when I landed a part in a Players' production in my first term. No mean feat, as Freshers, particularly of the female variety, were supposed initially to sweep floors, sew costumes or daintily hand out programmes before being allowed to tread the boards. Paul McGuinness, who was directing Edward Albee's *Malcolm*, had different ideas.

Businesslike, he auditioned me – James Morris and Sorcha Cusack were somewhere there too that day – and gave nothing away until I was assigned the role of the American, Eloisa Brace. The *Irish Times* critic waspishly placed my accent 'halfway between Boston and Brighton'. So what? I was in the thick of it all. Players was something else: loads of easy-on-the-eye guys with a curt way of communicating. The über-cool Andy Russell (are you still a bookseller in West Cork?); Tom Sanders; Paolo Tullio, the Malcolm of the play; Chris Meehan; Mike Colgan; Peter Coles … the list goes on. And young women like me, Maggie Stewart and Anne Adamson.

A skinny, flame-haired, flying-jacketed Irish American named Gavin O'Herlihy played Gus (he's now a real film star: *The Last Outlaw, Star Trek, Hidden Assassin*). A certain vertically challenged Chris Davison was wont to hang around too, pageboy haircut, endlessly strumming his guitar. He was forever being shooed off the stage when we rehearsed. Pop fame as Chris de Burgh with his 'Lady in Red' was yet to come. We were all acting. In fact, most of us never stopped. But singing 'Abide With Me' with that lot at the end of each performance and managing not to laugh was a Herculean task.

Every night after the play we'd get sozzled and throw an impromptu party, sometimes at The Old Stand, sometimes in Paul Scully's rooms. Khosrow Fazel, a wickedly lecherous Persian student, would invariably call by, or Gary Collier, or Donnell Deeny. Deliciously scandalous rumours were whispered about trust funds, gambling fortunes lost and found, false titles, illicit liaisons, drugs and debts and rustications. I was permanently breathless with the excitement of it all. But to this day I am mortified that when Paul suggested we enter *Malcolm* in some acting festival in the UK over the Christmas holidays, I demurred, saying I had 'too many parties, too little time'. Frivolity, thy name was Lucy.

And those party invitations kept flooding in. Helped in no small way by my debonair, darling brother, Dermot, whose suggestion I join him at 'Trinners' rather than some earnest British university was the main reason for its appeal. Dermot – memorably described in *TCD Miscellany*'s 'Valentines' column as 'Last seen walking down lovers' lane holding his own hand' – was also a party animal and going into his third year (Law) when I arrived. People who knew him (Veronica Aliaga-Kelly, Robert Neil, the American draft-dodging babe-magnet Regan brothers, Tom, John and Andy, who lived at the Intercontinental hotel, the MGB-owning, fur-wearing Letia Smith, Sheila Corr, Miles O'Donovan, Des Gilroy, Philip Myerscough) got to know me, too. Crossing Front Square without breaking an ankle on the cobbles – platform shoes were 'in' – demanded serious concentration as did greeting all the people you'd recently met (Michele Freyne, Tony Farrell, John Garrett, the gorgeous Roger Watts). Remembrance of people passed. Gilbert O'Sullivan's 'Clair' was top of the pops.

There were port parties and black-velvet parties. Flat parties, room parties and grand-house parties in Wicklow, Meath and Kildare. Lunch parties, tea parties, cocktail parties, Elizabethan garden parties, Knights-of-the-Campanile parties. Dinner parties in the Shelbourne, the Kildare Street Club, the Hibernian. Rugby parties in Davy Byrnes and The Bailey. And Boat Club balls and dinner dances all over the shop. Which stood out? So many, including a vicar-and-tarts party at the Hell Fire Club, in the Dublin mountains. Decadent? Naturally. And after, loads of us packed in a tiny car, driven by its owner

(Mike Stewart Moore? John Byers?) careered straight over the rocky mountainside by way of the boulders. The car was a write-off.

I also remember a mad and magical twenty-first at Tony Farrell's baronial hall of a house somewhere miles away in Westmeath. Everyone there was dressed in differing shades of velvet and I recall a gigantic moose head hanging down over the magnificent staircase, surveying the scene. But it might be my imaginings … and Aline Galvin's twenty-first at her then home, Loughlinstown House, notable to us – students, remember – for the unstoppable flow of Dom Pérignon and dancing around the floodlit gardens and pool. Other amazing weekend parties at Kit and Kirsty Hughes's Nash house, Gracefield, in Kildare, where we played Cardinal Puff and backgammon until the early hours. And later, a decidedly decadent party at the lakeside Luggala house in Wicklow, former home of Oonagh Guinness. It was about this time that Liz and I unwittingly gatecrashed the launch party for one of Jennifer Johnston's earlier novels. We were loitering in the much-lamented Hibernian Hotel having a drink and a chat (as one did) when suddenly we found ourselves slap bang in the middle of it. We acquitted ourselves on the literary talents of Miss Johnston's work famously. To be sure.

Did I do any work those first years? Not a lot. With only three seven-week terms each year, that was left for the holidays back in Blighty when I would catch up on some of the reading without my cool quotient suffering a bashing. But with the barn-storming, Yeats-loving Brendan Kennelly and devilish Joycean David Norris as my English lecturers, my conscience did, occasionally, prick. My despairing tutor (whose name escapes me) summoned me for a talk that first year because of my poor attendance. Did I have an excuse? Of course, but I couldn't tell him, sitting there with his grey suit and even greyer face. I was quite simply having the time of my life. Straight out of a Catholic English boarding school and a conservative family, all this unfettered freedom went to my head. TCD was just like some permanent pleasure trip. And I said yes to most of it.

I had a couple of semi-boyfriends that first year: Edward Cholmondeley-Clarke for one. Liz called him 'Chumly Bumly' when he wasn't within earshot, probably to put me off. We'd spend hours in his rooms in Botany Bay listening to his favourite music – Wagnerian operas, it so happens. One night, crossing

Front Square together late, we bumped into some drunken, boorish Boat Club members (Mike Mitchell, Mike Braddell, Bruce Walker … I mean you). And they hit on the great wheeze of trying to debag poor Edward. Somehow he proved a match for them and we got away with both his pride and trousers intact. Another person's face stares out at me down the years: a young, tweed-coated, beautiful nineteen-year-old called David Greenwood, who sent me hastily scribbled romantic notes across the floor of the Reading Room. That can't have lasted long as I was rarely there. I remember, also, someone called Seymour Cresswell. I don't think I even knew him. But I loved his fantastical name.

In our second year Liz and I lived with Maggie Stewart on Lower Fitzwilliam Street: the winsome Jane Marriott, who, like me, had a brother, Richard, at TCD, lived in the basement. That house was ideally placed as it was equidistant to Toner's pub and to Trinity, where most mornings we'd have a chat with Charlie Webb, our favourite porter, before picking up our mail. How I also remember, that year, zipping around Dublin streets in the late Mike McNamara's orange Mini. Mike was such a kind and considerate soul that he volunteered to 'stand in' for another student nervous about their upcoming driving test (this, remember, was pre-photo identities). Mike duly turned up at the North Dublin exam centre, took the test for his pal … and failed. I also remember prized invitations to Sunday lunches cooked by Kathy Gilfillan and Cathy de Hartog in their flat on Waterloo Road. Those two were cool with a capital C.

In contrast to their flat, ours was cold and crummy with dire furniture. Visitors to other flats were constantly ringing our bell, so one hapless night, Liz and I rashly decided to throw a full bucket of water out of our third-floor window onto the next offender below. We scored a direct hit – thinking of it now I am horrified – but back then, we didn't think, we just did. And the next thing we knew was when a drenched and burly Dubliner, deaf to our terrified apologies, tried to batter down our door, hurling blood-curdling obscenities at us. Murder was on the cards. A panicked phone call summoned student reinforcements in the form of Mike Stewart Moore, Chris Risso Gill, Johnny Byers and my childhood friend, the late Chris Arnold, whose combined brawn eventually saw the soaked man on his way. Later that year, some of those same students were hauled up in front of a Dublin magistrate for deliberately pouring Double Diamond beer from a balcony at Punchestown races onto the head of a plain-faced girl below. When asked if they had anything to say in their defence, one of them replied, straight-faced, that they'd merely been testing to see if Double Diamond really 'worked wonders'.

That next term at the end of January 1972 the unbelievable happened: Bloody Sunday. The anger and revulsion that swept through Dublin at the slaughter of innocents during a civil rights march was tangible. Our flat was just 150 yards from the British embassy. I remember watching the flames devouring the Georgian terraced building in Merrion Square in the dark. The vast crowds swelled hour by hour. Do I remember Dr Pittion, my saturnine French tutor, being there? I do. And the floppy-haired Dr Terence Brown, one of my English lecturers, pushing past me at some point? Absolutely. I also remember my brother Dermot clambering up on a cart for a better view and hauling me up beside him. People started singing 'If you hate the British army clap your hands' to the tune of 'She'll be Coming Round the Mountain'. We linked arms as the flames grew larger and jigged to the chanting, even though some were doubtless reflecting on the grand twenty-first birthday party for Nick Peck, son of the British ambassador, we'd attended weeks earlier. Many of us at Trinity were first-generation Brits (neither West Brits, nor Anglo-Irish as we were often mistakenly called) holding British passports. And in Dermot's and my case, our Cork-born father had served as a major in the RAMC during the Second World War. The inherent ironies, terrors and religious bigotries of those times were deeply troubling. We were duly informed that Trinity was to be closed in a national day of mourning. From then on, bomb scares in Dublin and within Trinity's walls became more frequent.

Dublin drizzled and we fell in love. By this time I had started walking out lengthily with Franz Waldburg, a gentle German who sheep-farmed and deerstalked near Glendalough. Oh the romance of it. Once or twice he came to lectures with me at Trinity, causing quite a stir, as he was in his mid thirties and I, just twenty. One night we threw a large dinner party at his crumbling house at Derrybawn in Laragh and somehow, without our knowledge, hash cookies appeared on the table with the cheese. Needless to say, those who ate them were flying. It was at this point that Liz, egged on by Julia Kennedy and myself, decided to deflate a well-known Dublin guest's ego by letting down the tyres of his swish new car. Sparks flew, but we never confessed.

Hollywood beckoned that year, from Ardmore Studios in the Wicklow mountains. Sean Connery and Charlotte Rampling were starring in the inexplicably batty film *Zardoz*, directed by John Boorman. Paul McGuinness was third assistant, or something, with zillions of film-extra parts for the grabbing. TCD students clamoured for roles, with Jenny Mullen and the late Ros Hill wrestling semi-naked in a mud bath. Others were encased in plastic or eccentrically outfitted as 'apathetics' (me) or as 'eternals' (Chris Arnold, Chris Rowley). I also got to live two unforgettable months that summer of 1973 in Madrid and Almeria with Oscar-winning film legend Lee Marvin and wife while he was shooting a Western.

Back for our final year, Liz and I moved into a smart three-bed mews in Heytesbury Lane with Julia and a Dublin couple who paid twice as much rent just for the dubious pleasure of the four-poster bedroom. A 'famous' writer, Brian Cleeve, lived next door and we drove him demented. Dobbin the carthorse lived on the other side with the twinkle-eyed rag and bone man, Paddy. There was a proper merry-go-round ride parked permanently outside on which streams of visitors would relive their childhood. Surreal wasn't the word. Our rent was a fiver a week each, which left a fiver over to live on. Even with our UK grants, our addiction to fashionable clothes, records and fun meant money was tight. So we had more part-time jobs flogging aprons to Brown Thomas and Switzer's or seating customers in Jonathan's on Grafton Street, courtesy of its irrepressible manager and lifelong friend Heather Gaye. We also accepted a lot of dinner invitations. The running joke was that a variety of Dublin men about town, such as the late Pat O'Brien, Peter Bunbury, Nick Bielenberg, Alan Scott, Louis Murray et al., would call to ask one of us out for dinner and whoever answered the phone first, got fed.

Despite the looming prospect of finals and the perils of the 'after' world, life was magical. It was *Teaser and the Firecat* time, Cat Steven's seminal album. We threw a summer party to say so long to all our friends and erected a tent in our walled, rose-clad garden. The disc jockey we hired for the night was Eamon de Valera (a grandson). There wasn't room to move with what seemed like the whole of Dublin trying to gatecrash. Brian Cleeve appeared in his nightshirt and nightcap, shouting wildly. How can one but look back and laugh?

So, so long to the Russell Hotel, where we would chain our bikes to the railings before sweeping in to their grand drawing room for tea; the Wicklow Hotel, where we were once asked, during Holy Hour, whether we would 'like a drink while waiting'. And Bartley Dunnes and the Brazen Head. And finally, so long, dear, dear friends and acquaintances from the seventies who are now pushing up the daisies.

PS: After all that laughing and living and lusting I managed a creditable 2:2 in my finals. My love of learning came later. That's life.

Lucy O'Sullivan (TCD 1970–4; Modern Languages, French and English) became a press officer in IBM's European HQ, Paris, before returning to London to set up her own Covent Garden press and PR consultancy, McCormick O'Sullivan Associates. After marriage and three children, she moved to Brussels to work for the European Parliament and European Commission. She finally returned to London and in June 2009 stood as an independent in the European Parliamentary elections for the Greater London region. Luckily, she wasn't elected.

ROUND TRIP

daniel reardon

IN DECEMBER 1969 I received a small envelope from Trinity College Dublin informing me that I had been accepted as an M.Litt. candidate in the English Faculty and that my thesis supervisor would be Eiléan Ní Chuilleanáin. This was thrilling news. I was aimlessly crashing around New York City trying to recover from the excesses of that crazy decade. My degree from Fordham University was deemed good enough to allow me to pursue academic immortality in the fabled city of Wilde, Joyce, Behan, Synge, Shaw and O'Casey. Dublin was also where my hero, Gerard Manley Hopkins, had died.

I arrived in April 1970 and met Ms Ní Chuilleanáin in her spectacular office in the Rubrics building. Such a heady, intoxicating discussion of Edmund Spenser, Colin Clout and *The Faerie Queene* I had never experienced. I reeled out of Front Gate and into O'Neills of Suffolk Street for further intoxication. There I met Brendan Kennelly and Michael Hartnett and was convinced I had found a Parnassian paradise. I was introduced to McDaids and Mulligans and The Bailey and wondered why I had waited so long. Ryans of Parkgate Street was another holy well on the way to the Phoenix Park and what was then called the Royal Zoological Society of Ireland. The zoo was my refuge, my *omphalos*, and had the splendid attraction of a members' bar that stayed open during Holy Hour. It wasn't all pints and snugs and modern poetry. My other sanctum was a carrel in the basement of the 1937 Reading Room in Front Square. There I read everything about Edmund Spenser's life in Ireland. That summer I made the pilgrimage to the idyllic ruins of Kilcolman Castle. I walked the shores of the rushy lake, trying to recreate the conversations between Spenser and his dashing visitor from Youghal, Walter Raleigh.

Back in Dublin there were poetry readings in the Exam Hall and the Senior Common Room where I was introduced to Seamus Heaney, Derek Mahon and Michael Longley. Upstairs in Synnott's my mentor Eiléan Ní Chuilleanáin held court every Thursday with Leland Bardwell, MacDara Woods, Pearse Hutchinson and Anthony Cronin. It was wildly inspiring and my own zoo poems were given airings in *Ariel* edited by Merrily Harpur and Margaret Hickey, and *TCD Miscellany* edited by Paul McGuinness. Elgy Gillespie, who had joined *The Irish Times*, used her influence to get my poem 'For the Flamingoes in Dublin Zoo' published in the prestigious Saturday poetry page. I was asked to read at Synnott's, in the Players Theatre and during Dublin Arts Week, when the music was provided by Tara Telephone, featuring Declan Synnott on guitar and an extraordinary singer and songwriter, Phil Lynott. There was a vibrant and exciting music scene with concerts and music sessions in the Exam Hall, Slattery's of Capel Street and O'Donoghue's, starring Christy Moore, Planxty, Sweeney's Men, The Chieftains and The Dubliners. And of course, the theatre – indelible memories of stunning performances from Micheál Mac Liammóir, Donal McCann, Cyril Cusack, Siobhan McKenna and Niall Toibin. The Abbey, the Gate, the Gaiety and The Olympia were magical wonderlands where Brian Friel, Tom Murphy, Tom Kilroy and Hugh Leonard cast their spells.

I had long been in thrall to the theatre. My school, Loyola, on Park Avenue and 83rd Street, is a five-minute walk from the Metropolitan Museum and Central Park. Just behind the museum is Delacorte Castle, its amphitheatre the site of the legendary Joe Papp's fabulous 'Free Shakespeare in the Park'. How could you begrudge standing for hours to get the free ticket that allowed you to witness stellar performances from Meryl Streep as Isabella in *Measure for Measure*, Martin Sheen as Romeo, Stacy Keach as Hamlet and George C. Scott and Colleen Dewhurst as Antony and Cleopatra? The Broadway theatres in the 1960s were still accessible on a student budget. I saw Richard Burton's *Hamlet*, directed by John Gielgud and presented (daringly at the time) in 'rehearsal clothes'. I was stunned by Paul Scofield as Thomas More in *A Man For All Seasons* and by John Gielgud and Irene Worth in Edward Albee's *Tiny Alice*.

At Fordham I was taken under the wing of the legendary theatre director Vaughn Deering who lived in the Lamb Club on Broadway and who made Mimes and Mummers one of the finest university drama groups in the country. Vaughn was a theatrical treasure trove as well as a meticulous stage craftsman. I was privileged to be in his shows from Shakespeare to Shaw, Aristophanes to George S. Kaufman. Through him I was introduced to the Provincetown Playhouse on MacDougal Street in Greenwich Village. I was allowed to watch rehearsals, help backstage and walk on in productions of Ibsen and O'Neill.

When I heard Trinity Players were planning a production of *The Tempest* I threw my hat into No. 4 and was thrilled to be cast as Gonzalo. Paolo Tullio was an achingly funny Glaswegian Trinculo, Michael Colgan an athletic Stephano and Roger Greene a nasty Sebastian. It was great fun and the production, co-directed by Donald Taylor Black, travelled to Cork for the Universities Dramatic Societies Festival.

Susan FitzGerald was appearing in *Black Comedy* with James Morris in the same festival, as was Jeananne Crowley as Ophelia in a production of *Hamlet* starring Patrick Drury and featuring Peter Caffrey and Paul Bennett as Rosencrantz and Guildenstern. Other Players' productions I appeared in were Pinter's *The Dumbwaiter* with Paolo Tullio, Goethe's *Faust* with Derek Chapman as a terrifying Mephistopheles, and the medieval miracle plays performed on flatbed Guinness trucks in Front Square. The most memorable was a full-on, big-budget production of Congreve's *Love for Love* with a brilliant cast: Jeananne Crowley as Mrs Frail, Louise 'Dillie' Keane as Angelica and Derek Chapman as Tattle. I played Sir Sampson, another 'old' character, and the production was an enormous success.

The big adventure after the run in Players was to perform for two nights in Mountjoy Prison. We were not prepared for the robust reception given to the play by the inmates, who responded uproariously to every Restoration *double entendre*, pun and piece of wordplay. The sight of the lovely young actresses in late-seventeenth-century costumes plus the high jinks and derring-do of Congreve produced a wall of wild sound from the truly captive audience. So loud was the constant hilarity the actors could barely hear their cues. At one point I delivered an exasperated plea as Sir Sampson: 'Why did I ever marry?' and from the stalls came a loud emphatic reply, 'Cause you're a filthy ould fucker, Reardon!' I knew the voice and spotted a stalwart of the infamous Saor Éire faction. He was shaking his fist at me and roaring with laughter. My fellow cast members looked at me more than a little suspiciously in the dressing room afterwards. How could I explain I knew the man quite innocently from drinking pints and discussing horses in Mulligans and that I knew nothing at all of his participation in bank raids and detonations?

Weeks later in the same genial pub I was in company with some of the cast. It was near Christmas and the place was packed. Suddenly we heard, 'Howaya, Tattle!' addressed to Derek Chapman. He turned to see a more than rakish young man smirking at us over his pint. 'And where did you see the show?' he was asked. 'And where do you think? I'm out on Christmas release and can't wait to get back. I have a fantastic lover and all the drugs I could want!' When we enthused about the knowledgeable reception for the play from the prisoners, this parolee was unimpressed. 'We might be dumb, getting locked up, but we're not thick.' The fact was that the Mountjoy inmates were by far the sharpest, most responsive audience we'd had for the entire run.

Meanwhile the groves of academe required attention and I was invited to run seminars and tutorials with the undergraduate English students. It was refreshing and illuminating reading the essays and papers of budding scholars and authors. The bestselling crime writer Ken Bruen showed great spark writing about English Romantic poetry. I toiled happily away on my thesis and was pleased with my insights on the life and works of Edmund Spenser. Unfortunately, an external examiner from the west of Ireland was not impressed. May she rest in peace.

But my inclinations had been turning away from the lecture halls and libraries – the pull of the actor's *métier* was becoming hard to resist. I auditioned for the Radio Éireann Players and was offered a two-year contract. I was able to listen and learn and act with such performers as Pegg Monaghan, Aiden Grennell, Eamon Keane, Tom Studley, Daphne Carroll and Brian O'Higgins. It was a joy to cycle out to the leafy Montrose campus, gather the scripts in the green room and pitch up in Studio Nine with Brendan Cauldwell, Seamus Forde, Colette Proctor and Breandan O Duill. We performed all the classics, expertly adapted for radio by P.J. O'Connor, Anthony Cronin, Tony Hickey and Hugh Leonard among so many others. Lee Dunne's *Harbour Hotel* became a fixture and *Strumpet City* got its first dramatization on radio with Brendan Cauldwell as Rashers Tierney, Tom Studley as Father Diffley and myself as Father O'Connor. After work I would call into the garden flat of the beautiful Vereker sisters, Margaret and Finola, on Wellington Road. Michael Deeny was the manager of the new, hugely successful Celtic rock band, Horslips. Here in the big front room all the new Horslips albums were carefully evaluated by the band members. Jim Lockhart would later work for RTÉ and Barry Devlin is writing films.

My slim volume of poems *In the Lion House* was published in 1974 to great acclaim (in the back room of Mulligans). I was asked to read one night at an arts festival in Monaghan town. It coincided with a Horslips gig in the town hall. Michael Deeny offered to give me a lift in his flash Mercedes convertible. It was a balmy evening and I perched in the back seat as he booted down the Slane Road. It was very rock and roll, like a scene from *The Great Gatsby*. Later on, while Horslips tore the roof off the place in front of a few thousand adoring fans, I read my poems to a half dozen Monaghan literati. One young critic was only too keen to share with me afterwards that while he 'kind of liked' some of the poems, others, he thought I made 'sound better than they were'. So much for trying out new material.

So from the great harbour of New York City to the bend of Dublin Bay, from the Lower East Side to Front Square, I made my journey. Now, 'by a commodious vicus of recirculation', I watch our daughters making the same trip in reverse. What else can be said but God bless and God speed?

Daniel Reardon (TCD 1970–3; M.Litt.) graduated from Fordham University in New York in 1970. He joined the RTÉ Radio Drama Department in 1974 as actor, playwright and producer until 2005. He wrote plays for radio, including the daily serial **Riverrun**. Stage plays include **The OK Thing To Do** (Abbey/Peacock); **Fun With Bamboo** (Winner, Bewley's Café Theatre Award); **Spenser's Laye** (Dublin, Cork and Edinburgh) and **Bleeding Poets (Irish Times** Theatre Award Nomination, Best New Play 2008). His poems, **In The Lion House**, appeared in 1987.

Stage appearances: **Philadelphia Here I Come** and **The Shawshank Redemption** at the Gaiety and the Pan Pan production of **Hamlet** at The Beckett Centre. Film and TV: **My Left Foot, Night Train, The Silver Tassie, Fallout, The Clinic, Fair City** and **The Tudors**.

IN SEARCH OF THE BEAUTIFUL PEOPLE

james ryan

OCTOBER 1970. Day One, Freshers' Week.

I walked in through the medieval portal, struggling not to appear like the rookie I was. Ahead was a jamboree of college society stalls, all jousting for new recruits. First on the right, seated at a small, fold-up table were the Marxist Leninists, every bit as grim as the Maoists – or were they Stalinists? – sitting directly opposite. I'd never seen a real-life, self-declared communist so I stared. A big mistake. I'd caught the attention of the fierce-faced, androgynous recruitment officer. Paralysed by first-day courtesy I became an unwitting victim of what felt like a show trial. All at once, I was back in my primary school, my attention piously focused on Sister Xavier as she led us through prayers for the conversion of Russia. The closing sequence of that routine, thirty-five tiny voices roaring 'Saviour of the World, Save Russia', resounded in my ears. I took courage and walked on, relieved when, in the same mechanical way, I heard that recruitment officer ask someone else if they were prepared to stand by while the proletariat remained enslaved and wantonly exploited by the capitalist machine. These were my first steps into the world in flux that was Trinity in the 1970s.

The ban on enrolling in Trinity without permission, imposed by the Catholic hierarchy on its flock, was lifted on 7 September of that year. Whilst it is very unlikely that the threat of eternal damnation was a source of anxiety for any of the 1400 Catholics on the books (approximately one-third of the student population), it nonetheless underlined the general disquiet, if not outright hostility, of the Irish Catholic hierarchy towards Trinity. One of the many consequences of this was to imbue the college with the allure of forbidden fruit, making it an attractive prospect for a generation at odds with the stifling conservatism of their era. Trinity, of course, had its own brand of conservatism, as many emerging would-be agents of change discovered, but crucially, that conservatism was, in the main, negotiable. Indeed, several of those who came to play significant roles in public life served their political apprenticeship challenging the guardians of college traditions. Whatever lay in store, the Front Gate with those heckling recruitment officers lined up beyond, marked the entry point to an exciting, diverse and often daunting world for the great majority of 1970 Freshmen.

It would be fanciful to imagine I'd decided to go to Trinity for ideological reasons. On the contrary, the decision was whimsical and, as would emerge, conflicted. On intermittent trips to Dublin during the school holidays – pilgrimages to buy some newly released LP or other, or, as was often the case, just the *New Musical Express* – I first spotted what until then I'd only ever seen in magazines; the beautiful people. There they were, floating in and out through the Trinity portal, nonchalantly happy, sometimes smiling, sometimes squishing their eyes as if taking in the world from an altogether different perspective. They were cool. I badly wanted to be a beautiful person, but just about everything militated against that possibility. For starters, I spent most of the year in boarding school in Tipperary. Short back and sides, complete with a chiselled side parting, were de rigueur. The summer holidays weren't long enough to grow even a semblance of the sort of hair I wanted. Despite this and other drawbacks, I believed that just by being in Trinity I might learn to float through that front portal, nonchalantly happy. There was, I should admit, a further and perhaps more compelling reason for wanting to be part of that floating show. I had the idea, generated from talk of free love and the like, that the beautiful people were directly connected to the permissive society. And that held out untold hope.

When it came to deciding which actual course I might take, a childhood ambition to be very rich, latent in the flower-power years, re-emerged. It might well have receded except for the appearance in the school grounds, just weeks before the deadline for applications, of a red MG. It was a sunny, Saturday afternoon in late October 1969. The roof was down and there was a meringue-like sex object with sunglasses in the passenger seat. The driver, older brother of a boy in my year, had called to visit. It was a James Bond moment. When it turned out that the MG owner had recently completed a business degree in Trinity, it became a 'course choice' moment. Business Studies it had to be.

Free secondary education, announced in 1966, was introduced the following year. Predictably, secondary-school numbers increased dramatically. The demand for university places would, when those numbers filtered through, rise accordingly. So too would entry requirements. However, for a student in the Irish education system hoping to secure a place in Trinity in 1970, those requirements were still far from challenging, probably downright risible to a current generation. Three Leaving Cert. grade Cs at higher level, four if you wished to study medicine. But – and this was a big 'but' – a student had to meet the esoteric criteria of the Admissions Office. While those criteria remained undisclosed, it can safely be assumed that a diverse student population, coupled with loyalty to the traditional feeder schools north and south of the border, and an age-old link with a wide array of UK schools and colleges, determined the decisions made. Those days were, however, rapidly drawing to a close. A nationally co-ordinated, grade-based points system of entry was about to kick in, ensuring that as the decade progressed the college would be increasingly populated by students who, in general, arrived with significantly higher grades than previous generations. As well as the work necessary to achieve such grades, these students needed to be well informed on such issues as subject choice before embarking on the Leaving Cert. programme, and indeed the complex workings of the Central Admissions Office. This led to a *perestroika* and subsequently *glasnost*, arguably symbolized by the breaking of a discrete entrance/exit onto Nassau Street. At any rate, meritocratic values had, at least in theory, come into play in the entry process and that, arguably more than any other development, shaped Trinity in the 1970s.

Happily, I was at a school which, partly through the international Catholic missionary network, partly through reputation, had a steady, if relatively small, flow of students from such far-flung places as Tanzania, Kenya, Barbados, former British Guyana and South Africa. Trinity, with its long-standing international reputation, was the university of choice for this group. It was also the university of choice for a second, marginally larger group, those of Irish parentage based in the UK or in the employment, further afield, of British multinationals and the British army. For one reason or another, some of these were ineligible for the exemption necessary to enter the other Irish universities without Leaving Cert. Irish, and consequently, Trinity was the only option open to them. These various factors combined to make Trinity an established option in my school. The dean of studies, Soapy Joe, was well up to speed on application procedures and equally well practised at writing apposite references. There was no mention of sin, mortal or otherwise, nor was there any talk of getting episcopal dispensation. I was one of ten students from my year to enter Trinity, five of whom, including myself, were set to study Business.

On the first day of Michaelmas Term the incoming Junior Business Studies class together with those from affiliated faculties, primarily Social Studies – well over a hundred in all – gathered outside Hut One. This long prefab bunker ran parallel to the Old Library in what is now New Square. Inside was a great expanse of collapsible desks and chairs with little or no aisle space. Used to the privileges of being seniors at school, it took a while to take on board that we were, once again, bottom of the pile. We were first years. Not everyone regarded this as a disadvantage. Elections for the class representative saw five or six candidates make an array of promises, all spectacularly outmanoeuvred by Pat Cox, who, with an already highly developed sense of political timing and an innate feel for the zeitgeist, denounced the opposition candidates as all being 'under the one umbrella'. There was an explosion of laughter, a mass release of the discomfort generated by the predictable rhetoric of some of the previous speakers. Cox had positioned himself as a champion of the changing order that was Trinity in the 1970s. When, many years later, the Progressive Democrats came into being, Cox and Harney, who would join the Freshmen ranks the following year, emerged as key players, bringing the same crusading energy that marked their debut into college politics.

It would be some time before friendship groups expanded to include people other than those from school. Years of the same routine, class all day, recreation and/or sports in the late afternoon and study all evening left us ill-equipped to deal with the large amounts of what we regarded as leisure time in college. Lectures ended at one. We had every afternoon off, or so it seemed. The result was that Mike Ryan, Paul McNaughton and I, who'd all been at school together, went to the cinema so frequently that by the end of the first term we had seen every film there was to see in Dublin. It was a while before we took control and headed for the individual paths on which we have, by and large, remained. Trinity was a privileged environment in which to discover those paths, a fact that was not as apparent then as it is now.

One of the oft-spouted generalizations is that change originates beyond these shores, reaching Ireland long after it has taken hold elsewhere. Although very questionable now, this notion had more than a little validity in the 1970s. Consequently, there was a palpable drive in the up-and-coming generation to 'catch up' with the rest of the western world. Nowhere was that drive more manifest than in Trinity. Here was a generation ill at ease in the prevailing moral climate. The exchange of views and ideas both formal and informal in college, travel, particularly the J1 programme to the US, access to an ever-expanding mass media and an all-out rejection of the still smouldering belief that suffering has its rewards, combined to ensure that many of the reforms the larger society would subsequently embrace were spearheaded in Trinity in the 1970s. Take for instance the appearance of a handwritten notice, propped against a big glass jar of blue, foil-wrapped Alka-Seltzer-like sachets in the SRC depot: *Condoms*. Was this the hand of Ian Wilson? Or Anne Connelly? Probably not, but they were the courageous instigators of many necessary and welcome changes that marked the era. It became something of a badge of complicity to explain that the reason that handwritten notice read *Condoms* and not *Condoms for Sale* was to avert the possibility of a raid from An Garda Síochána. Selling condoms was illegal, but, it was argued, supplying them was not. The implied contract, a donation to the cause – humorously called 'the ultimate protection racket' – was upheld by encouraging but watchful SRC personnel. Over a decade would pass before the sale of condoms ceased to be an offence.

The front steps of the Dining Hall served as a sort of Roman forum, as it still occasionally does, with a wide spectrum of issues raised for debate. This debate generally took place from about 1.30 to 2 pm. It was not uncommon to see the late Kader Asmal, key player of the liberal intelligentsia and indeed the Law Faculty, sail out from the staff dining room, smile at the assembled students, and ask those waiting their turn to speak, what was up for debate. Then, if the topic interested him, he would signal his intention to join in. A democrat through and through, he not only bridged the gap dividing students and staff, but implicitly schooled the assembled crowds in the art of impromptu rhetoric. Forty years later, Caroline Walsh, *Irish Times* literary editor, very rarely aka Mrs James Ryan, was in South Africa for the Franschhoek Literary Festival 2010. A group interview with Kader Asmal, author of a forthcoming memoir, was one of the highlights. The opening gambit came, not from one of the UK or Irish journalists but from Asmal himself and addressed directly to Caroline: 'Are you still married to the same man?'

To those of us who arrived in 1970, the Dining Hall steps debates were a novelty, but over the months that followed that novelty wore off because it became apparent that these quasi-impromptu gatherings ran to a definite pattern. One, two, three people would hold forth about a particular injustice, let's say, the prejudicial treatment of women by the college authorities. Typically, the first speech or two might be engaging, soon to give way to a spontaneous contribution from a member of the assembled group; some personal anecdote of injustice, heartfelt no doubt, but rambling and increasingly difficult to hear above the deepening impatience of the crowd. At this point, enter the doctrinaire pimpernel: 'I agree with the points made by the previous two speakers, but the injustices they're talking about will only be abolished when there's a thirty-two-county, socialist republic ...' Or '... will only be abolished when the workers of the world unite ...' And so forth. The mood changed, however, as the decade progressed. August 1971 saw the introduction of internment by the Stormont government. An opposition rally was organized as soon as Michaelmas Term began. Fiery speeches were followed by a circuitous march to the Dáil. Mega-phone-carrying stewards corralled us into a four-deep procession, all roaring 'No!' when, every few seconds, a steward barked the word 'Internment!' at us. When at the top of Grafton Street, UCD, Bolton and Kevin Street (DIT) marchers joined in, pals from summer travels, from school, from home, turned up.

Before long the protest began to lose momentum, soon to succumb to that mix of fraternity and fatalism embodied in the gently challenging anthem of the day, 'We Shall Overcome'. By the spring of the following year that challenge was no longer gentle. The students who filed out through Front Gate in their hundreds on 2 February would join an estimated 25,000 others on the streets of the city enraged by the Bloody Sunday shootings three days beforehand in Derry. The greater part of that march would converge on the British embassy, then in Merrion Square, and look on as petrol bomb after petrol bomb after petrol bomb was hurled at the edifice until fire engulfed the whole building.

To Southerners like myself, born into a republic that had all but factored out the North in the notion of Irishness it embraced, this violent action on streets we walked every day came as a real shock. It challenged our notion of ourselves, forcing a revision that in some ways is still ongoing. One of the many privileges of being in Trinity in the 1970s was the opportunity to consider that notion of Irishness, to interact with a wide spectrum of people who regarded themselves as Irish but did not fit the official version created several decades previously: a version memorably sent up by Joyce in his depiction of the Citizen in *Ulysses*. The diverse cultural milieu offered by Trinity in the 1970s facilitated the development of a broader notion of Irishness than was then current in the society at large. For my own part, a growing awareness of how damaging and hurtful the 'official' notion of Irishness could be, prompted consideration of the ambivalent position in which many primary-school friends who had emigrated to England found themselves when they returned home, in our case Rathdowney, County Laois, for their annual two-week holiday. A decade would pass before this awareness began to morph into a novel, *Home from England*.

Instances of cultural collision, an inevitable feature of rapid social change, abound. On a not-so-serious front, witness John Stephenson on the Dining Hall steps in May 1971. He's championing a reduction in the cost of Trinity Ball tickets on the basis that they're beyond the means of 'ordinary' students. Hear Stephen Navin retort, 'Most of us don't mind paying. After all we know we are going to have a jolly good night and that's the point.' Move on to a twenty-first party in Kildare the following year, a black-tie affair at which everyone seems to be trying to be everyone else. Watch young fogey friend from my year struggle to bridge what he perceives as a social divide. We're standing around in a group, four, maybe five of us. He addresses the very glamorous girl opposite, who, it has just emerged, was studying medicine at UCD. 'Oh. Medicine in UCD,' he honks. 'You must know my friend, my good friend, Sally Anne. Sally Anne Sheil?' She looks quizzically at him, then, somewhat irritated says, 'I am Sally Anne Sheil.' Suddenly, the rest of us are glugging whatever is in our glass, holding that glass to our lips in the hope that someone will say something that will allow the rest of us to breathe. But, no. It was all too obvious, too raw, too close to what any one of us, standing there in hired monkey suits, champagne flutes in hand, might nearly have said.

By that stage I had defected from Business Studies to Arts. Acquiescence from the folks back home had, after a few very tense weeks, been won by an undertaking to continue to take Economics. It was something of a bold move in those pre-modularization times – and fraught too, in that it created the illusion that I had a definite sense of what I was about. I must have felt obliged to uphold that illusion because how else can I explain that for the entire winter of 1972–3 I went about with Gabriel Josipovici's *The World and the Book* in one pocket of my large ex-RAF officer's coat and Dostoyevsky's *The Brothers Karamazov volume I* in the other? It is not beyond the bounds of possibility that I placed these in front of me every time I sat down in the Buttery. Either way, the defection worked out well. The History Department, with its gallery of wonderful, if anachronistic, lecturers, was a revelation. Chummy in that inter-war Oxbridge way evoked by Waugh, these lecturers were, for the most part, wholly immersed in their particular field of study, but managed, at the same time, to take a gracious interest in the development of their students. How well equipped some of them were to adjust to the changes taking place in college is open to conjecture. I can still hear the sound of thumping boots approaching the small Museum Building room, where the Tudor Propaganda tutorial for which I'd signed up was about to examine some fifteenth-century manuscripts illustrating Henry VIII's attempts to win favour for his reforms. The footsteps grew louder, more assertive. The door swung open saloon-bar style. The quietly spoken, timorous lecturer was terrified. The manuscripts were very rare, very precious. Anne Connelly and Carol Coulter stood in the doorway. Were they armed? Were they going to identify the manuscripts worth stealing just as Rose Dugdale had identified the Vermeers in the Beit collection? Gracious me. The moment passed, but the atmosphere remained tense. Connelly nodded amicably at the lecturer who gathered her gown tails and scooted out the door, all at once overly delighted to allow them the two minutes they requested to canvas for the forthcoming SRC elections.

I wasn't a great one for joining societies or clubs. I did, however, join the Film Society in Senior Fresh and remained a member until I graduated. The screenings were in Dixon Hall, a long, low, evangelical-looking building with a scatter of fold-up wooden tables and chairs similar to that in Hut One. Nouvelle Vague cinema with its often iconoclastic take on things was still relatively *nouveau.* So off I trooped on Tuesday nights – it always seemed to be raining – to Dixon Hall where a noisy projector, removed for some reason from the projection room and mounted on a chair on top of a table in the middle of the hall, created a subversive, clandestine atmosphere. This was reinforced by the makeshift screen and, of course, the smoke. Everyone smoked, creating a thick fug through which the work of Godard, Truffaut, Chabrol, Resnais and Varda flickered magically onto the screen. This I enjoyed enormously, so much so that I joined the UCD Film Society and headed out to Belfield for screenings on Monday nights, sometimes seeing the same film I'd seen the previous week in Dixon Hall, or vice versa.

During the summer of 1971, working as a relief dustman in central London, I had the good fortune, in the scramble for accommodation, to team up with a group of fellow students who would remain lifelong friends, among them the above-mentioned Mrs Ryan. Most of this group were in UCD so I found myself spending an increasing amount of time with them, worryingly comfortable with that brand of rebellion, self assured, dogmatic and faddish, particular to the sons and daughters of professional, blue-shirt (faded denim by then) families. The style was, by and large, anti-style, particularly among the more privileged, who felt obliged to mask advantage. There was no audience for the likes of MacDonald of the Isles who occasionally arrived to lectures in Trinity in a Rolls-Royce, no one prepared to debate the authenticity of his title – Baron. From the emerging US-style campus that was Belfield in the early seventies, Trinity was a place apart, a vestige of the *ancien régime.* That view, however, was voiced less and less as the decade progressed, increasingly associated, as it became, with an older generation, people who had failed to note how effectively Trinity had reinvented itself between 1970 and 1980.

Of the many very worthy aspects of the university to withstand the changes that decade brought was the exceptionally caring relationship that existed between teaching staff and students, particularly in the smaller faculties. Here, students were usually known by name from the outset. They were personally valued and encouraged to an extent that is just not possible now, given staff–student ratios. I recall my still very good friends Lucy Trench and Anabel Craig taking what seemed, at the time, the very sophisticated step of inviting their lecturers to their top-floor flat on Fitzwilliam Street for drinks following their conferring. Were there At Home invitations issued? Probably. One thing for certain, they would not have been called 'invites'. It was a grand occasion, parents, trailing admirers, classmates and notably the very formidable, but exceptionally personable, heads of the Italian and Art History Departments, Corinna Salvadori Lonergan and Anne Cruickshank. *Ní bheidh a leithéidí ann arís.*

And what of the beautiful people I'd seen loping through Front Gate on those visits to Dublin in the late sixties? I was destined, despite my cool line in accessories, Indian shirt, Moroccan beads and Jesus sandals, not to belong. Or at least, feel as though I didn't belong to that mirage-like elite. I was innately curious, inclined even to gawk. I had a country habit of making connections and 'placing' people. I was interested in everything. Anyway, by 1973, the memory of Woodstock (1969), or rather *Woodstock* the movie (1970), had begun to fade. The growing realization that it had been an end rather than a beginning, a final, all-out drawing together of the various threads that made up sixties' rock rather than the dawn of a beautiful new world, was rapidly hardening to fact. The sense of common purpose to which the civil rights and anti-Vietnam movements in the US had given rise was fragmenting. So too were the beautiful people. Some, already proponents of self-sufficiency, took up environmental issues and toyed with 'alternative' lifestyles west of the Shannon. Others, fringe no-hopers, stumbled from one high to the next, some never to return from the far side of the moon.

The majority, however, saw the writing on the wall and while they might have been slow to buy a suit, they were heading in that direction, albeit reluctantly. The first punks had begun to appear on Grafton Street by the mid seventies, so Crosby, Stills, Nash & Young were about to be drowned out by the Ramones, edging the 1970 Freshman further into the materially rewarding ranks of the status quo. My own trajectory, partly determined by sixties education gurus, Ivan Illich and Paulo Freire (John Holt would follow later), led to the H.Dip.Ed. and subsequently to a teaching position in the then very progressive Newpark Comprehensive. There I had the privilege of working on a series of innovative educational programmes with several people I'd known in Trinity, particularly Owen Metcalfe and Helen Jones. This interest prompted a return to college in 1980 to undertake postgraduate work, which after a year's course work, continued piecemeal until 1984. How things had changed. Hut One had been demolished, New Square had come into being as indeed had the Arts Block. Dons no longer appeared donnish, the swish of academic gowns in the cold, stone halls now rare, even a bit spooky: Professor Otway-Ruthven, doyenne supreme of that illustrious tradition, had retired. Kader Asmal had been replaced on the Dining Hall steps by Joe Duffy. Calls for a new world order had given way to calls for support for the striking Buttery staff – all of this happening against a backdrop of unemployment, emigration and the skeletal spectre of the H-Block hunger strikers. Gone were characters like Sam (Laski – I think that was his surname), the man with the rope bag full of papers who spent his days in the Hist Common Room, front line veteran, it was said, of the 1956 Hungarian Rising. Gone too were the Biba babes and the Judy Collins lookalikes. And where was hurley-flailing Joe Revington?

There were, of course, new myths in circulation, new arresting spectacles in Front Square, new poses being struck here, there and everywhere, all, no doubt, eye-openers for incoming Freshmen; a reminder for the initiated, like myself, that even if I had been so inclined, that great and profoundly formative adventure could not be repeated.

James Ryan (TCD BA 1975, H.Dip.Ed. 1976 and M.Ed. 1984; Business Studies). His first novel **Home from England** appeared in 1995. **Dismantling Mr Doyle** followed in 1997 and his third novel, **Seeds of Doubt**, in 2001. **South of the Border**, his most recent novel, was published by The Lilliput Press in 2008. He is a lecturer in the School of English, Drama and Film in UCD, directing the undergraduate and postgraduate programmes in creative writing.

OUR MAN IN NIRVANA

donald taylor black

'I started out on Burgundy
But soon hit the harder stuff.'
Bob Dylan, 'Just Like Tom Thumb's Blues', 1965.

WHEN I WENT UP to Trinity in Michaelmas Term 1970, I intended to divide my time between playing football for the 1st XI and directing plays. During Freshers' Week I joined Dublin University Players and scored a couple of goals in the Freshers' Trial in College Park; I still try and impress people by saying that it was a hat trick, but, on mature reflection, have to admit that it was probably only two. Although it was popular, football was distinctly unfashionable compared to rugby or the Boat Club, but it has always been massively important in my life. For a couple of months I trained with the senior squad under coach 'Big' John Colrain. Colrain was a tough man from the east end of Glasgow, who had achieved legendary status in East Belfast as player/manager of Glentoran. He won four trophies in his first season (1966–7) and, in the second, his side gained superb European Cup draws, in both Belfast and Lisbon, against Benfica, then one of the giants of world football, with Eusébio as their emblematic goalscorer. While John Colrain was coaching Trinity, his day job was as manager of St Patrick's Athletic in the League of Ireland. Sadly he died young, and almost forgotten, back home in Glasgow in 1984, at the age of forty-seven, which means that he was only thirty-three when he coached us in Trinity.

One of the best players in the squad was Pat Finucane, a skilful midfield player, who captained DUAFC in the two following seasons, 1971–2 and 1972–3. He was murdered by Loyalist paramilitaries in February 1989, who shot him fourteen times as he sat eating a meal in his north Belfast home with his three children and his wife, Geraldine, whom he had met in college. In 2003, the Stevens Report concluded that there had been collusion in his killing between the UDA/UFF and the security forces in the North. I played a couple of games with the 2nd XI in the AUL – home fixtures were in Santry – but soon realized that it was not possible to be committed to serious sport at university level as well as being deeply involved in a theatre group with such high ambitions and standards as Players. I don't know whether I would have been good enough to become a regular member of the first team but, in some ways, I wish I had given myself the opportunity. Terry McAuley was captain in my Junior Freshman year and he returned to Trinity in 1980, staying on staff until he took early retirement from his position as director of sport in 2009.

Despite my own early retirement from competitive football, I continued to play weekly for various social or 'drinking' teams, who didn't train, called after traditional Trinity names such as Moyne and Lecky: fellow team members included Denis Murray, later BBC Ireland correspondent for twenty years, and sometimes another Belfast man, Pat Abernethy, whom I directed in a number of shows in our small theatre in House No. 3. We took part in the five-a-side competition, held during Trinity Week, and I also enjoyed lining out for the T.T. West XI, both as an undergraduate and after I left. At least once I played (illegally) for either the Meath or the Adelaide in the Hospitals Cup competition, which is supposed to be confined to doctors and medical students.

At the beginning of the 1970s, those new to Players were conscious of the great reputation of its graduates from the previous decade who had gone to work in 'the business'. Our president was the wonderful R.B.D. French, my tutor, who had been a classmate of Beckett, and had written a book about P.G. Wodehouse. He was both wise and witty, with that particular upper-middle-class Dublin accent that has almost totally disappeared. Partly owing to the success of our predecessors, and partly because of our own youthful self-confidence, our ambitions were high, and during my time in Players the quality of the work remained reasonably good, and sometimes excellent. Our shows were regularly reviewed in national newspapers, particularly by David Nowlan and J. Kane Archer (both ex-Players) in *The Irish Times* and the indefatigable J.J. Finegan in the *Evening Herald*; Kane also wrote regularly, and positively, in the *Irish Tatler* and *Sketch*.

Roger Greene and I were campaign managers for Michael Colgan when he stood for election as chairman against Paul McGuinness, who was supported by the influential Donnell Deeny. Our candidate won narrowly, although votes could be bought quite legitimately, as any student who paid the annual fee of (I think) five shillings was entitled to instant membership. There were slightly more of these on Paul's side, as I recall, mainly because Donnell was a Hist person, rather than a Players one, and he encouraged a number of his debating colleagues to temporarily absent themselves from either the GMB or the Buttery bar to sign on for Players so that they could attend our AGM. Two years later, I was chairman myself.

Donnell and Paul had been in the same class in Clongowes as Eugene Murray, who was president of the SRC, 1971–2. One of his principal policies when he had stood for election was to remove the ban on female students living in college rooms and happily he was successful in this endeavour.

In my Junior Freshman year, Marjorie E. MacManus (Miss), the Warden of Residences, sent me to digs in Miss Fleming's at 117 Leinster Road, Rathmines. With 'shared room, partial board', it cost £5. 5s. per week in advance, and the food was appalling. Helen Fleming was bohemian and slightly eccentric and, whether it was loyalty to Trinity or snobbishness and hostility to the other place, she always called UCD 'National'. When she died in 1986, Richard Pine, who had also lodged there, wrote a loving appreciation of her in *The Irish Times*: 'Her Anglo-Irish background gave to her city life, a Bowenesque sense of her class's social role, subverted by a Somervillian sense of *atelier* mischief. She was only capable of suppressing the grossest outrages.'

Other former residents of 117 during her twenty-year tenure included Homan Potterton (later director of the National Gallery of Ireland) and Ted Smyth, whose house in Dalkey my wife Consolata and I bought almost a decade and a half afterwards. In the following years I lived in various shared flats or houses on the south side, including Belgrave Square (also Rathmines) and Pigeon House Road, Ringsend, until, as a Senior Sophister, I moved into rooms – or rather a single bedsitting room in the GMB, extremely convenient to the DU Co-operative Society shop in No. 27. It cost £50 'per quarter', plus an extra fixed charge for central heating, with gas and electricity measured by meter readings. I remember that students – particularly female ones – who lived on the top floors of period houses on such sought-after thoroughfares as Waterloo Road, Fitzwilliam Square or Lower Leeson Street had a particular system for when callers arrived for a late-night coffee, a nightcap, or even an assignation: the procedure was to ring the bell and then wait for an upstairs sash window to be opened and the key of the front door to be thrown down inside a sock.

I read General Studies but, having had a brilliantly inspiring English teacher at school, remained unimpressed with the majority of lectures that I attended. Compared with UCD, who had Denis Donoghue and Seamus Deane, Trinity's English Department was dull. The exceptions were two young lecturers: Brendan Kennelly and David Norris, both showmen in their different ways. Brendan enjoyed shocking convent-educated female Freshers with frank comments about sex, using language they would not have heard from the nuns. His passionate enthusiasm for Patrick Kavanagh (not long dead) sent me straight down to Fred Hanna's in Nassau Street to purchase the *Collected Poems*. David, only recently appointed as a junior lecturer, communicated his love for Joyce by acting out scenes from *Portrait of the Artist* and *Ulysses*, with the aid of a variety of accents. Later I was impressed by the quiet intelligence of Terry Brown and Eiléan Ní Chuilleanáin, who was supervising Danny Reardon's PhD on Edmund Spenser, alas never completed. My favourite member of the Philosophy staff was Peter Mew, who gave a brilliant series of lectures on Marx and his theory of alienation. However, I will not be remembered in Trinity for my academic career. My obsession with theatre and almost full-time commitment to Players meant that I spent little time in the pursuit of scholarship.

My third subject was Italian, which undergraduates, then, as now, could study *ab initio*. The tiny Italian Department was run by the serious-minded but kind Corinna Salvadori Lonergan, who was usually disappointed with my level of enthusiasm for grammar and syntax, although I put a little more effort into the literature. I failed Italian in my Senior Freshman examinations and therefore had to repeat the year. Whether as a punishment or as a genuine way of ensuring that I eventually passed the language in my finals, Mrs Lonergan advised me strongly to spend my final Hilary Term in Italy. Consequently, I went 'off College Books' from January to March 1975 and studied at the Centro di Cultura per Stranieri at the University of Florence. Of course, it wasn't a punishment whatsoever. It increased my love for Italian food and culture and gave me the opportunity of watching the talented twenty-year-old Giancarlo Antognoni play for Fiorentina in the year that his team won the Coppa Italia. I also watched dozens of films in the Niccolini, the Universale, Kino Spazio and the Casa della Gioventù, including superb Fellini and von Stroheim retrospectives. There was nothing like the Kino Spazio in Dublin then, before the Project Cinema Club, the Irish Film Theatre in Earlsfort Terrace and, much later, the IFI. I was also hugely impressed by a fascinating Mayakovski/ Stanislavski/Meyerhold exhibition at the Palazzo Medici Riccardi and attended a number of political demonstrations, including one against Pinochet and his military junta; perhaps the most charismatic of our lecturers was an enthusiastic supporter of the radical student-worker group, Lotta Continua, which had begun in the Fiat factory in Turin in 1969.

During my years in Trinity there was almost constant political violence in the North. Some students had strong views on either side, some held so-called liberal opinions, and others wished that it would stop, or merely all go away. Sometimes the violence couldn't be ignored or forgotten, and when Bloody Sunday exploded in Derry at the end of January 1972, this was one of those occasions. The atmosphere was extremely tense and, three days later, on the Wednesday, there was a national day of mourning and the British embassy in Merrion Square was burned down, following the throwing of hundreds of petrol bombs. A reported 30,000 people watched as the flames rose into the sky and parts of the eighteenth-century building collapsed. I was there amongst the crowd and, at one stage, was told to help direct traffic away from the scene. At the same time, a small group of English students were in hiding in The Old Stand, discussing whether they should leave the country.

Another of these major events was the day of the Dublin and Monaghan bombings in May 1974, when thirty-three people were killed. As the third bomb exploded in South Leinster Street, not far from the Lincoln Inn, at approximately half past five in the evening, Ingrid and I were revising in the New (now Berkeley) Library. It was the first day of Trinity Week. The blast was extremely loud and it travelled through the railings, across the cricket square, blowing in some of the basement windows, and shaking the building in the process. These acts were perpetrated by the UVF as a protest against the Sunningdale Agreement during the Loyalist Ulster Workers' Council strike. The UVF claimed responsibility in 1993, but it has been confidently alleged that British security forces were also implicated. Five months later, I attended the crowded Anti-Internment meeting in the Mansion House. Mary Robinson, then a senator for Trinity, was one of the main speakers, as was Joe Cahill of the Provisional IRA, who made a theatrical entrance, shouting, 'Magilligan is burning!'

This was also the year of the controversial British and Irish Lions rugby tour to South Africa, which broke the sporting boycott. There was strong support for the Irish Anti-Apartheid Movement, as it was co-founded by the late Trinity law lecturer, Kader Asmal. I was present at a meeting in the Museum Building on UN Human Rights Day, which was addressed by Proinsias Mac Aonghusa with a screening of a powerful new documentary, *Last Grave at Dimbaza*.

We rarely attended concerts but I remember Tara Telephone (with Peter Fallon), Dr Strangely Strange, the Consort of St Sepulchre, Supply, Demand & Curve, and Chris Meehan singing 'Hard Hearted Hannah, the Vamp of Savannah, GA' – and, on another occasion, with vocals by Anne Adamson. If that was the soundtrack, somewhere in the vaults of memory there are rusty cans of archive material containing raw footage of random sequences: I recall being taken by Susan Denne-Bolton to meet Ruth Buchanan, for the first and only time, as she was making her 1970 Christmas cake (and being permitted to lick the spoon); summer race meetings at Leopardstown, Baldoyle and the Phoenix Park; with Louise Keane (then Mirabelle to me) listening to *Déjà Vu* (Crosby, Stills, Nash & Young) in a borrowed flat in Haddington Road; Jack MacGowran's one-man Beckett show, *Beginning to End*, Mac Liammóir in *The Importance of Being Oscar*; John Arden and Margaretta D'Arcy's *The Non-*

Stop Connolly Show in Liberty Hall; Rosemary McCreery in the Victoria Hotel, Cork; meals in Gaj's, the Universal Chinese Restaurant, Bernardo's, Snaffles, the Coffee Dock in the Intercon, Captain America's, which had opened in 1971, and where Deirdre Bowen and Mary Broderick worked part-time, and (very occasionally) in the Hibernian Hotel, or the 'High Berinian' as Myles had called it; the long bank strike in 1970; Chris Clark 'borrowing' a bus from the Donnybrook Garage to drive home on a Saturday night; Seymour Cresswell being 'persuaded' to lead the singing of 'The Men Behind the Wire' in the bar of the Great Southern during the IUDA Festival in Galway; travelling on a Greyhound bus with Roly Saul from New York to Toronto to watch Mike Halliday and Chris Harte playing cricket for Ireland against Canada; tiny, but wicked, Mary Nessa Stanley proudly wearing her new boots in Clotilde Bowe's class; separating a jarred, obstreperous Ryan O'Neal from Chris Davison after a late night in the Squirrel's Nest in Lincoln Place; the entire Players' committee meeting for Mary Cakes in Bewley's ...

Paul McGuinness never held a grudge against me for campaigning on behalf of Michael Colgan rather than him. Towards the end of the Trinity Term in my last year, we bumped into each other by the Players' noticeboard at Front Gate and he asked me what my future plans were. I told him that I hoped to work as a theatre director and had a few projects at the planning stage, including a job offer from the Lyric in Belfast. Paul was then a successful assistant director in our slowly developing film industry and suggested that I join the Film and Video Section of the Irish Transport and General Workers Union (No. 7 Branch) and apply for a trainee assistant director's ticket: 'You could earn a few bob on commercials to keep you going in between theatre gigs. I'll arrange the signatures.' I accepted his kind offer and he got me in. Although I've never forgotten this gesture, I've never thanked him. Until now.

Donald Taylor Black (TCD 1970–5; General Studies) is a film-maker and writer. Since 2001 he has been head of Film and Media at the Institute of Art, Design & Media, Dún Laoghaire, where he is also creative director of the National Film School. After leaving Trinity, he directed plays at The Peacock, The Project, the Eblana, and for The Irish Theatre Company. His documentaries include: **At the**

Cinema Palace; Irish Cinema: Ourselves Alone?; Hearts and Souls; The Joy; Dear Boy: The Story of Micheál Mac Liammóir; and **David Farrell: Elusive Moments**. He lives in Wicklow with his wife, costume designer Consolata Boyle. They have a daughter, Katie.

THOSE WERE THE DAYS

anne connolly

IT WAS NEVER part of the game plan to go to Trinity – it just wasn't on my radar screen. My life was nicely mapped out in vague, but generally attractive terms. A degree in Social Science in UCD, followed by a nice job, doing worthy but enjoyable things. I left school the summer of 1970, a young, innocent, Mass-going sixteen-year-old. But one of those life-altering moments meant that I became part of the early wave of OISs (ordinary Irish students) entering that Front Gate, fifteen months later.

Like many of my fellow Irish students, I had never crossed the gates of the place. Nor did I think that particularly odd. I suspect few enough Dubliners would have in those days – it seemed such a world apart. I thought the year away had given me the confidence I needed to embrace this new life, but that cocky self-assurance evaporated pretty quickly once I hit Front Square. Freshers' Week was in full sway and everywhere there were large and loud groups of Brits, West Brits and Northerners, who all seemed to know each other and so clearly belong.

I was partly fascinated and partly repelled by many aspects of this arcane new world that existed within the walls of this gated community, so cut off from mainstream Irish life, despite being in the heart of the capital city. Coming from an all-girls Catholic school and a family that only allowed television at holiday time, I felt like the gawking bystander in those early days: the funnily clad porters at Front Gate, lecturers and the odd student rushing around in gowns, terms I had never heard of such as 'skips', JCR, SCR, SRC, Players, the Pav, the Buttery … I remember the desperate sense of wanting to fit in, at least blend invisibly into the landscape; to have the quick repartee those shouting salesmen at the Freshers' stalls all seemed to own.

Gradually, as I began to relax a bit, I came to relish many aspects of this peculiar world although the power to surprise lasted quite a while. I was meeting people who talked about appointments with their dressmakers for ball-gown fittings, others who were having flashbacks from the last tab of acid. I was getting invited to parties that took place in large damp basements in Fitzwilliam and Merrion Squares, with no parents present, and learning that some girls' parents didn't like them going to 'basement' parties – their preference clearly being for parties in manor houses.

There was the world of the Phil and the Hist, with more arcane rules and ceremonies and more gown-wearing. The most colourful and confident characters all seemed clustered in Players – a sort of natural habitat for all those West Brits with ascendancy lifestyles. There was a sports world that I knew nothing about, and never did find out about, except to know that the Rowing Club retained a ban on women members – that is until Jane Williams decided to tackle that issue. And then there was the world of politics, and student politics in particular. I think the psychologists would say I was subconsciously seeking attachment and this is where I found it.

Throughout my time at Trinity the place was alive with political fervour. The most evident manifestations were the almost daily 'mass democracies' on the Dining Hall steps. They were the focal point for whatever campaign was current – student fees, grants, catering prices, the oppressed peoples of some distant state. They started at 1 pm on the dot and finished at 2, in lieu of lunch for the most ardent supporters. They could attract an audience of as few as twenty for the less colourful events or as many as five hundred for the major ones. I vividly remember the cast of characters who took to the stage of those Dining Hall steps, in direct competition to whatever Players had on their lunchtime offer. People like David Giles and John Stephenson would expound on the reasons for the current campaign, while the Maoists, David Vipond and

Bláthnaid Ní Chinnéide, would educate us on the 'wrongness' of our ways and with redemptive fervour foretell the ultimate judgments of the people's tribunals against our transgressions.

Looking back now there appears to have been an informal schedule for the campaign year. Typically there was one major Trinity-based campaign, one major USI march and then occasionally an occupation either inside Trinity or with other colleges, in places like the Department of Education. The USI marches focused on issues such as funding of higher education, more equitable access and fee increases. The internal campaigns focused on fees, library hours, catering prices and quality of food. Did any of them accomplish anything? Not from memory. However, while it is easy to be cynical with hindsight, there was outrage at the inequities in the system, and the protests did reflect a genuine desire for change.

One of the most memorable of the external protests, and for me the first major public march of my life, was to the British embassy to protest against Bloody Sunday. The crowds outside the embassy that day were really angry, looking to avenge the appalling murder of thirteen people in Derry on that fateful Sunday of 30 January 1972. Half the crowd there roared their support for the torching of the building in the carefully orchestrated 'spontaneous outrage', while the other half, me included, looked on with a certain amount of bourgeois horror as huge lighting torches were hurled through the windows by men scaling the balcony outside.

Other parts of the political world began to intrude into the semi-independent republic of Trinity. Dick Burke, Minister for Education in the Fine Gael/Labour Coalition government, announced in 1974 that he intended to bring in legislation to create three university groupings – Trinity, UCD and NUI (comprising UCC, UCG and Maynooth). UCD, for very obvious reasons, strongly supported the measure. Trinity, for equally obvious reasons, didn't. To protect its long-term interests, Trinity began an unseemly scramble to offer degrees to a range of courses in a number of Dublin Institute of Technology (DIT) colleges: Kevin St, Bolton St, Cathal Brugha St as well as to the National College of Art and Design.

What was interesting was that it appeared to be something of a wake-up call within the upper echelons of the college. By then, F.S.L. Lyons was provost and clearly saw the need to address Trinity's political isolation, its positioning as an essentially British institution, third choice after Oxford and Cambridge, associated with Ireland only by virtue of its geographic location. He argued the need to bring it into the mainstream of the Irish academic and educational policy world. As deputy president of the Students' Union at the time, and therefore a member of the board and Academic Council, I was able to see up front how he set about developing and implementing a highly sophisticated and effective strategy to reposition Trinity. Despite protests from traditionalists such as R.B. McDowell and others, Lyons set about communicating a new message to the outside world, drawing attention to Trinity's important contribution to international science, literature, Irish cultural and social life, and to Ireland's reputation internationally.

McDowell didn't take it all lying down. At one unforgettable board meeting in 1975, we were discussing how to ensure the safe transportation of the Book of Kells to the USA as our contribution to the bicentennial of the American War of Independence. There was an air of great solemnity as we addressed the risks of moving this vital national treasure. A special squad was to enter Trinity after midnight, transfer the book into a high-tech air-conditioned container, take it in an armoured vehicle to Dublin Port or Dún Laoghaire, bring it out to sea in a safe vessel and then transfer it to a waiting US submarine. We were all terribly mindful of our custodial responsibility and bound to secrecy. R.B. was appalled. 'Provost – what are we doing? Risking the Book of Kells for a ceremony marking a number of minor skirmishes and the ultimate defeat of the Empire?'

Occasionally he surprised. The campaign to extend library opening hours, which had garnered sufficient support for a two-day occupation, got his wholehearted support. He could just about defend a Christmas Day closing, but would have pushed for 24/7 opening hours had he heard of the term. Like many others, I had the pleasure of being taught by him, but was constantly frustrated by the fact that he started the lecture some ten minutes before arriving in the lecture hall.

At the time, Trinity was the only college in Ireland with people living on campus. This gave it the aura of a small village. You didn't need to stir from campus if you had a mind not to: shops, pubs, theatre, companionship, all were within the gates. There was always something happening, whether in the Buttery, the Phil, the Hist, a party somewhere, the Pavilion. My memory is of endless cups of coffee during the day, plenty of unhurried time to gossip and debate, and enjoying Trinity's distinctive cuisine – the famous chocolate-biscuit cake and chicken-and-mushroom vol-au-vents. Supper could be a few pints of Guinness and a packet of crisps, all looked over by Matt the wonderful barman, who missed nothing.

Pints were essential in those early days of the women's movement. We formed invading swarms of 'liberationists' who targeted pubs known not to serve women pints. We would go in groups of five or six, order pints, be refused, order the same again in shorts and then refuse to pay for them until the pints were pulled. Those were the early days of the movement. The easy availability of the Pill in Trinity through the College Health Centre, and condoms through the Students' Union shop supported a transition from 'nice girls don't' to 'nice girls can' and ultimately 'nice girls do'. 'New' women crashed the Trinity Ball in jeans and looked in horror at their sisters all dressed up in Edwardian finery, different dresses for each occasion: the Elizabethan garden party, College Races and ultimately, the ball.

Mind you, the Trinity Ball was changing too. As the role of the Ents (enter-tainments) officer grew and particularly once it was a full-time sabbatical post, people like Ian Wilson and Ciaran Owens were becoming serious players in the world of music promotions. They were able to attract big names in punk or whatever else was in vogue. The formality of an evening-dress occasion was gradually eroding. One year a Chair-O-Planes was installed in Front Square and the following morning there was a memorably perfect circle of vomit on the ground where the machine had stood – not repeated the following year.

This was the period also when the gay liberation movement began to take shape, powerfully led by the young David Norris, then an enormously popular lecturer in the English Department. His courage and leadership really helped so many people in 'coming out'. During that time he set up the Hirschfield Centre and the gay helpline offering a safe place for those transitioning into an openly gay life and who wanted more than Barclay Dunne's as a place to hang out. He and others such as Ciaran Rose were powerful role models for those understandably more hesitant.

They were heady days of personal freedom. The sexual revolution was alive and well. Women became entitled to rooms in Trinity, though in separate houses. The college authorities were gradually giving up the battle against overnight stays in rooms for members of the opposite sex. In fact when authorities in other colleges ordered newly installed condom machines to be torn down, Trinity turned a blind eye. The Students' Union began openly selling condoms in the shop. The wonderful Violet Taylor, a woman in her sixties who ran the shop and impressed us all with stories of her pink-gin lifestyle and regular foreign cruises, meeting eligible and not so eligible men, was completely relaxed when we asked her about introducing them into the shop. 'Darlings, I may sell Panama hats, but I don't have to wear them,' and then sought to see if she could swap *Gay Pride* magazine for condoms.

With hindsight, I am sorry I didn't put in more of an appearance in the classroom. We had some wonderful lecturers. Some in particular stand out. Professor T.W. Moody was a gentleman and a Quaker and a very liberal force on Academic Council. He supported efforts to have Trinity divest its investments in South African companies and backed Students' Union proposals to enroll Chilean students arrested or at risk in the Pinochet regime for their opposition to the overthrow of Allende's government in 1973. David Thornley was a wonderfully opinionated and engaging lecturer, when around. He was one of that new batch of left-wing Labour Party members who became elected to the Dáil for the first time in 1969 and again in 1973. Aidan Clarke had a bewitching, mellifluous voice and gave fascinating lectures in American History.

Tutorials, when you went to them, were intimate groupings of six to eight students. I took some time to get used to the idea that your tutor, in contrast, was not someone who lectured you, but was there to support you and keep you out of trouble. We memorably abused this system once, when a group of students were locked up in the Bridewell following an occupation of the Department of Education and one of the group trying to secure their release bravely decided to call the late Kader Asmal at 3 am to see if he would post bail. The lovely Kader, despite being woken from his sleep, just asked gently if it could wait till the morning.

What I value most about that period and didn't fully appreciate at the time was that it was a wonderful environment for a more vocational education than the curriculum suggested. I think of so many people who honed the skills, not just the knowledge they needed for their chosen careers. Mary Harney surely learnt the art of political survival and persuasion by tackling the barriers to becoming the first female auditor of the Hist. David O'Sullivan, who later became secretary general of the EU Commission was not just a great debator within the Hist, but led an intellectual foray into other arenas and began challenging for a 'third way' within the Students' Union – not the natural habitat for Hist members in those days. People did brave things too. Val Roche, who later became the manager in the Students' Union, had been to the forefront in leading the protests against the overthrow of the Allende government. She made various visits to Chile to connect with those challenging the Pinochet government. She was imprisoned in Montevideo on her return from one such visit and to her jailors' consternation went on hunger strike – a weapon they hadn't seen used before and which successfully ended her incarceration.

My own apprenticeship was somewhat less heady, but still invaluable. It ranged from braving the crowds on the Dining Hall steps (an essential prerequisite to standing for the Students' Union elections) to organizing protest campaigns, the art of pamphlet writing (every march had to have one), endless hours at the filthy Gestetner machine in the back office in the Students' Union, negotiating bulk-purchase agreements on everything from cauliflowers to condoms for the Students' Union Shop, attending board and Academic Council meetings and watching masters in the art of persuasion and politics – John Bristow, Martin O'Donoghue, Gerry Giltrap and the wonderful F.S.L. Lyons himself. Up in the garret of the Brunswick Chambers, there was life in *Trinity News*: everything to do with putting a newspaper to bed, from typesetting, cutting and pasting, writing and ultimately editing the paper.

If I was to name one thing that most encapsulates the time – the heady politics, the razor-sharp wit, the cast of characters, it would probably be Damien Kiberd's lament in *TCD Miscellany* to the passing of Chou En-Lai on 8 January 1976:

> In Memoriam
>
> So, farewell then,
> Chou-en-Lai.

You've gone to that commune
In the sky.

You were a great man
While on earth
And you always wore
That same grey shirt.

Among your friends
An unbreakable bond
Nixon, Brezhnev,
Heath, Vipond.

Anne Connolly (TCD 1971–5; History and Politics, Students' Union 1975–6) established the Well Woman Centre, and had a varied career with **Magill**, Léargas, and Kingspan, her own consultancy practice. She now runs the Ageing Well Network.

A FORETASTE OF WHAT IRELAND COULD BECOME

carol coulter

TRINITY in the early 1970s prefigured in many ways what Ireland was to become thirty years later – liberal, multi-denominational, sexually emancipated, multicultural. Despite its reputation as 'the Protestant university' there was no attempt on behalf of any Protestant denomination (the Church of Ireland being the most likely suspect) to dominate its ethos, and, apart from a few relics like grace before Commons, there was little evidence of any religious presence. Each of the Christian denominations had its chaplain, but they were there to minister to those students who maintained a relationship with their church and made no attempt to impose themselves on anyone else.

This was in marked contrast to the regimes that pertained in the universities of the supposedly secular NUI. One friend of mine was sent home from UCC for a term for editing a magazine that was less than deferential to the then Catholic bishop of Cork, Cornelius Lucey, and another was one of a dissident minority on the editorial team of the UCD newspaper, *Campus*, when the majority agreed to the university's ultimatum that they issue an abject apology to the Archbishop of Dublin, John Charles McQuaid, for his unflattering portrayal on its front page.

There was no such religious censorship in Trinity and among the student body one's religion truly did not matter; no one asked or cared what religious background you came from. For Irish students, almost all of whom had come from a fiercely segregated secondary-school system, this was a great liberation, and friendships and romances were forged unselfconsciously across denominational barriers.

It was also a place where it was taken for granted that many if not most students were sexually active, thanks largely to the enlightened policy of the Student Health Service, which prescribed the Pill to any woman student who asked for it. There were therefore few noticeable unplanned pregnancies in college – those that did occur ended in a trip to England for an abortion, often assisted by discreet advice from the Students' Union. While I'm sure many students were not sexually active, just as I'm sure many students were practising their religion, the face that the student body presented to itself and to the world was a secular and sexually emancipated one.

Trinity was always special among Irish universities, in that it had a cosmopolitan character. Recollections of the 1960s suggest an absence of southern Irish students. But by the end of the 1960s and early 1970s this had changed. Though Archbishop McQuaid's ban was not lifted until 1970, many Catholic students were already defying it by then. Of course, his writ did not run in Northern Ireland, so some Northern Catholics, beneficiaries of the eleven-plus, were already there, side by side with their Protestant fellow fortunates. There was also a noticeable sprinkling of English grammar-school boys and girls, who had none of the sense of entitlement of their more aristocratic compatriots. Often of Irish ancestry, they were popular for many reasons, not least their generosity in buying drink for the rest of us, which they could afford due to their princely English grants.

By then the proportion of upper-class English students had decreased significantly, and they no longer dominated student life. Indeed, many viewed them rather condescendingly as the scions of the British upper class who were too intellectually challenged to get into Oxford or Cambridge and who came to Trinity instead, from which they would depart in due course armed with their pass degrees to dabble in something or other. In addition there was a generous sprinkling of students from Africa, Asia and the US, adding to the international atmosphere.

Trinity was changing in other ways. The exclusion of women from many college activities, and of their physical presence from the college itself at night, was crumbling. The Elizabethan Society, set up to provide a debating society for women who were excluded from the Historical Society, ceased to exist when the latter finally admitted women to membership. Yet a casual sexism persisted, especially among certain lecturers, who behaved towards female students in a manner that today would produce charges of sexual harassment. I recall one younger male lecturer, known for his dalliances with female students, approaching me with the line, 'You have one of the best brains of any woman in college.' As a pick-up line it failed, but he was always prone to antediluvian exaggeration.

Thus by the end of the 1960s Trinity was poised to participate in the international wave sweeping universities across the globe. It was a ferment of political activism during the years I was there, though the emphasis shifted from a concern with international politics in the late 1960s to a focus on issues closer to home in the mid 1970s.

On my first day in Trinity during Freshers' Week one figure stood out among those lined up beside stands as they recruited members for the various societies. Tall, with long curly red hair and a red beard, law student Greg Murphy loudly exhorted new students to join the Fabian Society, which I did. This formerly rather sedate institution was soon to rename itself the Socialist Society and become a cauldron of ideological debate among different brands of Marxism, though it was dominated by Trotskyists. The Maoists had their own organization, and rivalry between the two groups was fierce.

A year later Greg ran for the presidency of the Students' Representative Council on a ticket with fellow law student Michael Forde, who ran as deputy president. They undertook to take office together, and if only one of them was elected he would not take up the position. Greg did win the presidency, but Mick did not win the deputy presidency, so the student body never had the experience of being led by the flamboyant figure of Greg Murphy, later to become a criminal lawyer. He died in 2002 at the age of fifty-three.

But I had come to Trinity to study English Language and Literature, not politics, and my interest was divided. I had also joined the English Literature Society in the expectation I would be exposed to great creativity and brilliant critical insights. However, I found myself mainly subjected to excruciatingly bad poetry from over-earnest young men (there were no aspiring female poets there at this time, despite the earlier example of Eavan Boland) and my personal poetic efforts did not survive my own critical eye, so this society proved a disappointment.

Yet exciting (at least to an eighteen-year-old) discussions of literature and life were to be had in spades in the Coffee Bar in No. 29, where both the conversation and the chocolate-biscuit cake made it the preferred place for English students, rather than the rather more raucous environment of the Buttery. The latter, however, had the added attraction of alcohol during opening hours, and a wider selection of students could be found there, among them the politicos.

Later in the evenings we would be found in O'Neills of Suffolk Street, where somehow someone always had enough money to buy a round. Restaurants were few, and Mrs Gaj's in Baggot Street, with its Hungarian goulash as well as its standard fare of hamburgers and chips, seemed exotic.

So my earlier years in Trinity (I spent nine years there in all, staying on to do a PhD) were rather schizophrenic, divided between the worlds of English literature and socialist politics. The English department in Trinity had never embraced the Marxist literary criticism of Raymond Williams, and Terry Eagleton, then making a name for himself as an up-and-coming critic in Oxford, had not hit its radar. The category of cultural criticism had not yet emerged as a distinct discipline, and it was still frowned upon in Trinity to see social context and ideology as relevant to the study of literature. One of my lecturers told me sharply after my Mod Part I (third-year) exams that I would have done better if I hadn't wasted so much time on politics.

But how could I not? – 1968 had just happened. It is impossible to describe to young people today what it was like then to feel part of a global movement of young people certain the world was going to change and that our generation would do it. We were eighteen, nineteen, twenty years old and we felt we could bring down the governments of the world and bring in a new order. That was not as far-fetched as it now appears – in 1968 the French and Czech governments did come very close to collapse in the face of mass demonstrations sparked by students, and within a few years the Americans would leave Vietnam and the Salazar regime in Portugal would fall. Events just a short distance away in Northern Ireland suggested similar things were happening here.

This unrest at the very end of the 1960s and in the early 1970s made Trinity, along with other universities, a very political place. Few weeks went by without a mass meeting being called on one subject or another on the front steps of the Dining Hall, usually attended by at least hundreds of students in Front Square. The cobbled Front Square, bounded by the Exam Hall, the 1937 Reading Room, the chapel and the Dining Hall, must have formed a sort of amphitheatre as the voices of those speaking off the steps carried even to the students at the back of the crowd. The subject matter ranged from issues of immediate concern to students to questions of national and global import.

By the mid 1970s global events were paying second fiddle to more local concerns among students, and the Students' Union, which replaced the Students' Representative Council of earlier years, debated issues like improvements in catering for students, affordable accommodation and food and a comprehensive grants scheme. It also provided a number of student services including, controversially, advice on abortion for women students who sought it.

Postgraduate students, of whom I was one, occupied an ambiguous position. As graduates, they were deemed to have moved beyond the concerns of most students. Yet they were still studying and were struggling to make ends meet. Some, like me, were supplementing their grants or college research awards by teaching seminars in their departments, or by leading experiments in the science laboratories, but this was poorly paid.

A number of us, including Ann Wickham and Nick McDonald, came together seeking to improve out lot and we joined the union ASTMS, which organized some third-level teachers in other institutions. We also set up a Graduate Students' Union to campaign specifically for improved facilities for postgraduate students, and I was elected its first chairperson, with Ann and Nick as secretary and treasurer respectively. We threatened to strike in support of our demand for a dramatic increase in our hourly rate of pay, and succeeded in having it more than doubled. All this, as well as the issues mobilizing the general body of students, involved many meetings on the front steps of the Dining Hall.

I then decided to run for the presidency of the Students' Union, jointly with Anne Connolly, about to graduate in history and later a leading figure in the feminist movement, who ran for the vice-presidency. She was elected, I was not, but I remained on the executive of the Students' Union. The following year we campaigned together again, this time for the presidency and deputy presidency of the national students' organization, USI, with John Daly of UCC standing for the position as education officer. We were defeated by the incumbent machine run by Official Sinn Féin, which elected Eamon Gilmore as president. We considered it an honourable defeat as we had obtained about a third of the votes despite lacking any of the patronage at the disposal of the incumbent machine.

If this gives the impression that our lives were filled with earnest but ultimately trivial political discussions, it was not so. The Union's entertainments officer, Ian Wilson, ensured that the best bands around played in college. The Irish traditional music scene was vibrant both inside and outside Trinity, with music festival Éigse na Tríonóide attracting some of the best traditional musicians in the country, and regular sessions taking place in a number of the pubs within walking distance.

Trinity Ball remained the highlight of the social year, but was available only to those who could afford it. On the night of the ball those without tickets had to be off the campus by 6 pm. As deputy president of the Students' Union Anne Connolly had a room in college, and on the evening of the ball held a small and quiet party, from which the guests sallied forth about midnight to join the action.

All this meant, of course, that my PhD thesis received only sporadic attention, usually prompted by a deadline delivered hesitantly by my supervisor, the shy and gentle Professor J. K. Walton. His undemanding supervision provided a benign example of 'light touch regulation' long before the phrase was invented. My pleasure at the eventual acceptance of the thesis by the panel of external examiners was at least partly due to relief that his faith in my ability to finish it had not been misplaced.

The five years spent on it, albeit intermittently, convinced me, however, that this was not my vocation. Though I enjoyed the in-depth examination of my subject, the prose and plays of Sean O'Casey and their European context, footnotes and I are not natural bedfellows. I also learned I only really work when faced with a deadline. Journalism was therefore a natural fit.

I was lucky enough to find work, first on a freelance basis with *The Irish Press* and later with *The Irish Times*. Both are within a stone's throw of Trinity, so I have spent all my adult life within that square mile bounded by the Liffey on one side and Nassau Street on the other, punctuated only by brief spells working in the *Irish Times* office in London and Belfast.

Journalism has its limitations, and I have been fortunate in being able to indulge my interest in writing in more depth by being asked to contribute academic articles or write books around issues relating to culture, feminism and social issues. This has given me an excuse to return to Trinity for days at a time, to walk across the cobbles of Front Square to the Library, to find a spot to sit and read the assembled pile of books, to experience again the pure pleasure of reading in that place.

Thus the memories have remained fresh, and walking across the cobbles I have felt again the sense of freedom, the intellectual stimulation and the intensity of the friendships that marked the experience of being a student in Trinity during those years.

Carol Coulter (TCD 1967–71; English Literature) went on to study for a PhD on Sean O'Casey, which she finished in 1976. She began working as a freelance journalist and joined **The Irish Times** in 1986, where she is currently Legal Affairs Editor.

MY YEAR AS A FASCIST

peter kavanagh

JUNIOR FRESHMAN YEAR was the usual stuff. Knocking down walls between student houses in Hatch Street so one's eighteenth birthday could be celebrated in style. Streaking out of the Burlington Hotel toilets at closing time, racing round the lobby, traumatizing guests before flying out to freedom: except that the Burlington locks its lobby doors at eleven. A night in the cells. Fines. Threats of suspension or rustication from men with bald heads. The usual good-natured tosh.

But then between my first and second years disaster struck. My romance with Isabella, the Spanish au pair living opposite my parents in Belfast, ended. Her father recalled her home. I hadn't seen it coming. I was inconsolable, and became one of those familiar gloomy, haunted figures you'd see sweeping in through Front Gate, wafting Munch-like, spectrally, toward the Buttery.

So there I was, bruised, angry, tormented, lugging my rucksack of Mod. Lang. Lit. back down south. Entering college, I hear a politico on the distant Front Steps and the recurring words 'Spain' and 'fascist'. Paying attention for the first time, I hear about the torture and deaths of thousands of communists and anarchists in the Civil War. I realize that Isabella's father, a highly placed general responsible for 'security' under Franco, must be authorizing that.

I listen on. Colonial Spain's crimes in Latin America. This is what I need to hear. I desperately want to join in on this pillorying of Spain and its fascists, but I need a vehicle. I found a play by Arrabal, the Spanish Absurdist dramatist: *The Labyrinth* is set on a Spanish estate owned by a shadowy general figure. The grounds are strewn with clothes lines laden with dirty laundry. In the middle of the park an innocent man lies, chained to a toilet, unable to find his way out of the maze.

I brought the play straight to the Players committee, avoiding, naturally, my personal take on the subject, and delivered a blazing resumé. A month later we're deep in rehearsal, wrestling to give life to *The Labyrinth*'s mind-numbingly crude allegory. It's sounding as dramatic as a reading of a Marx-Engels tract on Front Steps. But that's ok with me. Local response on the first night is understandably mixed, but the *Sunday Times* drama festival critic, hungry for regional material, invited us to London to perform onstage at the Royal Court.

So there we are, droning Arrabal's platitudes to the habitués of London's most sophisticated theatre venue. As I lie half-naked, chained to an unplumbed, unstable Armitage Shanks at the back of the set, I gloat. Wait till those fuckers in Madrid hear about this! London's theatre world finally exposing the regime! I imagine Isabella's father, toking on a fat Cohiba, choking on his brandy at the news. Then I learnt that Isabella has taken up with an English officer stationed in Belfast, and I raced back down south and through Front Gate for another hit of diatribe. As I listened I obsessed about Isabella. Her father had been a fascist, her Brit officer by definition also. I recalled an article I'd read in *Sight And Sound* about Latin-American movies exploding onto London's art-house screens. I had found my next mission.

Six weeks later I was on the Film Soc. committee and running for the post of chairman. It being the seventies there were no females, just blokes. It was all very matey and non-combative. So with my ass on fire, my championing of a season of Latin-American movies won me the job. Soon I was spending my day racing between calls to London distributors from an unsupervised phone in Front Square and the 'free' photocopier in the SRC office. En route I'd take a Damascene detour via Front Steps to soak up restorative rhetoric. And as my pain around Isabella intensified, so my film programme radicalized.

We met over a crate of Guinness to discuss the brochure and the blurbs I'd written. '*Hour of the Furnaces*,' read aloud the vice-chairman, 'a four-hour clarion call to liberation movements worldwide, tracing Argentina's break with colonial Spain …'

They looked at me, fearfully. A beat.

'Ok, so where are the stills?' asked Publicity. 'They need to go to the printer by Monday.'

'Stills? What stills?'

Next weekend the committee, mates, girlfriends, and a photographer career round Dublin's hinterlands in a minibus. We're constructing our own publicity stills for our brochure. First stop, Sandymount Strand, where an SRC luminary and better half pose as drowning lovers in *Hasta La Victoria Siempre.* Against a dry-stone wall in Monkstown, the deputy treasurer appears to cower before a barking mastiff to promote *Viva La Muerte.* On the road south the treasurer and fiancée decapitate an H. Williams chicken for *Die Like A Dog (As My Ancestors Died).* It's all great fun, everyone's stoned and pissed. Our love of film and our friendship revives. In Enniskerry, shot in contrasty black and white, we sprawl in a lane as the massacred strikers from *The Hour Of The Furnaces.* Finally as night falls we steal into the grounds of a Roundwood church and pose on the steep rockery below a life-sized, very kitsch crucifixion. We're fearless Tupamaros, in torn T-shirts, waving farm implements. The flash pops. We cheer. *Guns of the Trees* is in the can. A police siren sounds. We abandon our weapons and flee.

The brochure looks great. The season, however, is a disaster. Beginning in November it spans some of the coldest months on record. Another oil crisis has turned Dixon Hall into an icebox. Winds from the sea sweep in across the polar wastes of Trinity's cricket and rugby pitches. Twenty or at most thirty people, gloved and swathed in duffel coats and blankets, listen to the excited Front Steps rhetoric of my introductions, then watch as suns blaze down on Mexican, Bolivian and Brazilian landscapes, scenes of unspeakable carnage and mutilation.

In the piping-hot projection room the committee look as frosty as the fields outside. Even without sub-zero temperatures, wouldn't Costa Gavras's mainstream revolutionary hit *Z* have packed in a hundred at least? But I'm smiling, my face pressed to the viewing window. Although not many, our members are getting a chance to witness the climax of *Die Like A Dog (As*

My Ancestors Died): the generalissimo being impaled on his golf umbrella. My hurt around Isabella has finally been slaked.

After Michaelmas break I am held to account. On our way to the committee room, my last remaining ally, the liaison officer, warns me: 'They're not happy. Your season almost bankrupted us.' And it's true. I feel as if I'm facing a Phalangist firing squad. I duly promise that never again under my stewardship will the Film Soc. showcase a season of gonad-numbing political epics.

'What we need now is a season of independent, experimental underground classics.' Beaming, I summarize classics from the alternative filmmaking canon. Like *Zorn's Lemma*, Hollis Frampton's ingenious trawl through the alphabet, replacing all twenty-six letters with an arbitrary image.

'Is that it?'

'No, then the climax! A couple walk through a winter field for twenty-five minutes reading a mathematical proposition … It all comes in just under an hour. So we can make it a double bill with Michael Snow's masterpiece, *Wavelength*, a 35-minute single-shot zoom into a postcard pinned to a school classroom wall.'

The groans turn to cries of despair.

'Though the chief reason you should re-elect me …' I shout over angry yelps, waving the brochure, 'Is this – a crowd-pulling Warhol season, opening with his eight-hour *Empire*, a static shot of the Empire State building at night. The climax is at fifty-eight minutes when the arc lights come on and you can finally see it!'

The AGM is set for the following week.

'It's over,' my liaison mole tells me. 'You're toast. And it's the treasurer's turn for chair. That's how it works.'

'What are you talking about? Miles does Business Studies. He'll never go for Warhol. Or Stan Brakhage, or Peter Kubelka.'

'And he's right! Let it go mate. Humble pie. You've had your stint.'

'Miles is a counter-revolutionary, a treacherous …'

'Miles is a decent guy, who'll do the job well and return us to profit.'

'Never! This season will happen. It has to. We owe it to our members.'

I'D SPENT the Easter break holed up twelve hours a day in Paris' Cinématique watching experimental films, when I should have been outdoors sightseeing with my new girlfriend. But she'd left me. I was back in that dark place. And when in pain, like some Evangelist I'd recite the names of my film-maker saints: Maya Deren, Jonas Mekas, Paul Sharits, Bruce Baillie. And their films: *Meshes of the Afternoon, Castro Street, Back And Forth, Reminiscences of a Journey To Lithuania, As I was Moving Ahead Occasionally …*'

Except my season may not happen. These luminous, numinous, life-changing masterworks may not get an airing. I telephoned each committee member, but no one returned my call. I reread the Film Soc. constitution, and discovered that ordinary members could vote at our AGM. I rang friends who were members, but no one liked the sound of Brakhage's *Mothlight*, with its moth wings glued to each frame of celluloid. I called friends of friends. But Kubelka's *Unsere Afrikareise* – its big-game hunters' utterances swapped for those of the wild beasts they kill – may have been a masterpiece of alternative nature documentary, but it wasn't buttering parsnips here.

Looking at the Society's register I found four members registered at the same address. I dropped round on some pretext, then casually turned the subject to life in Ireland, Dublin's provincialism and its worst symptom – the schlocky disaster movies then monopolizing Irish cinema screens; films like *Jaws, Towering Inferno* and *Earthquake*. They sighed. I asked, didn't everyone wish that *Anticipation of the Night* or *The Lead Shoes* would get distribution? Everyone agreed, but asked if Clint Eastwood was starring. I trawled the Buttery. I sat by the door, nursing a chocolate log, watching out for movie buffs I might persuade to attend the AGM. 'Please come! Support a return to the alternative, authentic stream of film-making dating back to the Lumière brothers, before entertainment and financiers hijacked the tradition.' No interest. The only person who heard me out was the magnificent Angela, mother to us all, with her cherubic lips and crash-helmet cheekbones. 'I'll come and vote for you, love, and your radical whatever it is.' Even I could see that co-opting Angela was not a recipe for success.

IN THE LIBRARY I carried a pile of historical biographies over to a blue vinyl-covered desk and leafed through the lives of visionary but long-serving leaders who had held onto power. So many, but who really endured, who had clung on right till their death, preferable from natural causes? If only I'd studied history instead of classics I would know this stuff.

First up, the communists: Tito, that hardy perennial, still going strong at the time. Stalin, ah Stalin had died happily, and in his bed, but only after exterminating all his political rivals and hundreds of thousands of his own people. Lordy. Ditto for Pol Pot who was still hanging in there – looking closer, his modus operandi appeared even less right on.

And on the right? Pinochet was still alive and of course torturing and brutalizing his own. Greece's fascist General Mataxas died a natural death after a short rule. Mussolini had lasted twenty years, but what a way to go. And the hated Franco himself had just expired peacefully in his sleep before I could get over there and tear out his dark heart, worse luck. Otherwise the two sides sounded alarmingly similar. I found a definition of fascism, which, among other things, 'seeks the cultural rebirth of a nation ... through the imposition by strong leadership of one man's irrational will ... *he-llo!* ... using culture ... and education ... *yes* ... rejecting decadence and suppression of opposition ... through violence if necessary ... sometimes arising from a sense of lovelessness in early childhood, compensated for by sense of omnipotence.' *Oh gosh.* And then this quote below the picture of Franco: 'Fascism entails a revolutionary aim to transform society, politically and culturally. This was never Franco's goal.'

Franco wasn't really a fascist?

I looked at a picture of his family; and his daughter, the one Isabella had been called after. Staring out of the window, their beautiful morphed faces stayed imprinted on my mind and seemed to hover over Back Square. I felt my loneliness return. Who out there gave a damn about experimental films, and who gave a damn about me? I'd made the error of many a dictator. By not finding love with one person, I'd needed to be loved, or noticed, by everybody. So Franco wasn't a fascist. But I was. I packed my bags for Belfast and went home.

Peter Kavanagh (TCD 1970–5; Modern Languages). After reviewing for **In Dublin, The Irish Times, The Guardian** and London's **Evening Standard**, he moved to Paris to appear, often subliminally, in films by directors including

Polanski and Molinaro. He learned his craft, first with James Morris in Dublin, then with the BBC in Belfast and London, was appointed drama producer in radio, and won many awards. As a director, he made five films, one winning a Bafta and one, written by Kathy Gilfillan, starring Bono. He also directs theatre and musicals, and writes plays, screenplays and reviews for, among others, the **TLS** and **Dazed & Confused**. He never got round to a formal graduation, and seeks other veteran graduands for a late-autumn flowering.

SLIDING DOORS AT FRONT GATE

ruth mccarthy

LIKE MOST of the Irish students I was all of seventeen years old. Dublin-born and Wicklow-convent educated – a product of that typically patchy, mildly eccentric, good-enough-for-girls education. (For example, we studied *Macbeth* for two solid years. Why? Because nobody noticed.) I know it was not as good as the equivalent boys' education because I was sandwiched between two brothers being educated by the Jesuits, and what they did was different. They experienced more comprehensive, challenging teaching, which was reflected in their writing and their results. Basically the school ethos could be summed up as, 'Be good sweet maid, and let who will be clever.' Most of us were good through lack of opportunity and clever despite the education, and inevitably the majority of us were greener than grass. Almost culpably naïve. So Trinity became *An Education*.

And Trinity was on a cusp. Traditionally, until then, a large number of students from England and Northern Ireland arrived every year, creating that unique and accidental mix of increasingly impoverished Anglo-Irish families, Home-Counties public-school Oxbridge rejects, Bogside Catholics and polite Malone Road Protestants, plus the big new entry post-1968; the Dubs, south and northside. When I walked through Front Gate in September 1971 I was entering a new world that was paradoxically just about to melt away. During my four years (1971–5) the Fellows' Garden disappeared under concrete, the shiny new Arts Block soared into being and in 1976 undergraduate numbers doubled almost overnight.

This new old world included a group of school friends scattered between Hon. Mod. Lang. (like me) and those who'd defied the stereotypes and opted for grittier Economics or Law. It became clear that honors students took exams at the end of the summer, rather than in June. Those September exams were a poisoned chalice. Admittedly I had a blast during four consecutive Trinity Weeks in June with no thought of essays or revision – but then paid double the price in sweaty August, sitting at home cramming arcane texts and chocolate biscuits while everyone else earned huge tips waitressing in Martha's Vineyard, or swanning around the Riviera crewing yachts. Or canning peas in Goldhanger.

What were we thinking about – how did we think? For that first full year I thought there'd been a shocking mistake. I sat in tutorials with A-level students from English and Northern Irish schools trying to understand what they were saying. Struggling to keep up with forensic discussions about Eliot and Baudelaire and Maupassant and Joyce, I felt clueless and tongue-tied in the presence of so much confident knowledge. There was a huge gap between where they started from and where I found myself – at least two years of in-depth reading and critical thinking. I couldn't define the difference, I just fell straight into the gap, because it's fair and true to say that no one had ever taught us to think: thinking for yourself wasn't at all a desirable feature in Catholic young ladies of the time, and was actively discouraged by the nuns.

At least during year two I discovered other things to read and discuss, woke up to nascent feminism, was mesmerized by *Spare Rib* and Germaine Greer's *Female Eunuch*, annoyed and stimulated by Jean-Paul Sartre and Camus and *Private Eye*, by Simone de Beauvoir and Kate Millett, and began to think for myself: to think about what was happening in Ireland, which was still holy and Catholic (even if we were finally allowed to go to Trinity) and still stuck in the dark ages, if you were female. In fact it occurs to me now that at that time TCD was possibly the best place in Ireland to be if you were female. Lurching towards equality.

The local students all lived at home, then as now, and travelled in every day. Living in Blackrock with my family, I walked up to the Stillorgan Road every morning to catch the bus into town. Hitching during a (pretty regular) bus strike an amazing black vintage Rolls once stopped and picked me up – it was de Valera's driver, on the way into town after dropping the ancient ex-president home from church as he did every day. He dropped me at Front Gate, and I longed for someone I knew to be there and see me – but no luck. The 46A was a critical factor in my Trinity life. On the top deck one morning I taught myself to smoke, mainly because the guy I was interested in smoked and I thought it would help to further the rapport – it didn't, but I went from zero to twenty a day in a week. Born to smoke. Rothmans, Major, Benson and Hedges (Gold Bond, anyone?), trendy stinky Gauloises. I enjoyed every single one – I felt I was so good at it they should have been paying me. (I gave up equally quickly, in London five years later, when an evil genius GP sent me for a chest X-ray to the geriatric hospital in Kensington: by the time the result came through I'd stopped smoking forever.)

Slowly, so slowly working out how it all worked. Realizing that the Northern girls who came by bus and brought in their own sandwiches all lived in digs in Raheny and Crumlin, and the Northern girls who drove cars lived in nice flats in Ballsbridge – they didn't seem to know each other. Starting to hear so much more about the North (hitherto the source of Opal Fruits and cheap butter): listening to Bernadette Devlin and Ian Paisley, watching appalled as Bloody Sunday exploded, marching behind coffins and banners to the British embassy in Merrion Square.

Just as important as politics and feminism – what were we all wearing? This was the early seventies, the decade taste forgot, so it was chocolate brown and burnt orange, flares so wide they hid your platform clogs; crushed-velvet hot pants and peasant blouses. Cheesecloth and jeans for everyone, T-shirts and desert boots a must. And then there was a lot of dressing up. In the last days of this particular Raj, the public-school mores were a given on any formal occasion, from the Knights of the Campanile to Trinity Week and Regatta – black tie and long dresses, even morning coats. The phrase 'West Briton' was new to me but if you joined in with the dressing up and the cricket matches, the Pavilion teas and the boats on the river, then there was a good chance you'd hear it.

And then there was Commons. The peculiar pleasure of sitting at those long tables, not because of the food, or the stale stout, but because it felt so exciting to be collegiate, to wear a gown and to be part of that cacophonous, historic whole. And to know that only a few years before women weren't even allowed to be there, or anywhere on the hallowed male territory after 6 pm. Yet there we were.

Who made an impression? The legendary McDowell still strode the Squares, talking animatedly to himself or anyone who engaged with him. Tommy Murtagh teased young women with existentialism and French philosophers in the Rubrics and eventually married one of them. David Norris was brilliant about life and wildly funny about Joyce on a weekly basis, while poor old Dr Shields of the oddly green complexion droned on lugubriously about phonetics at 9 am every Friday to an almost-empty Chemistry theatre (we took turns to go and sign everyone else in, I don't think he ever looked up). Intellectual buccaneer Brendan Kennelly set fire to poetry and young minds, challenging the conventions and demanding response: many years later he kindly acted as referee for my Master's application in London, proving that Trinity blood is thicker than water. (On Yeats: 'Writing like this has to be the second best thing in life.' Innocent that I was it took me days to work out what he believed to be the first.)

Tall Northern Sean was brilliant in every sense: bored by his regular studies he took to translating French texts into Sanskrit in the Reading Room every day. A nameless tall lean guy in a black leather jacket looked the epitome of cool lounging around Front Square dealing drugs to those in the know; then one winter evening he knocked on the door of a friend's rooms in Botany Bay and as the door opened he quite literally fell face first onto the floor. After twenty minutes of resuscitation he was being walked round the square in the fresh air, after ten more I was off for the relative safety of the inevitable 46A. Quite off-putting, hard drugs-wise.

In my second year I became a much more regular night-time *habituée* although I still needed to catch the last bus home. It meant I got to see a lot more of what was going on, from mild toking in the ladies' loos to major excesses around Botany Bay. A standout story: Jeremy Kimber and Philip Bradley 'found' a small bulldozer late one night, wired it up and drove it furiously around the tennis courts until it took a wrong turning down the slope to the Buttery. The dauntless pair shot off into Philip's rooms nearby and jumped into bed, still fully dressed (including boots). Moments later the Skip and assistant dean rushed in, to the sound of loud snoring. Shaken awake, with much yawning and complaining, and invited to explain the astonishingly black and greasy condition of his hands, Jeremy looked at them in bafflement and said, 'Oh, that! That's nothing. I just ran my hands through my hair ...'

They came from Harrow and Shrewsbury, Charterhouse and Fettes; they were confident, cliquey and seemed thoroughly at ease. They were good fun and completely different, a tad patronizing and a bit fascinating – and the public-school girls were the same but much prettier. They seemed so sophisticated, older and up for anything, so of course I fell in love with one of them and it was like moving to a different country.

The fixed points on the new map included The Old Stand, Mulligans, The Bailey, The Unicorn, Davy Byrnes, Dobbins restaurant, the snug in Ryans of Parkgate Street, and occasionally the new nightclubs in Leeson Street. There was money – from their families, or the trusting UK government, and when it ran out we could cook something on the basic two-ring burners in rooms. When funds were really tight the last resort was a takeaway curry on St Stephen's Green, a vile mess of unidentifiable objects blanketed in thick brown spicy effluent. The Chinese restaurant in Wicklow Street wasn't much better – we ate something they called sweet and sour pork that looked like small golf balls deep fried in yellow rubber and tasting equally of pineapple and gristle. Our own *haute cuisine* included deep-frozen corn on the cob, sausages, tinned spag and large bottles of Hirondelle, a wine guaranteed to give you a headache as soon as you bought it.

In my final year I moved with Lynette Dobbin, veteran of Trinity ski trips and surely one of the world's funniest women, into 9.0.1 on the left side of Front Square. It took a little while to get used to the sirens and street noises; no time at all to adjust to independent living and freedom from the dreaded bus route. The main doors were always open; I remember much borrowing of clothes, sharing of food and alcohol, late-night excursions to a dodgy mini-market round the corner, raking through the freezer for something vaguely edible, ideally identifiable. Electing a 'Word of the Week' and pinning it to the wall in our rooms – like 'serendipitous', 'commensurate' and good old 'existential' – each trying to use it more often than the other, crying with laughter because it was so pretentious and so funny.

Much frenzied reading in the subterranean levels of the Reading Room. Occasional requests for rare books of any ilk so that I could head to the eyrie above the Long Room for a bit of peace and essay-writing. Realizing that my grasp of French grammar was truly appalling and not knowing what to do about it (nor did my examiners, who reconciled the fluency of my spoken French with the idiocy of my written language by awarding me a 2:2 overall, for which judgment of Solomon I still thank Professor Hickman). Grasping the opportunity, finally, to spend time reading long novels and poetry – the time that wasn't spent being in love, being in the pub, being on the Trinity squash team, being in France.

My last Trinity summer was also spent in rooms, in 3.2.1, above the HQ of the DU Players. The plan was to save travelling time and to study hard; that might have worked if I hadn't chosen to share with Caroline Orr, then glamorously studying for her second-year exams and a powerfully distracting influence, not least because of her flame-to-moth capacity for attracting gentlemen followers. One of them insisted on a glass of whiskey – a proper drink – when he called by, so bought one, and left it with us. We must have refilled that wretched half-bottle a dozen times during the six weeks.

None of that is surprising: what does surprise me is how little thought we gave or were encouraged to give to the subject of what we would do next. I remember the milk-round interviews with Unilever, Boots, Marks and Spencer and others as embarrassing episodes of mutual incomprehension. I'd had lots of holiday jobs (the first in the marvellously named 'Gaywear', and in various shops and hotels in France) but I didn't have the first idea about industry. I knew nothing about business or even about working in an office before going in, I knew very little more coming out. IBM and ICI were wasted on me. In some ways I think it's taken me most of my life to catch up.

Those Sliding Doors that opened into Front Gate gave me four years in which to grow up, at a time that in retrospect was largely optimistic – post-sixties, pre-boom. We didn't know it then but we really were living the final years of the old Ireland – de Valera's and John Charles McQuaid's. And I did know how beautiful Trinity was – the warm red of the Rubrics and the shining grey of the cobbles after rain, the clean lines of New Square, the surprising green curve of College Park in the heart of the city, the high rake of the seats in the Chemistry building, the low lamps over desks in the Reading Room. The contrast between the noisy clamour of Dame Street and the privileged peace within the walls. The funny little co-op shop on the corner of Botany Bay where everything was on tick till the end of term or possibly till the end of time. How lucky we were.

Ruth McCarthy (TCD 1971–5; Modern Languages, French and English) worked for fifteen years in London book publishing and journalism. She married and has two daughters. In 2002 she took an MA in Critical and Cultural Studies at Birkbeck College, University of London, and went on to qualify as a 'Time to Think' consultant and facilitator. She is co-chair of the Ireland Fund of Great Britain and a fellow of the RSA.

A CRASH COURSE

ian wilson

IN 1971 a public-school boy from Belfast arrives at Trinity with little or no experience of sex and drugs and rock and roll, and just over a year later I was Ents (entertainments) officer. My first big gig was with the future of folk and Irish music, Planxty, and what I hadn't known before then became obvious pretty fast.

January 1972, the start of second Hilary Term, brought Bloody Sunday and the huge backlash against all things British. Needless to say, Trinity students were among those who firebombed British premises. There was also real concern that the atmosphere made TCD a target, especially when the Bloody Sunday march passed by the front of the college the following week. Wiser heads, most likely the secretary, Gary Giltrap, took heed of what the Students' Representative Council said and duly hung a huge banner out of the JCR window over Front Gate, declaring TCD students' revulsion at what had happened. And as the march passed by, Front Gate swung open and at least 2000 students poured out to join the tens of thousands heading to the British embassy in Merrion Square.

May 1974 and South Leinster Street, just by the Moyne Institute, was the site of one of the Dublin bombs. The bonnet of the car that had carried the bomb landed on the cricket pitch in the middle of stunned players. One of the senior microbiology students was in a lab fronting onto the bomb site and miraculously sitting behind a pillar when the windows and Venetian blinds disintegrated around him. Had our class in the lab next door not finished early, it being virtually the end of term, we would have been in the line of the blast.

I was running the music at the Trinity Ball and our regular Trinity Week open-air concerts in College Park were on the following week. Should we cancel these shows as a mark of respect or for safety concerns? Vice-Provost David Howie was adamant that we should not be seen to cave in before such intimidation, so our lunchtime shows went ahead. But every British-based act booked for the ball cancelled over the next week. Not surprisingly, although a less-than-full event, the ball happened nonetheless.

By now 'Ents' was a machine still staffed by unpaid volunteers from officer down – including the Yeats sisters, Siobhan and the late Sile, John Dick, Sue Barrett, Quentin M. Roantree and many more, with a Friday-night Exam Hall show and a weekly lunchtime concert in the JCR. We developed the first viable college music circuit as commercial promotion more or less collapsed due to the problems in the North. Al Stewart, Tír na nÓg, Stackridge, Jonathan Kelly, Stefan Grossman, John Renbourne and Jacqui McShee (Pentangle), The Woods Band, Paul Brady, Bees Make Honey, Supply Demand and Curve with Brian Masterson and the late Jolyon Jackson among others.

At the end of Summer Term 1973, we started the Trinity Week open-air shows on the Dining Hall steps. Spud, led by fiddle player and Trinity student Don Knox, were the highlight, later to be managed by another contemporary, one Paul McGuinness. The following year, we moved the shows to College Park, where they continued into the 1990s before sadly petering out. And of course, there was the whole Trinity Ball music organization, which I took over from the late, lamented and extremely talented Bill Graham in 1974 and with which I remained involved for the rest of my time in college.

The SRC was the theatre for incessant infighting among the left groups – Official Sinn Féin, Labour and various ultra-left oddities. Topping the pile were the Internationalists/Maoists led by the pugnacious orator, Foundation Scholar and research chemist, David Vipond. Master of the Dining Hall steps, he led the clashes in the Dining Hall. This fracas ended up with the Gardaí clearing the Dining Hall, one of the front doors being ripped off its hinges, and, last but not least, one Garda hat in my possession.

Already looking like an interesting summer, it got even more interesting as David took it upon himself to object to the awarding of an honorary degree to the president, Erskine Childers. As the procession moved from the Provost's House to the Exam Hall, Childers was verbally abused by David in the vein of 'You are a traitor and the people of Ireland will hang you for it!' Given the state execution of Childers' own father, the whole pantomime went nuclear: big splash on all the front pages, total panic by college authorities. There was some physical contact as well, leading to Vipond being carted off the premises for a while.

Michaelmas had Vipond back in the driving seat, and we blundered into the by now recurring event, the catering boycott, whereby we protested the constant price rises by effectively removing all custom by picket and persuasion – and supplying a rough and ready, but edible, alternative. Unlike other previous boycotts, we were well organized and by the second week, the boycott was biting. A Dining Hall steps meeting was called to buoy up the masses and as Vipond was doing his thing, the Dining Hall doors opened and out walked the catering staff en masse. They simply said that they were going to be laid off if the boycott continued. It collapsed on the spot – we had been roundly humiliated and outmanoeuvred by the college. It also marked the effective end of David Vipond's motivation and interest in the SRC presidency, leaving me on my own again.

At the same time I was treasurer and and had to implement a proper accounting system as required by the Capitation Committee. The CSC paid a considerable grant to the Hist and Phil for provision of daily papers in the GMB reading rooms. The papers were delivered by a newspaper vendor based in a stall at the bottom of Grafton Street, and they exasperatedly approached the new CSC treasurer, solicitor Peter Lennon, to find out why they were owed over £1000 or so – and this in 1975! In effect the Hist and to a lesser extent the Phil had siphoned off the money for the papers over a two-year period for other uses. All of a sudden, the Hist and Phil were having their accounts taken apart, their grants cut to pay the debts and in the following year's CSC election, there was a clean sweep by the new order. By that stage we had also stacked up the Trinity Week committee with new blood such as the effervescent Gerry Ryan, a natural showman, just cutting his teeth at that stage. The days of control of funds being held like a sword of Damocles over the Students' Union was gone.

Trinity was no friend of the Union of Students in Ireland (USI), which had for most of the seventies been controlled by a succession of Stickies (Official Sinn Féin) or close associates – Pat Brady, Pat Rabitte, Kieran Mulvey, and the then president Eamon Gilmore were all well-known figures. Trinity Students' Union had long railed against this hegemony and were treated as outcasts in the USI fold. Given all this and the general dislike of anything that smelt like Sinn Féin in TCD at the time, it seemed a no-brainer to pull TCD out of USI. So, in autumn 1976, a well-coordinated national strategy to dismember USI was launched, with TCD the big prize. Mark Turpin and I waged a guerrilla war against the disaffiliation campaign and we were first out of the traps, to their complete surprise. The campaign against disaffiliation became the acronym CAD, and the slogans poured out and onto posters all over college: 'Don't be Mad, be a CAD'; 'It's not bad to be a CAD'.

One Sunday evening we met Eamon Gilmore in USI headquarters and asked him two things – to give us material support and to let us handle it in TCD. He made the opening for me to meet Gordon Colleary, the businessman behind USIT. Colleary knew the lie of the land. At the same time we launched our campaign of change from within, of constructive engagement, and in a ludicrous gesture, I went up against Eamon Gilmore for election as USI president: doomed to failure, of course.

It was decided to have one big debate and vote in the Exam Hall. The meeting went ahead at lunchtime and just to rub it in, we organized a march from the science end with 500 or so arriving behind a CAD banner. I spoke last and, producing a banana from my pocket, which I waved at the overflowing Exam Hall, explained that I had just paid thirteen pence for a banana in the Buttery, which I could buy 'outside' for five. The vote was decisively in favour of working for reform within the USI, effectively ending the disaffiliation movement for several generations of students.

It was not lost on me that the presidency of the Students' Union was there for the taking. Brian Murray, Paul Tipping and I went in a joint ticket for president, vice-president and Ents officer in the elections in Trinity Term 1977. The only other candidate for president was Des O'Neill, medical student and now one of Ireland's best-known geriatricians. Des graciously withdrew just before the elections, meaning I was elected unopposed, something that had never happened previously.

And so to autumn 1977, the era of punk. Not to be left out, Paul Tipping was very keen that we should have the most current bands playing Trinity. We booked The Clash. It was a bit like having The Beatles playing TCD in the sixties. The two shows in the Exam Hall sold out in less than an hour, with students queuing in the morning for the SU shop to open. The college didn't know what hit them as the circus of kids in black bin bags, safety pins, torn jeans, tartan trousers and spiky hair queued at the Front Gate to get in. We followed this up with two shows from The Stranglers, a fortnight later, but only one show was allowed in the Exam Hall and a show booked outside the college failed to happen for insurance reasons. By now the issue of use of the Exam Hall had become a hot potato and the Senior Dean, J.V. Luce, was given the job of reining us in. His strategy was that noise levels were likely to cause damage to the fabric of the Hall, so he set a rather arbitrary noise limit.

The Buttery bar had been closed on a Saturday for at least a year due to lack of business, and we were determined to get it open. The election of Senior Dean as chair of the Societies Club was a mere formality, or so the college thought and we simply used our inbuilt majority on the committee to counter-nominate the SU president. Then to rub it in, Paul launched the new Saturday nights in the Buttery with a full live band, a disco and a nominal admission charge. The first night the queue stretched to the Front Gate and hundreds were turned away. The Buttery had its biggest night in years. The college was gobsmacked: we had out-manoeuvred them politically and in one stroke made the Buttery viable again.

During the second term the row over the concerts came to a head at a show with the iconic New Wave band, the Buzzcocks. Sound levels were monitored. The next morning I received a rather terse phone call from the Senior Dean, informing me that the following Friday's concert in the Exam Hall was cancelled due to a breach of the agreed sound levels. Somewhat unwisely, he neglected to check who was playing, and so Monday's Dublin evening papers carried a small note that The Chieftains' concert was cancelled. By Tuesday morning, emblazoned on the front pages of all the national papers, were pictures of The Chieftains with headlines such as, 'Chieftains too Noisy for

TCD', 'Chieftains to damage Exam Hall'. It was a PR disaster for the college and the concert went ahead. The late George Dawson (in many ways my mentor) was deputed by the board as peacemaker since J.V. Luce was barely on speaking terms with us by now, and the board appointed their first press and PR officer, former *Times* editor Fergus Pyle.

As the campaigns moved on and were successful in their own terms, we attracted increasing attention from the rump of the ultra left in TCD, and especially a new and shadowy group called Revolutionary Struggle, who seemed to have some contact with the INLA, the most extreme and dangerous of the Republican paramilitary groups. They and their followers hijacked a meeting and proposed a vote for 'an occupation' to further the 'struggle' and won the vote. This had the effect of binding us to take such action, even though there was no purpose and no objective to be achieved. Under pressure I had no choice but to implement this and came up with a plan to take over the college treasurer's office. This ill-fated occupation was set to happen on a Monday morning but on the Sunday we experienced the heaviest snowfall in many years, effectively closing the college. I made it clear that the occupation was no longer on, but the more extreme elements went ahead anyway.

As expected the closure of the treasurer's office hit the college hard as this effectively froze its share and investment portfolio. There was no reasoning with the occupiers and eventually we had to reassert control. On the Wednesday we held a huge open-air meeting where we won the vote to end the occupation. The fact that we could do this scared the college even further and clear blue water between the Students' Union and these elements was positive for us, but it did blunt our radical cutting edge a bit. A couple of years later, a British Leyland executive was shot in TCD while giving a talk and it was generally believed that Revolutionary Struggle were behind this. Certainly, this was not the kind of cutting edge we needed.

With the end of our year in office came one of our other rituals, the row about the ban on 'overnight guests of the opposite sex' as it was quaintly phrased in the regulations. Somewhat pompously, I announced my intention to invite the incoming president, Sue Jameson, the first woman to hold the post, to spend the night in my rooms in college. We had a field day with the press. To be fair, the college responded with more guile than before, placing notices around campus stating that 'If the President of the Students' Union feels it necessary to announce publicly his intention to have a female staying overnight in his rooms, then we suggest he has rather more need of the services of a psychiatrist than of the Deans of Discipline.' Clearly they had learnt something from us along the way.

Ian Wilson (TCD 1971–7) studied Science and held various posts in college including entertainments officer, vice-president and president of the Students' Union, introducing the first open 'sale' of condoms in Ireland. He worked for **In Dublin** and joined RTÉ Radio 2, producing **The Dave Fanning Show** for ten years, and instigating Larks in the Park, Beats on the Street and Ireland's first 'rock' showcase, Cork Rock. In 1997 he was appointed chairman of the European Broadcasting Union's Eurosonic group. He is producer-in-charge of alternative music and music production for 2fm and of live broadcasts for events such as Oxegen and the Electric Picnic. He is also a husband of one and father of four.

Trinity Week, 1973, Spud on the college Dining Hall steps.

DICK SPRING'S LEGS

ingrid craigie

DICK SPRING'S LEGS. Coming out of rooms. Dark-blue shorts, carrying a rugby ball. The memory is so vivid, it must have been in my first term. Perhaps it was the element of surprise, the unexpected pleasure, a long-limbed gazelle in a sea of jackets and jeans. And like a ten-second cine film, it still reruns in my mind any time I cross Front Square.

I think I'd always known I'd go to Trinity. It was exotic and familiar at the same time. My father was there in the late thirties. A Knight of the Campanile, his Trinity was all about sport. My brother was there in the late sixties. Political factions, the end of the ban, the burning of Mao's *Little Red Book*. Fun. I knew those years were special, would change us and bind us. My plan was to read English, join Players and become an actor. That was what I wanted, passionately, although I had only the vaguest notion of how I might make it happen. But I knew it was a credible route into the profession. In my final years at school, I often went to productions in Players. It was the first time I saw Sorcha Cusack on stage. I wanted to be her. And if I couldn't be her, I wanted to be like her. So I had to start at the beginning.

My introduction to academic life was through my tutor, J.D. Pheifer. Over a glass of sherry – I thought I was in a Noël Coward play – he gave a magnificent piece of advice. 'Get involved in the life of college, do a certain amount of work and leave the rest to Big Brother.' It was wonderful because, coming from a rather structured school system, it could be quite daunting to be left to your own devices. The British students, of whom there were still a good number, had been through A levels and were really a year ahead of us in every way.

J.D. looked and sounded like an English don of the thirties, though I was told he was, in fact, American. His delight in *Beowulf* was almost infectious. In my third or fourth year, when I was secretary of Players, he took over from R.B.D. French as honorary president. The committee invited him to dinner in the Guinea Pig restaurant to celebrate, where I had sweetbreads for the first time. A decorous, charming evening. At our tutorial next day, when it came to my turn to translate, he enquired solicitously if I was up to it. He would understand completely if I was too tired.

I still have Prof. Walton's notes on Shakespeare and Harden Jay's on Anglo-Irish literature. From them I learned how to approach a text, how to read a script, how to unlock what lies behind and within the words. Lecturers wore gowns. I remember Harden Jay's occasional distressing coughing fits and, on several occasions, her saying, 'As I'm not wearing my gown, you may smoke.' Which meant she could too. David Norris and Brendan Kennelly, our star lecturers, dazzled and beguiled us; respectively a showman and a charmer, passionately committed to sharing their joy.

Because I was taking an honors degree, examinations were in September, to give us time, not to study, but to read through the summer months. This was awful, in one way. They were always there, lurking in the background but the upside was you could enjoy term times to the full and take part in the life of college, as recommended. It was not until the end of my first year that I gained enough courage to audition for Players. I had done a play for Mod. Lang. but Players was my goal. It was run by second-, third- and fourth-year students, most of whom seemed to be English or have been in school in England. They all had grants, seemed older, confident and worldly. I was in awe of Dillie Keane and terrified of Deirdre Bowen, now an undoubtedly fearsome casting director in the States. But in 1973 I got the part in *After Liverpool* by James Saunders, directed by Donald Taylor Black. We started going out and were together for the next four years. I met a great nucleus of friends in that first production – Donald, Karen Callaghan, Pat Abernethy, John Mulligan, Andrew Leonard,

James Hickey and our beloved and much missed Rupert Murray.

Second and third year seemed to be all about Players, including bringing a production to the Student Drama Festival in St Andrew's and another play to the Lyric Theatre in Belfast. On that occasion the atmosphere in the North was very tense. Our southern-registered car was flagged down at an army check-point. A British army officer approached. Andrew Leonard was driving. He rolled down the window and said, 'Ah, Plowden.' Plowden looked like he was going to faint. It turned out they had been at school together in England. We drove on.

While we were rehearsing *The Cuchulain Cycle*, the wooden floor at Front Gate, which was made up of large oak blocks, was being replaced. We acquired several of these old blocks. Wilde and Beckett must have crossed over them. They became the severed heads of warriors in *The Only Jealousy of Emer*, before which I performed a fairly erotic dance, choreographed by Karen Callaghan.

Dick Spring would go on to become a very significant figure in Irish polit-ical life. At the other end of the spectrum, I have a photograph taken in my first year of President Eamon de Valera at Trinity races, dressed in morning coat and top hat. He was approaching his ninetieth birthday and was in his last month as president, in which capacity he attended the races. But the person who most influenced my political and social consciousness is Mary Robinson, then a law lecturer, practising barrister and Trinity senator. In a politically desperate period of intense violence and raw emotion, she courageously and passionately upheld human rights and doggedly pursued change and justice, whether speaking out against internment or campaigning for social equality, not just for Irish women but for all Irish people.

Each memory of Trinity brings another. Most study was done in the Reading Room. Every time the door opened, everyone looked up to see who was coming in. I remember Tim Palmer sloping in, his coat draped over his shoulders, a louche, elegant Prince Hamlet. I don't think he ever stayed long. He just wandered in to leave his books or find someone, his girlfriend, a Biba cloud of blonde hair. And there was a beautiful English lecturer, who came just for a term, I think. Her subject was Anglo-Saxon. Quietly spoken, she had long, straight dark hair, with a fringe, always dressed completely in black – miniskirt, tights, boots, jacket – except for a white high-necked shirt. I think we were all a bit in love with her. And then she went. Donald and I used to save up to go to a really good restaurant once or twice a year and I still recall the thrill of eating in Snaffles and The Soup Bowl for the first time. But the darkest memory was the Dublin bombings. I was in the New Library when one of the bombs went off, just outside, in Lincoln Place.

Towards the end of third year, two things happened. We formed our own company, rented Players for the summer and put on a season of plays, which were reviewed by all the papers and periodicals, such as *Hibernia*. Players was taken seriously as a fringe venue and people in the business came to see us. Then Michael Colgan, who had graduated before I arrived and was a stage manager in The Abbey, met me in Front Square and asked if I'd like to be a walk-on in a production of *The Vicar of Wakefield*, starring Cyril Cusack. That meeting and Players led to my being invited to take part, in my final year, in a summer-long course for young actors at The Abbey, given by Patrick Mason. At the end of the summer, he cast me as Emily in *Our Town*. We closed on a Saturday, I sat my finals the following Monday and I was invited to join the Abbey company. I developed a bad rash on my hands and feet. I didn't know, at the time, that it was stress. I was having too good a time.

Ingrid Craigie (TCD 1972–6; English Language and Literature), actor, was a member of The Abbey Theatre Company,1976–81, and worked as a freelance actor ever since in Ireland, the UK, the USA and Canada in world premieres of plays by many writers including Brian Friel, Tom Kilroy and Sarah Kane. Television includes the Bafta-winning **The Ballroom of Romance**. Film includes **The Dead**, directed by John Huston. In 2007 she received the Special Tribute Award at the **Irish Times** Irish Theatre Awards and the inaugural Alumni Award from TCD for her contribution to Irish theatre.

Ingrid Craigie and her brother Duncan.

A UNIVERSITY OF LIFE

mary harney

TRINITY in the early seventies was for me a new and exciting place to grow into adult life. Having been raised on a small west-Dublin dairy farm, Trinity was definitely another world. It was inhabited by people whose ideas, background and language seemed very far away from those I was used to at Coláiste Bríde convent secondary school in Clondalkin. I was the eldest of five children in a traditional Irish farm household where Catholic values were taken as given and the virtues of hard work were instilled in all of us. My parents had moved from Galway to a Land Commission farm in Newcastle when I was an infant and having had to struggle to establish a life for themselves they were determined to give their children a good education. All of their own generation in Galway had had to emigrate, my father's brothers and sisters to Chicago and my mother's to Manchester. The decision to send their eldest daughter to university was grounded in this reality. In the early seventies only a smaller number of secondary students went on to third level, so I knew I was in a privileged minority.

Trips into town had formed my first impressions of TCD, with its impressive main facade overseen by the statues of those leading statesmen and graduates, Henry Grattan and Edmund Burke. The bishop's ban on Catholics attending Trinity had just been lifted so I was among the first group of students of that background to go through its impressive portals and the first Catholic chaplain, Father Heffernan, had just been appointed. Notwithstanding its long history, Trinity was then a relatively small university and there was a sense of knowing everybody at least by face. There was a large contingent of students from Northern Ireland at college. Having befriended people from both Northern communities I became educated in the complexity of the differing perspectives there and these insights stood me in good stead in my later political life. One of Trinity's great strengths was that it brought people together from a wide variety of backgrounds and was therefore a perfect laboratory for development of new ideas and new perspectives. Although right in the centre of Dublin, when one walked through the archway into college there was a sense of being in a different world – old in its buildings and history but ultra-modern and vibrant.

Freshers' Week was in full swing when I arrived in late September 1972, and I was immediately confronted by an amazing choice of activities in which to become involved. It was easy to resist the temptations of rowing, mountain climbing, archery and so forth and I straightaway joined the Hist, having been a keen debater at Coláiste Bríde. Unbeknown to me then was the fact that it was a natural breeding ground for aspiring politicians. During my time there we debated everything from Northern Ireland to apartheid, gay rights, divorce, and, of course, the futility of the Vietnam War – being young we were blessed with the conviction that we knew the answers to all of these issues and problems!

Given that I had come from a conservative Catholic family background, I immediately took a liberal stance on the social issues of the day. In those days there was no divorce, homosexuals were regarded as criminals and contraception was illegal, thankfully a far cry from today's openness. Being sometimes obliged to debate on the opposite side to one's own views honed our capacity to see the world as others do. The Hist was attractive in other respects. Its home was the Graduate Memorial Building (the GMB) with its comfortable drawing room and free daily newspapers – a particular advantage for cash-strapped students. In those days before instant worldwide communication media, institutions like the Hist were able to attract a regular flow of prominent people wishing to promote their ideas or politics.

I was inherently involved in the Hist and its affairs throughout my college career between 1972 and 1977 and found the variety of people, the eloquence and frequent passion of debate and, of course, the labyrinthine internal politics enormously appealing. I was put on the committee during my first year and remained there in various capacities, including as treasurer, until I became auditor in 1976. I was, as it happens, the Society's first-ever woman auditor. I like to think of this as my first exercise in mould-breaking. At the time (perhaps to this day) it was customary for the auditor of the Hist to be elected to membership of one of the clubs on St Stephen's Green. This perk was not accorded to me; with casuistry that would not disgrace a Jesuit, it was explained that the failure to elect me was not because I was a woman but because I was not a man! That particular mould, too, has since been broken.

The Hist helped to broaden my horizons, not least through trips to other universities for debating competitions in Ireland and the UK. As you might expect, my term as auditor, the guests I invited and the whole tone of the Society were of a political bent. I brought to debates my friend and mentor Jack Lynch, John Hume, and the British Liberal leader Jo Grimond amongst others. I had, I believe, no great difficulty in controlling the 'House', having been an attentive apprentice to my predecessors over the last three years. My years at the Hist had equipped me well for a career in political life, upon which I had already embarked as I left Trinity. During my first year and with the encouragement of my economics professor, Martin O'Donoghue, I joined the college Fianna Fáil cumann because I admired Jack Lynch. The Cumann was relatively new in Trinity as understandably the Fianna Fáil tradition had not featured strongly in its history!

My joining coincided with a period of some turmoil as many members tendered their resignations in protest at amendments to the Offences Against the State Act recently introduced by Des O'Malley. In this transition, and because there were so few people left, I was made an officer at my first meeting. It was an era of political agitation and university students were actively involved. One meeting of the Hist in 1974 developed into a riot as a group of Internationalists and Marxist-Leninists objected to 'fascists' being given opportunity for 'free speech' – the 'fascists' included the then Minister for Justice due to speak at that evening's debate. Gardaí had to be called in to restore order – a source of great excitement to students. Fianna Fáil had gone into opposition in 1973 and in the last years of my college career a process of renewal was vigorously pursued by Jack Lynch and Séamus Brennan and this included a push to broaden the role of women and young people – a familiar theme even today. Having taken ESS (Economics and Social Science) at Trinity I focused on economics from second year onwards and then enrolled for the H.Dip in 1976 and spent a year teaching mathematics, economics and debating at Castleknock College. Teaching was not for me because instead of taking the Dip exam in June 1977 I acceded to Jack Lynch's invitation to be a candidate in the general election.

Looking back at the hectic life we had in Trinity I now wonder where we fitted in any time for study. The politicking of the Hist and Fianna Fáil were absorbing but I also found myself involved with the student Society of St Vincent de Paul. I and fellow students used to visit an inner-city area of great social and economic deprivation where families lived in large tenement housing and where conditions were worlds apart from nearby Trinity College. This served to convince me further of the need for lasting and radical change through political action, and was another example of how the broad Trinity experience gave opportunities to students for a really rounded education.

My years at Trinity coincided with Ireland's accession to what was then the EEC, although I was not personally involved in the campaign for membership that predated my involvement in politics. It was a time of great change, transformation and hope with our membership of this reforming European project. I was lucky to be one of about thirty students taken on a fact-finding mission to European institutions in Brussels, Luxembourg and Strasbourg by the then senator and law lecturer, Mary Robinson. She was far-sighted in ensuring that we understood how these institutions, which were to play such a huge role in Ireland's future, worked. Little did I know that fourteen years later I would represent my country at ministerial meetings in these very places. Even then Mary Robinson was clearly a woman apart and an articulate champion of minority causes; she was highly respected and admired, particularly by us young women.

During my first years at college I travelled every day on the 68 bus from Newcastle to Dublin and so missed out on some of the atmosphere of Trinity and activities that went beyond 10.30 in the evening. However, I had the privilege of living in rooms for my last year. My room at New Square was my first home away from home and it did not seem to matter that a number of students had to share bathrooms and kitchens. It was a liberating experience and wonderful to live right in the centre of town, sharing the campus not just with other students but with academic staff who lived there at the time. We self-importantly hosted dinner parties for our friends, which featured different variations on the theme of spaghetti Bolognese and wine served from value cartons. Highlights of the social calendar were the Trinity Week garden party where ladies sported long dresses and large hats – the Elizabethan era seemed alive and well – and the ball, which even then was a raucous all-night affair, followed (money and physical stamina permitting) by breakfast in the nearby Hibernian Hotel.

Trinity has a proud tradition of educating some of the most outstanding people in our history ranging from Wolfe Tone, Thomas Davis, Edward Carson and Douglas Hyde to Conor Cruise O'Brien, Dick Spring, Mary Robinson, David O'Sullivan and the late Brian Lenihan. College was so very exciting in the seventies because it was in the process of evolving as an institution to become a broad-based Irish university, growing rapidly in both stature and numbers of students. We students were encouraged us to think for ourselves and have the courage to challenge fixed ideas and the status quo. It was never boring and always great fun.

Mary Harney (TCD 1972–6; Economics and Social Science) enrolled in a Higher Diploma in Education in 1976. She was appointed to the Senate in 1977 and elected to Dublin County Council in 1979 and has been a member of the Dáil since 1981. Founder member of the Progressive Democrats with Des O'Malley in 1985, and Minister of State with Responsibility for Environmental Protection, 1989–92, she was elected leader of the PDs in 1993. Voted **Irish Independent** Woman of the Year in 1996, she was tánaiste and Minister for Enterprise Trade and Employment, 1997–2004, tánaiste and Minister for Health and Children, 2004–6, and Minister for Health and Children, 2006–11. Given an Honorary Doctorate from Lynn University, Florida, she was voted **Irish Tatler** Woman of the Year in 2005. She is married to Brian Geoghegan and has four stepchildren.

A LONG TIME AGO

eithne tinney

I NEARLY DIDN'T make it to Trinity at all. My plan was to go to Paris when I left school, to study the piano at the Conservatoire Nationale de Musique. My second instrument was the flute, which I studied with the formidable French principal flautist of what was then the Radio Éireann Symphony Orchestra, André Prieur. He was himself a product of the rigorous Conservatoire, and convinced me of the merits of its disciplined system. It appealed to my business instincts that if you won a place there you paid no fees. I didn't realize that this was the theory, but that in practice pupils were expected to take additional weekly lessons privately with their professor, which was probably very costly indeed.

In any event, my mother insisted that I was too young, and too much of a wild child, to be unleashed to my own devices in Paris. First, I must spend a year at university. She had already put a stop to my runaway gallop a couple of years earlier by changing my school and forcing me to repeat fifth year, which I deeply resented at the time. A quirk of circumstance meant that I had entered secondary school at the age of ten, and was poised to leave at the age of sixteen. I was looking forward to this as I detested the boredom of school and couldn't wait to leave it behind.

But my mother was immutable when she had made up her mind, so off I had to go to Loreto College, St Stephen's Green, to do what was then a two-year Leaving Cert. cycle. As my mother was a professor at UCD I opted for Trinity to put space between us. I loved her dearly, but we had a tempestuous relationship when I was growing up and the last thing I wanted, now that I had achieved relative freedom, was to be proximate to either of my parents. Since it was only for a year I decided to apply for General Studies and nominated English, French and Music as my subjects. When the Leaving Cert. results came out I received a charming letter from Trinity inquiring would I not prefer to pursue an honors degree? I kept it for many years, as its courtesy pleased and flattered me – can you imagine getting such a missive from the CAO? But I stuck to my original plan.

In my two years at Loreto I had become very friendly with a girl named Marie-Louise Savino. She had dark, Italianate good looks due to her father's antecedents, and we shared a love of music and of debating. She had a really wicked way of annihilating the competition, and our team was very successful. She was also really funny, a quality I deeply admired. She became ill in our final months there and sat her Leaving in hospital, but we were all too young to understand the significance of that. We simply thought the chapter was closed when she came out of hospital. She and I were the only ones from our class to go to Trinity in 1972. It was still quite unusual for Catholics – whether lapsed or not, as I was – to choose it over UCD. Term started in October, and we both joined the famous TCD Choral Society, conducted then, as it had been for many years, by the inimitable, eccentric Dr Joseph Groocock.

One day in November Marie-Louise and I were making the long climb up No. 5 in Front Square, which housed the Music Department, to the lecture room right at the top of the building, where choral rehearsals were held. We were chatting, and then she went quiet. I realized she was out of breath. This made me anxious, although she brushed it off. Within a week she was back in St Vincent's hospital, and this time there was no coming out. The last time I saw her she was semi-comatose. I sat with her for half an hour or so and then tried to slip out silently. As I reached the door of her room I heard, 'Ethna'. I turned around, and she smiled very sweetly at me and said, 'Don't worry about me.'

A few days later her mother rang around 8 am. I was still in bed but when told who was on the phoned I lurched downstairs as fast as I could. Her mother told me she had died a couple of hours earlier. I had never asked Marie-Louise what was wrong with her because I sensed she didn't want to talk about it. So I said, 'What did she die of?' and Mrs Savino replied, 'Massive pleurisy of both lungs.' I was none the wiser, but asked no more questions. Marie-Louise was an only child and her death broke the hearts of both her parents. Her funeral in the Church of the Three Patrons in Rathgar was the saddest I have ever attended. She was buried in Mount Jerome Cemetery and within five years both her mother and her father had joined her there.

The sadness I felt was ameliorated by all the wonderful things I discovered at Trinity – partial freedom, intellectual stimulation, great music and above all an abundant social life. This gyrated between the Buttery bar in Front Square, O'Neills public house in Suffolk Street, and the Central Hotel in Wicklow Street, which had a magical Bloody Mary cocktail that could rout the most dismal of hangovers. As we Irish would say, you will not encounter its like again: I certainly never have, though I searched long and wide. Having taken the hair of the dog, it was off to Bewley's in Grafton Street for a hearty 'breakfast'.

In the midst of all this it is a wonder any of us got to our lectures and tutorials, and indeed I confess I missed many a lecture. But I loved the life at Trinity and so decided that Paris could wait. Under those circumstances, when I secured my General Studies exams in June of 1973, I asked permission to sit the honors exams, then held in September, in English and French with a view to going straight into the second year of a BA moderatorship. Permission was granted, I swotted hard, passed the exams and proceeded with the change of course.

Of course the unremitting socialization had to be funded, and so I always had an eye to the main chance. In the summer of 1972 I had already built up a stash of cash by working for five weeks on the evening shift in Batchelor's factory in Cabra, which in those days was connected to my family home in Rathgar virtually door to door by the number 12 bus. The work was monotonous, but the women who worked the shift were great fun. They called me 'love', and never got to grips with the notion of college, although I tried to explain it to them. They would ask me from time to time when was I going back to school.

The first job I secured in Trinity itself was a small stipend to sing as a soprano chorister in the Chapel Choir, which performed during term-time at Evensong on Wednesdays, and the Sunday morning service. I wasn't really a soprano, but Professor Brian Boydell brushed that aside since no one else wanted the job, and I was employed. The choir was conducted by Malcolm Proud, who soon roped me into his other choir, Trinity Singers, albeit as an alto. Malcolm was a superb musician, and although my background was steeped in music, he introduced me to a whole new land of composers such as Josquin des Prez, Orlando di Lasso and William Byrd. There were also fabulous a cappella works by Bach, Brahms, Poulenc and Britten, and I derived intense pleasure from the year I sang for him in both choirs.

I wasn't the most punctual attendee at rehearsals, however, which used to drive Malcolm crazy. In the summer of 1973, Singers attended a choral festival called Europa Cantat in Autun in France where choirs of all sizes assembled to present joint concerts as well as their own individual recitals. We were participating in a performance of Gabriel Fauré's *Requiem* but Malcolm was naturally most concerned about our individual concert. After a night spent seriously on the tiles I failed to get up for the requisite rehearsal, despite the urgings of my female fellow Singers, with whom I was sharing a dormitory.

During the rehearsal break, at approximately 11 am, a furious Malcolm stormed into the dormitory and accosted me in the bed where I was peacefully slumbering. As he was a mild-natured man this was seriously out of character. I took the arrogant view in those days that I didn't need to rehearse, since I could read almost all the music we performed at sight. It was only years later, when I founded the orchestra Classical Graffiti, which I both conducted and managed, that I came to realize how insanely frustrating it was to deal with mavericks, no matter how talented. So Malcolm, if you are reading this, I apologize.

When I arrived in second year I got a job serving on Commons. This was an evening meal that was free to fellows and scholars of Trinity, and any other students who could afford the fifty pence to pay for it. For two hours' work, five out of seven days a week, we were paid well enough for our trouble with the added perk of a free meal. Proceedings were presided over by one Mrs Betty Pickering, who really should have altered her first name when she married. Why not recast herself as Elizabeth, or even Lisa? Despite her pleasant, slightly aloof nature she was inevitably referred to as Petty Bickering.

I also undertook some evening work in the newly opened Pavilion Bar, which was all right as long as you were serving, but became something of an ordeal when you were sent out to hassle the students into drinking up. Separating any serious drinking student from his last pint (and in the Pavilion they were overwhelmingly male) is not for the faint-hearted. I didn't last long there. Besides, study called. I had set my sights on winning a Foundation Scholarship. As well as nightly Commons, scholars had their fees paid and free rooms in Trinity, bang in the centre of Dublin, which could last for quite a number of years if you went on to do postgraduate studies.

To achieve this you had to get first-class honors in a special 'schol' exam that was held in late April of your second year. This was something of a stretch for me, as I had not really distinguished myself in my first year, but I became very fond of the 1937 Reading Room, where most of the arts students did their work, and I ran out with a worthy 2:1, which meant I was exempt from the September exams. The only person from our year in Arts to achieve 'schol' was Jo Shapcott, an exceptionally good-looking English girl who had an additional exotic aura due to the fact that it was known she was an orphan.

We became firm friends, not least because I asked her the first time I met her what had happened to her parents. She told me no one had ever asked her that in Trinity before, which is quintessentially Irish. People all spoke about it when she wasn't there, but never to her directly. In that regard, we are a strange people.

We were both free that summer because of our 'schol' results, and we went off on separate adventures but met up in Paris in September to participate in the annual French grape-picking harvest, the *vendanges*. It was one of the worst harvests in living memory. Jo and I were holed up in a hostel in Paris, with little left in the way of funds, for an unanticipated ten days of teeming rain. We whiled away the time by attending a festival of James Bond movies, as we were both keen on Sean Connery.

When the harvest was finally declared we were assigned to a farm near Villefranche, where we spent sixteen days of the hardest work I have ever endured. Our employer issued us with Wellington boots that did not fit as we never thought to bring our own, and the earth mixed with the incessant rain to make a cement of several pounds that we had to drag with us. We worked dawn to dusk to get in the grapes as quickly as possible before they rotted on the vines. Even in the best of weather grape-picking is not at all romantic. The grapes are so low down that you are crippled by the day's end and secateurs are used to cut them off in bunches. You end up with seriously cut fingers, which are infected by the insect poisons sprayed on the grapes. I was extremely shocked at the state of my hands at the end of the sixteen days, but they healed quickly enough.

After that holiday the Freshman years were over and it was time to knuckle down to serious work. We had some brilliant lecturers, people of such communicative power that they could make a dictionary sound interesting. I particularly remember Brendan Kennelly and David Norris in the Department of English, Barbara Wright in the Department of French, and Brian Boydell in the Department of Music.

As well as my academic work the piano was looming again, as I knew I wanted to pursue the study of it after my degree, so as well as long hours in the 1937 Reading Room I spent many on the top floor of No. 5, where there was an ancient but still useful grand piano. I used to practise there at night when the place was quiet. When I was finished, and particularly if funds were low and socializing was not an option, I would listen to LPs in the tiny library annexed to the practice room, listening to music, dreaming of the future and smoking cigarettes, which in those days was not *verboten*. Two recordings I listened to over and over again, gazing into a deserted Front Square, were Sviatoslav Richter's live 1957 Sofia performance of Mussorgsky's *Pictures at an Exhibition* and Dietrich Fischer-Dieskau singing '*Mache dich, mein Herze, rein*' from Bach's *Matthew Passion*.

The facility to practise the piano proved significantly important when I moved out of the family home into rooms with Jo in my final year, which was devoted solely from the Trinity perspective to the study of English Literature. I embarked on a novel self-imposed regime where I decided I would read no critical works at all. I would immerse myself in the texts and rely on my own critical faculties. It worked up to a point, and I exited in the autumn of 1976 with a BA Mod 2:1 in English and French, ready to pursue a new adventure in the Royal College of Music in London, which proved to be quite different from what I expected, but that is another story.

When I look back on my four years in Trinity I feel privileged to have had the experience. The combination of freedom and rigour suited my temperament, and it was an intensely sociable place where there were no boundaries of gender, race or religion. Only a fraction of the size it is now, it was a very cohesive community, where some of the staff interacted closely with some of their students. I wonder can that happen now? Are there invitations to the Senior Common Room, to the Provost's House, to the Fellows' Dinner? I wouldn't want to return, as some of my contemporaries have done, to pursue postgraduate studies, because I think I would find a very different Trinity, which I could not love so much.

Eithne Tinney (TCD 1972–6; BA moderatorship), pianist, conductor, teacher, impresario and broadcaster, joined the staff of RTÉ in 1999 as a producer with Lyric FM, where she is responsible for **The Lyric Concert** and **Operanight**. A non-executive director of EBS, she lives in County Limerick with her husband Billy Fox, and a family of horses, dogs and cats.

MEMOIR OF A FASHIONABLY DRESSED SOCIALIST

godfrey deeny

I NEVER REALLY felt that many of the people I met during my time in Trinity got me, or if I got Trinity that much myself. Though with hindsight the place did leave an indelible mark. For the interests, and obsessions I developed during my time in college were to mark out my career, choice of countries, romances and particular peripatetic journey through life.

Before starting in September 1973, I had walked through Front Square a number of times with older brothers while I was still studying for my Leaving Cert. in Clongowes Wood College. While they saw it as a shining temple of learning and wit, it struck me as a badly defended fortress, surrounded by spear-tipped wrought-iron fences, with gates where polite but self-important porters wearing odd jockey-style hats made sure the hoi polloi did not enter.

Nonetheless, when I won a place in the Department of Economic and Social Sciences, I was excited at the thought of intellectual jousting, and the chance to finally sit in a class with a member of the opposite sex – something that had been denied me for the first seventeen years of my life. I had expected Trinity would be an elegant melange of *The Glittering Prizes* meets *Jules and Jim*, where posh dandies in tails would joust with existentialist lefties in polo necks on the great issues of the day, where I'd fall madly in love with a leggy gal, who would dump a dull rugby player for my *bon mots*, dance moves and the chance to listen to my collection of soul records.

Instead, on my first visit to our famed debating society, the Hist, I was pained to discover that the Dublin bourgeois, newly ascendant over the formerly dominant Anglo-Irish, had banned the wearing of dinner jackets to debates. All the speakers dressed appallingly badly and everyone came across as obsessed with how their record would appear if they ever became cabinet ministers. No one seemed to really want to live in the moment.

On the great issues of the day, the Troubles, Israel/Palestine or joining Europe, these teenage politicians blithely repeated the official positions of the governing parties. It all sounded so middle-aged ahead of its time, in particular one 'officer' of the Hist called George Birmingham, a sparrow-like figure who favoured long prison sentences for anyone even suspected of being a terrorist. A decade later, returning to Dublin from my job as a sportswriter in Rome, I chuckled on listening to RTÉ during an airport taxi ride to discover *piccolo* George's public rubric included being some sort of Minister of Youth. Youth, they usually say, is wasted on the youth; these folks didn't even have the good sense to fritter it away. So, despite, being a debating champion at boarding school, I never once addressed the Hist and fairly promptly skipped its moribund debates.

I forget how I found my digs in Terenure, but though the landlady was civil and the breakfasts of black pudding ideal in the dank Dublin mornings, I hated having to wait in the rain for the bus. Was it the number 15A? Lurching around corners in an irritating daily commute to Trinity did not do it for me, and I quickly resolved to find a flat from where I could easily walk to Front Square. It was a lesson I learned for life, and in any city where I have lived since then, from New York to Milan, Moscow to Paris, I always lived within walking distance of my office.

Happily, at New Year I took a 'pad' at 40 Pembroke Road with my nearest brother Arthur and our pal John Doona and began to enjoy the shabby gentility of decayed Georgian Dublin. The wind literally whistled through the aged windows, the carpets were threadbare, the beds absurdly uncomfortable, and one needed a ten-pence coin to fire up the boiler for a bath. Yet its peeling plaster, smoky turf fires and ornate doors had great charm – an ideal locale for distilling pint bottles of Arth. J. Guinness or our favourite tawny port as we discussed the affairs of the day, played poker or bridge or simply just got stoned and discovered music.

Most of my friends read *The Irish Times* for free in the Phil drawing room after lunch, but my reading centered on regular supplies of the *New Musical Express* and *Rolling Stone*. The great musical expert of our era in Trinity was the late Bill Graham, who sucked in his breath when he laughed and had an encyclopedic knowledge of music. In our digital era of iPods and iTunes the idea of building a record collection has been lost, as has the wonderful art form that was designing album covers. But by the end of my first year, I'd amassed what I thought was a great collection of forty-five dance records, soul classics and avant-garde obscurities, mostly acquired second-hand in Pat Egan's tiny downstairs store near Front Gate. But my assortment suddenly appeared pitiful to my eyes after our first visit to Bill's wee flat near Keoghs, the first place I heard Miles Davis or Stockhausen. Man, did Bill know his music.

Our first meeting was tinged with a certain confusion, as I thought he was the one and same Bill Graham, the legendary promoter, who staged the great gigs at Fillmore East. Not! A decade later when I saw Miles play like a god in Perugia Jazz in 1985, I thanked Bill in my mind for the introduction, only then realizing that he had opened a certain vista, that a youthful fellow from a provincial town in Ireland could move across the universe through writing about his passions – be they music, art or style. And when I heard of his death in the mid nineties, when I had achieved a certain success in my *métier*, thanks in many ways to the help and advice of wiser, older heads like the Godfather of Fashion John Fairchild or Kaiser Karl Lagerfeld, I realized that Bill, albeit in just a few meetings, was my first mentor.

A key part of Dublin DNA for me has always been live music, and no week was complete without a concert, whether Freddie White in some pub, Genesis or Rory Gallagher in the decrepit National Stadium, or, best of all, my big brother Michael's band Horslips, whose brand of Celtic rock inspired me almost as much as their totally over-the-top ethno-glam clothes. Quite why no one has ever done a fashion retrospective on the 'Lips beats me.

It was a time when we all DJed, fighting to put the next single on some crappy Dansette, to bop madly in a crammed student pad. I never did manage to become a 'real deejay', though that's partly because of my habit of exiting modern DJ booths as soon as I have launched a track to hit the dance floor myself. I have had to literally fight other DJs out; clubs you see, like nature, abhor a vacuum. But the love of dancing and the quirky imitations of Mick Jagger and Fred Astaire that I developed in Dublin 4, the chance to hold and twirl a girl that had caught my eye, never left me.

Trinity was also a college full of talk; though as time moved on I decided the conversation of non-students was, well, more intriguing. A far better audience could be found outside in the pubs of Dublin, which became the salon that I never found inside College Square. My favourite pub became Smyth's of Haddington Road, located close to Pembroke Road and the flat of my final year; my favorite abode in Dublin, 40 Lansdowne Road. There, to my surprise, I met 'country people', who referred to me as 'our Trinity scholar', which was, technically speaking, not correct. Like many students it took me several attempts to develop a taste for the succulent bitterness of Guinness, but after I did my taste buds were hooked for life, and even today, once a month, I search out a pub somewhere near the fashion circuit and down a pint or two of the plain. In Smyth's, the key word among non-Dubliners was 'genuine', meaning were we really being honest with each other, rather than just striking a pose. And it's a lesson that stayed with me all these days, especially in the *faux cul* world of fashion, where what fashionistas say is rarely what they mean.

Back inside the walls, I recall that politics was the main topic of conversation, even if this often bordered on the absurd. In disgust at the pomposity of student politics, my witty brother Arthur even founded his own party, the Free Catholic Anarchists, or FCA, to run for president of the Student Union. Its brief week of existence included an inaugural 'rally' on Front Steps, the 'assassination' of our leader, and his 'resurrection' the following day when we marched him across the campus in a coffin before his miraculous revival. To his credit, Arthur even got 300 votes, narrowly beaten by a Maoist, or perhaps through the fog of political war, I confuse two elections.

I had read Chairman Mao's *Little Red Book* and agreed with his view that the intelligentsia needed to get their hands dirty, at the very least in their youth, and join in the productive struggle. So, each summer, I'd head off to London, seeking out pointedly working-class jobs on building sites, or driving trucks.

Despite those endeavours, most people classified me as a pinstripe socialist, which I rather liked, as it indicated I took care over my appearance. The money I earned went essentially on three things – clothes, a car, and buying drink and drugs to share with girls. The rest, as George Best wisely put it, I just wasted.

My first car was a modest wee Mini, costing the princely sum of £300, and it changed my life. For true genuine authenticity, you see, nothing could beat an actual trip to the country, especially to the Wicklow hills, or down the coast to the massive beach at Brittas Bay or wandering around the racetracks of Leinster, dipping in country pubs along the way. In today's Ireland of non-drink driving it would be impossible, and rightly so. But I cherished our own private road movies, properly beginning an hour out of Dublin when the drink and drugs began to take hold. With hindsight, our dabbling with drugs seems so innocent. Once a month we used to 'score' a modest lump of Moroccan hash, shared among my flatmates. Making that last a full four weeks helped develop the skill of husbanding resources; and compared to the self-indulgences of my thirties in Ibiza and New York, it was all rather tame. And rightly so, for little learning can be achieved when wrecked.

Though I had edited a magazine in Clongowes, Trinity was where I first got a title – film critic of *TCD Miscellany* – and I discovered that people actually read and cared and were indeed infuriated or charmed by one's words. My rudimentary prose and cocky opinions now seem so jejune, but at the time I held my opinions passionately, and later as a magazine editor the first thing I looked for when hiring staff was whether they were really consumed by what they did.

Fortunately, I was a modestly decent student. Getting an honors degree – albeit only a 2:2 – despite reading way off the course incessantly; with my favourite cubbyhole for study, the basement of the New Library, tucked away among the dusty compilations of Irish newspapers and obscure government records. Years subsequently, when an American girlfriend insisted I suffered from ADD, I realized that's why I hid away two floors below – I am forever too easily distracted.

A course in economic geography led me to discover Le Corbusier and Buckminster Fuller, and develop a lifelong love of architecture. Part of the appeal of my profession is the never-ending search by design houses for intriguing spaces, whether beautiful museums, giant disused factories or historic palaces. Yet, the architecture that I have continued to prefer is the grand Georgian style of central Dublin, echoes of which grace my Directoire home in Paris. When it came to design the Protestant ascendancy knew what they were doing, and the Celtic Tiger never caught up.

Curiously for a man so obsessed with sports I was strikingly unathletic. Rugger-hugger girls never gave me the time of day, the rowing club crowd had never heard of Kurosawa and I broke my nose playing squash in a bloody moment, so mine was not an exercise-filled four years. However, I can boast of one sporting endeavour – winning the Trinity croquet championship three years in a row in New Square. My team changed each season – the Hist, remarkably given my views, one season, the FCA the next, the Phil the third. Okay, it's not quite Michel Platini being *Capocannoniere* in Série A three years running, or Barcelona winning the triple. But I still felt proud when I broke three consecutive hoops to seal my triple, especially as croquet is an unforgiving, ruthless sport in a quiet sort of way – rather like fashion.

Plus, I liked the way people dressed for croquet, odd in an era when to be well attired invited angry accusations that you were gay. Every few months some lumpy rugger fan or pimpled youth insisted I was an 'effing queer', largely, I surmised, on the basis of my dress. Not many lads wore polka-dot velvet jackets, or silver suede platform boots, but so what? It was later in life in the bohemian splendour of Manhattan's Lower East Side that I was to realize that when the gays noticed your style, the girls always did too.

Sexually, Trinity was far too often for me an era of missed opportunities, or fumbled seductions. I slept with six girls in four years and only had sex with three of them. There were far too many nights when, even after getting into bed, women simply refused to take off their underwear. I was, and am, incurably, romantic, but that era in Trinity when condoms were still banned throughout the Emerald Isle was unbelievably frustrating. You simply could not buy a rubber Johnny anywhere. Marijuana was easier to come by. No wonder the *cailíní* of Trinity were so demure. If anything drove me out of Ireland it was the lack of sex, its scrotum-tightening sexual famine. Still, I loved the back and forth, the banter of Irish women; they way they bought their round – not something that happens much here in France, or Italy, or Russia.

I even loved their occasional upbraiding: having read Engels, Germaine Greer and Simone de Beauvoir I was, of course, a feminist, yet recall the brutal slagging one day because of my rock-n-roll habit of referring to women as 'chicks'. I'd like to thank those gals for their quite rightful anger.

I did finally fall in love in my final term with Gina McGilligan, a philosophy student who had never heard of Kurosawa either, but was happy to discover him; a delicately featured girl with an enigmatic blonde beauty, someone who made me laugh all day. We first kissed during a walk along Sandymount Strand, years before I had read Joyce, and I can still recall that unique churning feeling in my stomach with pleasure, and regret.

Reading F. Scott FitzGerald's *The Great Gatsby* before I even entered college, I was struck by the author's remark that the athletic Tom Buchanan was never to achieve the success in life he had accomplished in university, describing him as 'one of those men who reach such an acute limited excellence at twenty-one that everything afterwards savours of anti-climax'. I was determined that no one – especially me – would think that of my Trinity days.

Yet even if they were far from being my best days, they were a fine and largely gentlemanly first course – *un amuse bouche* – in life before the cosmopolitan years of America and the continent. And they were days imbued with the happy sense that life was blessed with potential, hours where the biggest lesson I learned was the absolute necessity of leaving time and space for the impromptu and unexpected. That's still what keeps me most sane today.

Godfrey Deeny (TCD 1973–7; Economics), international fashion critic, is former editor-in-chief of **Vogue Hommes, Women's Wear Daily**, luxury magazine **W**, Dow Jones Milan correspondent and European editor of **Fashion Wire Daily**, and men's fashion critic of the **Financial Times**. He lectures in Moscow State University's graduate business school and the Paris Fashion Institute. He is the editor-in-chief and joint owner of **Achtung**, a German fashion magazine, and **Sepp**, a football fashion magazine.

ALL CHANGE AND NO CHANGE

caroline preston

I FIRST WALKED into Front Square as a Fresher, with my father, who, though an undergraduate himself as war broke out, had not been inside the gates of Trinity for over thirty years. He was a big man of military stature and fond of storytelling. I was therefore not paying much attention to his new story about a character he had known when he was at college, who was then Junior Dean. I was naturally more concerned about giving the impression that I already belonged. When we reached the Campanile a small man in several dirty coats who was talking to himself with conviction appeared from the shade. My father, already considerably shaken by what appeared to be the ghostly reincarnation of a man he assumed long dead, was astonished when the famed Junior Dean lifted his more famous pork pie hat and said, 'Ah, Orr! How are you?' Professor McDowell's recall of his former students was clearly as remarkable as his propensity to appear from the shadows, often when one least wanted to see him.

What strange place was this? I had been brought up on a diet of Trinity stories. Was my time here to be filled with stories and jolly japes to recount to my grandchildren? I was the third generation of my family to attend Trinity. My grandfather, a man born in the last century but one, was a Methodist who hugely disapproved of drink. His story of witnessing a young man entering

Botany Bay in broad daylight, far from sober and clearly unable to distinguish one side of the Bay from the other, was a long-time favourite in our household. The Square was grassed at the time and in it were planted three small trees. The weary traveller struggled as his legs swung in wild circles in search of a foothold and made progress only in ever-decreasing circles. Miraculously, in his futile journey to find his rooms, he crashed sickeningly into each tree in turn, eventually thumping to the ground and declaring himself, 'losht, losht in a bloody forest'.

My father, in his turn, in a reversal of the usual narrative of his exemplary youth, was particularly proud of being arrested outside Front Gate as he inadvertently threw a punch at the constabulary (his words), believing him to be a student from the National University during the course of a Trinity Week provocation that got out of hand. His short time in college was spent making better use of his long reach on the cricket pitch and in Jammet's before what was naively referred to then as the 'fracas with Hitler' cut short this happy existence. It is no surprise therefore that, in his later years, and especially at the dawn of my college career, he threatened to return (with me) to finish his degree, a prospect that filled his daughter with horror.

As the generation that came after the sixties, we felt, perhaps, that we had missed something of the boundary-busting glamour of that decade. Trinity could no longer be described as the alternative to Oxford and Cambridge for the self-confident and eccentric public-school men and women with generous allowances. Ireland and, more particularly, Dublin had claimed it. There remained the vestiges of the strong connection with the English. I hesitate to admit that I attended a couple of meetings of an organization, the focus of which was to support the Conservative Party, usually hosted by the aforementioned Junior Dean. The sherry was free and the boys wore dapper bow ties, one of whom, I suspect, was the reason for my new-found interest in British politics.

There was, of course, a considerable cohort of Northerners, thought by many to be a breed apart. This, I suspect, was simply a reflection of the secret view held by the wider population in the Republic that they would prefer it if the North and its Troubles would just go away. I was determined not to be considered one of them, which, of course, genetically at least, I was. I managed this in part because I did not sound like one. My Dublin friends, largely to rile me, maintained the view that I was 'not really Irish' – not because I was from the North but because I was a Prod (aka West Brit), a jibe that then as now ignites a red hot rage.

The early seventies were a time of transition from the racy eccentricity of the previous decade. Jammet's was no longer, the Hibernian was in its death throes. Dublin was down at heel, albeit with a genteel shabbiness: it had few restaurants and almost none we could afford. There was little entertainment, save the theatre, which was almost always beyond the student budget. We made our own music and theatre, and eating was not high on the agenda. I loved the unstructured, often crazed exuberance and humour of life in Dublin, the ever-present irreverent banter, the sweet bitter smell of roasting hops from the Guinness Brewery. I loved the pink evening light on wet streets. I loved the sheer familiarity of it all.

I was soon lost in (and thoroughly enjoying) a heady combination of no parental control, an entirely unchallenged drink culture and the emergence of sexual freedom – which, for the most part, was just confusing. Many of my fellow travellers also appeared to be under no constraints at all. Dillie Keane and the late, much-loved Mandy Walker held court in a mews off Ely Place complete with two cats named Toothache and Gumboil. These two highly intelligent and crazy ladies rocked back and forth between being best friends and dangerous, albeit short-lived enemies. Returning from another late night in The Bailey with one of them (I forget which) we were met with a grisly sight: a much-loved teddy bear strangled with the loo chain, from which he hung, tragically, a bread knife through his head. Recovery days – and there were many in Ely Place – started at about noon, inevitably with a traipse to H.W. Williams for whatever cure could be afforded, usually still in our nightclothes.

Being in the wrong clothes for the time of day became somewhat of a theme running through my college career. The ritual of pints on the docks at 7 am after the Trinity Ball didn't do much to lift the reputation of undergradu-ates with the working men of Dublin, not only because of the often foppish and always dishevelled evening clothes, but because most of us were by this stage speechless with drink. If able, we adjourned to The Bailey, a favourite haunt, to down Death in the Afternoons, apparently drunk by Hemingway as Dutch courage in the Spanish Civil War. Perhaps it was such romance that prompted an impromptu trip to Galway, still wearing the finery of the ball attire, in which we returned four days later, not so fine. Otherwise I was fond of sporting a peaked cap and an *à la* Bardot short skirt with striped socks and clogs. What was I thinking?

A goodly proportion of the student budget was lost in The Bailey, I am ashamed to say. It was the meeting place of a ragbag of characters with not much in common other than that lectures and tutorials were not of high priority. Roly Saul, propping up the corner of the bar, his giant shoulders and splendid red beard shaking to the tune of his thirsty laughter. Tony Sheridan, a man who reputedly never paid for his accommodation throughout his entire career in college, was always wrapped, summer and winter, in an extremely 'high' bearskin coat, rescued from an ancestral attic in Athboy. One could be forgiven for thinking that Tony lived in The Bailey where he drank black pints for most of the day, sucking the foam from his luxuriant moustache and reading the London *Times* from cover to cover. His decision to join the Irish Guards when he finished his 'studies' came as a shock to all of us and indeed he was almost unrecognizable when cleaned up for his new career.

Charlie Hickson, whose party piece involved, at a critical stage of inebriation, standing on a table and sing an entire movement of Beethoven's Fifth. Don Neligan, who commanded much respect, having shot his television set, amused himself and the rest of us by accusing a charming and amiable fellow (who later married my cousin) of having '300 years of upper-class inbreeding'. Naturally no harm was meant by the description. Neligan doubtless thought it was a compliment.

My father loved to think he might return to read Law again, insisting that he was entitled to a year's credit, given his military service – an extraordinary example of the Trinity mindset of the age, if true – and he often engineered to be in Dublin at party time. In my second year, I shared a flat in Belgrave Terrace with Tessa Tulk Hart, Jane McFarlane and Louise Lloyd Carson, who were natural magnets for partygoers. My father gatecrashed one particularly dangerous party where, as was common, the bottles of paint stripper (Hirondelle, I believe) were thrown into a black bin with whatever industrial alcohol could be found or fecked. On the upper floor thin young men with pale faces were studiously manufacturing carefully constructed joints. Intense concentration was applied to produce the thinnest, the fattest, and ones that you smoked from the middle. Thus emerged a work of art of immense proportions containing a veritable fortune's worth of the magic weed. In a moment of paranoia it was feared that the old geezer downstairs might have a problem with the activity being conducted on the upper floor. I suggested they should test the theory by offering the same old geezer a puff. Unaccustomed to the etiquette of these matters, my father smoked the entire contraption. Whether or not the old man realized what he was smoking remains a mystery; but such was his determination to be a Trinity student again, he would have smoked mackerel skins if asked. To this day I am not sure whether I was delighted or mortified at the sight of the military man, who normally presented himself with an old-fashioned clip, engaging in long and rather tortuous conversations, which described all manner of things as 'groovy' and 'far out'.

Sport in Trinity of the early seventies was largely for the boys. We obliged by being enthusiastic supporters, especially of the rugby team, which was enjoying a purple patch with such luminaries as Donal Spring (Dick's brother), Mick Fitzpatrick and Ollie Waldron, then the old man of the team known as Eaten and Oxford, having obtained a Master's from the latter and had his ears chewed to earn the former. He was at this time doing an LLB, I believe, at which I was also making a rather halfhearted attempt. My contribution to the Trinity rugby effort was to take notes for him after one famous Colours match as his hand had suffered from serious connection with the UCD front row. Nor were the Knights of the Campanile, that ancient Society for the sporting elite, for the ladies, or so it seemed. An occasion confined to men only, then as now, sponsored the fighting spirit. Nothing would do but for my great friend Ruth McCarthy and I to don sports jackets and ties, and painted moustaches ... not our finest hour, nor our best shot at emancipation.

In my final year I acquired the job of secretary of 'Diversions' on the Trinity Week committee under the indulgent and wise supervision of Professor Ian Howie. This was time for serious nonsense. Mixed rugby formed part of the programme. In another misguided attempt at sporting equality, the women determined to play the men. I will long cherish the sight of Donal Spring without his teeth (a man devoid of vanity), upon tiring of swatting the ladies out of the way, and afraid of hurting anyone, simply lifting the diminutive

Louise Lloyd Carson and touching her and the ball down for a try. Similar challenges arose on the river. Club fours, a Trinity Week competition, was the only opportunity for women to row in those days (Jane Williams was to change all that most effectively a couple of years later) and involved mixed fours racing a short distance at Islandbridge. A sensible plan seemed to be to put each woman behind a man (who could be assumed to have some additional experience of these matters). We simply went round in a circle, a parable for much of our lives at the time.

'Diversions' included in its brief an encyclopedia of dares and forfeits, many of them involving the hapless Professor McDowell. Clingfilm on the loo seats and the light bulbs removed from the jacks in Botany Bay ... and worse. Spare a thought for the unfortunate American tourists, all blue rinse and see-through plastic macs, who came to see 'Kelly's Book'. During Trinity Week they were considered fair game and tour companies duly warned of latter-day Dick Turpins terrifying the visitors and holding them up with water pistols in the interests of charity. Such activity today would earn an immediate arrest.

So, did we miss out on the heyday of Trinity? Perhaps some of the sheer madness that thrived in a community of visitors had tempered a little. However when I think of the pressure put on my own children during their university careers, I have no doubt that we were blessed with a time in our lives when we could be push the boundaries without too much downside. Unlike today, college was a very small community. Every face was familiar. Most of us who were not from Dublin lived in rooms for at least a year. Whereas those who had not come through the Irish education system sometimes felt treated as outsiders, the critical mass of the previous decade allowed us not give a damn, and did not prevent us making our own stories. On the plus side we were growing towards being an integrated community with a rapidly emerging common culture, and a co-joined sense of who we were and where we were going.

I had never wanted to go to any other university and have never regretted my choice. I'm afraid I didn't learn very much, cramming for the exams in September and avoiding work as much as possible for the rest of the year. Two theses entitled 'Joan of Arc and her relevance to contemporary female medieval mystics' and 'Stolypin land reforms in pre-revolution Russia' have had little practical value for the rest of my life. I did, however, acquire an ability to drink large amounts of whiskey, a love of late nights and late mornings, a combative mind, a distaste for research, a sense of the ridiculous, a skill for walking on cobblestones in platform boots and clogs, and richly textured and lasting friendships and memories of incalculable value.

My brother David followed me a few years after I graduated. He also had a golden time and got into many scrapes, some of which involved his lawyer sister visiting the Bridewell in the small hours to mollify miffed Gardaí who were apparently no longer tolerating students as they once did. His son, Patrick, a young man brought up in England, is determined to make it four generations. I hope he gets in. He too will doubtless have a golden time and learn the tolerance and humour of the three generations of his family who preceded him.

Caroline Preston (née Orr; TCD 1973–7; History and Political Science) joined A&L Goodbody Solicitors in 1980, was a partner, 1986–2008, and head of the Goodbody Litigation Department, 1997–2003. In 1994 she was appointed Solicitor to the Attorney General. She currently chairs the board of governors of St Patrick's University Hospital. Married to Punch, they live with their two children in County Meath. She was Master of the Westmeath Foxhounds for eighteen years.

REVOLUTION IN THE BUTTERY

arthur deeny

I REMEMBER the Buttery. Other graduates can recall the classical proportions of Front Square and the contest of wills in panelled committee rooms, dank with instant coffee. My world revolved around the Formica table tops patrolled by Angela and her imperious trolley. Then, as now, an architectural black spot, it was my arena and my living room. Matt's lugubrious face behind the bar scanned the ranks of drunken Northerners, mysteriously smiling girls, plotting Maoists, postering Ents (entertainments) officers, Kerry politicos, hearty Med. students, poets, poseurs, cadgers and chancers. Most of us couldn't afford a pint and hadn't a hope of getting off with anyone but we lingered on in the hope of one or a bit of the other. We were young and we knew we had time and wasting it was the sweetest of pleasures. We all thought of ourselves as desperadoes because we bunked off lectures to drink the odd glass in the daytime and share a spliff while we laughed at the careerists (that was the worst thing you could call anyone back then). We were having the Revolution and we were damned if we were going to be miserable about it.

We forcibly occupied the Senior Common Room one night in a protest against something terribly important. The reality was that many students failed to appreciate the necessity for revolution and the Students' Representative Council was reduced to protesting about the catering, because that was the only thing that would draw a crowd. This was at a time when you could buy a filled roll in the Buttery for a shilling and sixpence!

I was deputed to gather bedding for the revolutionaries that night, so we wouldn't freeze to death while destroying bourgeois capitalism. I knocked on doors in Botany Bay and one was answered by the impossibly blond Rupert Murray in a cloud of incense. 'I don't have a blanket, but I do have this,' he said, plucking something diaphanous from the back of a sofa. 'It's a flow,' he explained, demonstrating by waving it gently in the air, as though it were a dragon kite, before donating it to the cause.

I was never a proper hippy myself, what with being so politically active that I reached the dizzy heights of travel officer in the SRC. Politicos weren't supposed to be stoners. Though Bill Graham's vice-presidency was shrouded in smoke, he still spoke with machine-gun rapidity and laughed at your jokes the moment you thought of them. Always quick on the uptake. I suppose that's how he discovered U2.

It was palpably evident to us that the old order was tottering on the brink of collapse. Back in the twentieth century, Irish political parties were still defined by the Civil War, men wore ties to work and they even played the Angelus bell on television every night. Imagine it!

Not everyone shared our millenarian perceptions. Especially not the Young Fogies; not real young fogies, just Irish imitations. We were short on national self-confidence and everything from *The Irish Times* to the Irish Grand National was an imitation of something bigger and better in another place.

When I followed my brother Donnell from Northern Ireland to Trinity in 1972, the posh English had largely abandoned Dublin University and so it was necessary for somebody to impersonate them. There was no shortage of volunteers. One of our lecturers did a passable Malcolm Muggeridge in tweeds and gown. Apparently he was from Chicago. Then there was the Baron, *mar dhea*. I remember him taking the committee of the Phil on a picnic in a fake Rolls. They wore black tie. Some of them went on to be cabinet ministers. All I can say of the students I knew who have gone on to high political office is that they were as middle-aged then as they are now.

My personal style was described at that time by my brother Godfrey (later to become editor of *Vogue Hommes*) as looking like a cross between a UCD engineering student and Gary Glitter. Platform boots had an irresistible charm for the vertically challenged. Notwithstanding that, I managed to lose my virginity.

'I know a lot of people who know you, Arthur Deeny, and they all say you're a bollox,' a little blonde informed me. So, of course, I fell in love. I did that a lot. I am not claiming to have had hundreds of amorous conquests. I just had a Wodehousian tendency to fall in love with people on the slightest provocation. This was particularly anachronistic of me, because we were also having the sexual revolution at that time. The liberated women understood this well and regarded the whole affair with great calmness and maturity. The Irish boys, by contrast, tended to retreat behind the refuge of their six packs before the monstrous regiment of new women.

I did my best to come to grips with the situation but you must understand that Trinity was a yearned-for paradise after a ghastly adolescence in mono-sexual boarding schools, playing filthy games in the rain. So I generally behaved like a kid in a sweet shop. Fortunately the girls involved were as wise as they were beautiful. I am grateful to them all for their kindness, tolerance and discretion. I know that sounds merely silly, but I am sincerely thankful to those good women and to Trinity for giving me some of the best years of my life and other good things besides. Most of all I am grateful to my dear old dad. He put six children through various costly universities. Technically speaking, my school leaving results qualified for a grant. After a good deal of work on the part of Harry, our accountant, the UK taxpayer was persuaded to part with 300 quid. Sadly, Harry's fees for his Herculean labours came to 320. That's fatherhood for you.

I repaid my father's love and kindness in the traditional manner of sons, by crashing his cars and drinking his money and failing the exams about which he cared so much. Did I mention that I was supposed to be a medical student? Cutting up dead people isn't as icky as it sounds, but there are hundreds of bones in the human body, and we were expected to know an insane amount about them. Edward the lab assistant could identify a metatarsal from a meta-carpal with his eyes closed. I couldn't, so I flung myself on the mercy of the School of English and Brendan Kennelly.

'What will you do if I don't let you in?'

'Drive a van, I suppose.' I'd never driven a van in my life, but Brendan took pity on my implausible improvidence.

The study of English was meant to make me a writer, in the way that medicine had been meant to make me a doctor. I'd read *The Lord of the Rings* too young and it quite turned my head. Many years later I learned that Tolkien was one of the academic loonies whose antediluvian theories meant I had to spend three years studying Anglo-Saxon. '*Swa thaes middengeard, ealra dogra gewham, dreosath und falleth.*' That bit about this middle earth, dropping and falling every day, sticks in my mind because, when I became a Junior Freshman for the second time, I felt my best days in Trinity were behind me. I'd already done most of the fun stuff. I had written a waspish column for *TCD Miscellany* and played the lead in Players in Mayakovsky's *The Bath House*. Unfortunately the performance ended with a particularly unconvincing explosion, leaving the stage in darkness and the audience nonplussed, until a voice from the cheap seats gave us our denouement: 'Deeny has farted again.' So at least we left them laughing.

Because debating was the only tolerable thing about school, I had followed Donnell into the Hist. David O'Sullivan, later to become the most powerful civil servant in Europe, was auditor and he badgered the committee into awarding me the Maiden Speaker Prize. But I was protesting about something and declined to accept the honour. Yes, I was that much of a dick. I'm fairly sure I joined the Resources Protection Campaign around this time with my best friend Culdaff. I think I was made secretary or something else above my competency level. We didn't succeed in nationalizing Ireland's mines but we did have proper meetings at which nobody was stoned. Una Claffey was our guru.

Culdaff's real name was John Doona and his father was a jarvey in the Gap of Dunloe. My father had once been Master of the North Armagh Harriers and this fact may have been mentioned when the subject of horses came up. So, when I visited Killarney with John, he put me up on his dad's youngest horse, when it was raring for the stables at the end of the day, and gave it a lash of the strap up its arse. The beast tore off along the tarred road like a student at a movie matinée fleeing the cinema after the picture had finished and before the playing of the national anthem could stop him in his tracks. If I hadn't known how to ride a horse I'd probably be in a wheelchair now and it would have served me right.

I had other Kerry friends. If Trinity meant shades of Oxbridge to an earlier generation, to me it conjured up the mists of Abbeyfeale, Knocknagoshel and Druagh. The poets and the cute hoors all seemed steeped in a national authenticity that the scion of a mere province could only envy. As a boy I had thought the worst thing about being from Northern Ireland was that, though you were in a sense both British and Irish, you were never really either.

Of course, after 1969, it turned out there were much worse things about Northern Ireland. While we were having the revolution in Dublin over the price of sandwiches, people were tearing one another's hearts out in Lurgan, my home town. The civil rights movement decayed rapidly into an old-fashioned military rebellion that seemed to me as prehistoric and insupportable as Elvis and the Holy Hour in pubs.

The potent demographic of a million queen-loving Prods ensured the rebellion was always going to be a pointless, hopeless, bloody mess. Which didn't stop it going on and on for year after bleeding year. I was that unimportant creature, a pacifist revolutionary, who always viewed the slaughter of civilians, by whatever army, on whatever pretext, as shameful cowardice. When we heard the bombs go off in Nassau Street, the Northern girl I was chatting up in the Buttery knew what it was, and we both knew there was nothing we could do. Just like the time I had gone shopping in Robinson Cleaver in Belfast with my mother and, afterwards, for a gin and tonic in the Carlton Bar. As thirteen bombs went off that afternoon, one after another, everyone in the bar would flinch and dodge, then sit up straight again after each report and have another drink, in the unspoken agreement that rushing out to investigate was a good way to get blown up.

For years thereafter I endured from countless Southerners variations on the Five-Pound-Note Story. This generally involved lengthy accounts of death-defying feats, such as buying a packet of biscuits in a sweet shop in Belfast, paying with an Irish fiver and getting all their change in sterling, then escaping rapidly before they could be eaten alive by blood-crazed zombie Loyalists. It wasn't until the dawn of the twenty-first century that I began to meet people in Dublin who had been to Northern Ireland on their holidays, just as though it was an ordinary place, like Knocknagoshel.

It was probably one of my Kerry friends who suggested I stand for election. The revolution had turned sour. The Maoists, under David Vipond, had taken over the SRC. They believed themselves to be the real revolutionaries, and they all spoke in a flat broad North of England accent they were said to have adopted from their founder in the sixties.

One day I was doing my best to impress girls in Front Square with my swordstick, the way you do.

'This should be prove useful,' I bravadoed, 'come the Revolution.'

'Come the Revolution, Mr Deeny,' intoned Vipond, *en passant*, 'you'll be on the wrong end of one of those things.'

For my part, I remained, like those old revolutionaries who wrote the Constitution of the United States, dedicated to the pursuit of happiness. So, naturally, when it was time to elect the new president of the SRC I stood as the Free Catholic Anarchist candidate and Brian Curtin, my running mate, wore a parrot on his shoulder. My assassination on Dining Hall steps and resurrection under Front Arch were *coups de théâtre* and we got enough votes to make a balls of the election for the serious candidates. It was something to do with history repeating itself as farce. Perhaps, more accurately, it was my largely unthought-out attempt to reverse the trend to dull common sense that would lead inexo-rably to the conniving, triumphant banality of the era of Haughey, Reagan and Thatcher. Afterwards I felt I had done well and was entitled to a prize. Sure enough, my prize came to the party in Godfrey's rooms. Síle Connaughton asked me how I'd done in the elections, wearing a most unpolitical grin. So I fell in love again, for the last time.

We mustn't forget the music. Steely Dan played the soundtrack to our lives. I remember seeing The Clash, the Rats, Horslips and, of course, Bagatelle singing 'Summer in Dublin' (still the best encapsulation of those times). It was at a gig by Stepaside in the Project that I asked Síle to marry me and she consented. On that, or on some other evening, I bumped into Kathy Gilfillan. She had graduated some time before and was in flying form. 'I've become a copywriter,' Kathy declared.

'What's that?'

'I don't really know.'

Perhaps she remembers it differently. Presumably everyone does. It was a very long time ago.

Síle went to the college doctor when she got symptoms. He told her it was stress and gave her two aspirin. Today her symptoms have grown up to be finance director at MTV. Though I was a father at my Commencements I was still some way from being a grownup. I had always known the real world was lurking outside Trinity's walls like a hungry wolf. Others had more sense. Peter Murtagh went from being editor of *Trinity News* to editor of real newspapers people pay money for. Damien Kiberd morphed from Trotskyite agitator into a veritable media mogul. Today, as a matter of journalistic record, he insists that he saw me once leap head first from the balcony above the debating chamber in the Hist down to the argumentative crowd below. Maybe he's right. Perfectly pleasant people, who had gathered together our fivers to help us buy hash, moved on to heroin, became tedious, dangerous, incarcerated and eventually dead. Good friends went on to be judges and have been judged in their turn. In time I was able to shelter from the real world, in the playpens that are called creative departments in various ad agencies. I'm still unsure what a copywriter really is but, whatever they are, I'm one of them now.

I may be wrong about everything but I seem to remember climbing to the top of the Campanile on builders' scaffolding to look down on dear old Dublin and seeing it press hotly round the walls of Trinity, more like a lover than a threat. I remember Paul Tipping saving my life in College Park, by kicking the boy from Newry who was swinging an iron bar at my head, and the night I saved the melodious Chris Mullane from a flying pint glass outside Players. And everyone remembers Ian Wilson wearing a cow on his back and a dress to every party. I remember the good days and we had many of those in Trinity. I also remember, many years later, keeping the score at a cricket match and calling out, 'Bowler's name?'

'Vipond,' came the response. Afterwards we shared a pint and a few blue jokes but nobody mentioned the war, or the Revolution.

Let me finish with the memory of a bus stop in Ballsbridge. I was acting the eejit to amuse Anis Sadek, with whom I was sharing digs, because he had the biggest smile in Egypt and it was fun to make him laugh. An old man got on the bus after us and insisted to the bus conductor that he would pay our fare, because we'd made him laugh too. 'If there was more of that, and less of the depredation ...'

In the 1970s, there was more of that in Trinity than anywhere else on earth.

Arthur Deeny graduated in 1978 (he thinks), raised a family writing copy and jingles for sundry ad agencies. He has done stand-up comedy and written plays for BBC Radio 4 and the Edinburgh Fringe, as well as writing, producing, directing and performing in award-winning short films. He is married to art historian Síle Connaughton-Deeny, and their three daughters, Leda, Shaula and Cordaella, all went to Trinity.

Arthur Deeny and Síle Connaughton at Trinity Ball.

SAKI GOES SOCIALIST

patrick guinness

I HAD a few perceptions about Trinity before I entered in 1975. In the 1960s my parents had entertained a huge variety of Irish society, and the Trinity student slice was freshly scrubbed, self-confident and wore tweed jackets. They were invariably jolly and several had unfashionably short hair. The academic side was represented by the voluble Professor R.B. McDowell, often invited to the same lunch or dinner with Professor Kevin Nowlan, his counterpart at UCD. In the background I was vaguely aware that my family had sponsored many of Trinity's newer buildings. Whenever walking past the fine Georgian facade I noticed that the doormen wore riding hats and a uniform. Then I was at school in England, 1970–4, and my exam results allowed me to read law at 'Trinners'. By then my London-based cousin Catherine had studied there and apparently had enjoyed herself.

Despite this perspective I had never set foot in the campus before registering in late 1975, and so, like many of my class, I entered in a state of complete ignorance. I rather expected to be given a room in college but this was by now a rare commodity. The Law Faculty was based in the hideous but efficient new Arts Building. I recall my surprise at learning that until the 1970s Irish Catholics were forbidden by their church to attend Trinity at all. This with recent overdue educational reforms meant that the college was struggling to cope with about 5000 students, compared with about 1000 in 1960. Gone were almost all the tweed jackets, and the tyranny of fashion now dictated that we all wore anoraks and jeans. Portrayed to me as an island bastion of gentility in the big city, it had just taken on a suitably demotic air, along with massive government subsidies.

In a class of about forty, my fellow students divided instantly into those who were from legal families and those like me who were not. The former knew what desk they would occupy in Uncle Jack's office in four years, or they routinely met judges and lawyers at their parents' drinks parties; some even wondered aloud what the rest of us were doing studying law. I knew next to nothing about law and even had to look up what a mortgage was. I had heard of mortgages in a vague sense but money wasn't a subject my family ever discussed.

Within days we had to elect a class representative to the Law Society committee, and I decided to run, only promising a barrel of Guinness to be shared by my electors. This parody on real politics was accepted with good humour and I was re-elected in following years. On the committee I met the late, already voluble and personable Gerry Ryan, who was in the year above me. We remained friends in later years. Gerry had a band, I ran a mobile disco, and both of us wanted to play at the committee's annual balls. Naturally we voted to hire each other whenever the matter came up.

The faculty was outstanding, but few would be famous outside the legal world today. Mary Robinson lectured us crisply on European Law, with a minimum of waffle. At the time she was famous for taking the only first in Law at Trinity since 1945, or so the story went. She was prominent in arguing for feminist and gay rights that are norms today. At some point she set us an essay with the promise that the best half of the class would go on a tour of EEC institutions in Brussels, Luxembourg and Strasbourg. I made it onto the list but her budget was short by £1500. I asked my grandfather Bryan to help, and he did so at once, but his kindness was countered by Mary commenting drily that he could, of course, write it off against his tax bill. Having an income of £3000 at the time with which to support a young family, I considered his gift most generous.

The first night of the tour in Brussels was marred by the Ulster students, who were apparently unused to air travel and promptly drank their duty-free whiskey. A bedroom had its furniture smashed up. Empty bottles were thrown down five storeys onto the street, aimed at the windscreens of cars parked below. The rest of us heard the noise and stood by horrified. Mary appeared in a sensible nightgown and quelled the mayhem in two seconds, but her unshaven shins were noticed and the miscreants christened her 'Hairy Mary', a moniker which unfortunately stuck. She was later elected president of Ireland and became a breath of fresh air in the cynical and often corrupt world of Irish politics.

The other Mary was a sprightly blonde bombshell who lectured us in Criminal Law in shortish skirts and sexy leather boots. Compared to the male law lecturers in their uniform grey suits Mary McAleese was a sight for sore eyes, but we soon learnt that unfortunately she was already married. She has also served as president of Ireland. The barrister Willie O'Dea lectured on tax, explaining that it was a flexible area where the letter of the law was often a starting point in negotiations. He was a practical man who became famous in Irish politics for regularly and uniquely receiving two 'quotas' in elections. The most able student proved to be the late Brian Lenihan junior, the next Trinity law student after Mary Robinson to take a first-class degree. Brian happened to be the son of Robinson's presidential election rival in 1990.

On the left wing was the late South African Kader Asmal, thought by us to be surely a communist and known to be an important member of the African National Congress. To him New York was not an exciting place but a centre of oppression. Though a gifted speaker, he mispronounced 'entrepreneurial' as 'entreprennial', making it seem like an aberration. When lecturing us on unfair dismissal laws he might compare Poland's system with the British or Irish laws, as if its one-party state was fully comparable and a natural reality. I often wondered what he thought of the Polish Solidarność organization that took off after I left college. I spoke at some anti-apartheid meetings at his request, feeling that it was only natural and logical, as Irish people can be as insular and xenophobic as the British. I could not tell him that my godparent Clementine Beit also had staunch anti-apartheid views; she was married to Sir Alfred Beit, whom Kader would have seen as one of Africa's evil arch-capitalists. Rather like Kader himself, the Beits had left South Africa after the National Party success in 1948. The main socialist argument often fails as too many capitalists are progressive. Kader went on to become a minister under Nelson Mandela.

Other more moderate socialist research students were unfairly labelled by us. Tommy O'Connell admired Gramsci, not Lenin, but was called 'Tommy the Commie', and the labour rights specialist Ferdinand von Pronzynski became known as the 'Red Baron'. These were law school opinions, more affectionate than rude. From examining old laws and then drafting new statutes, lawyers are sure that they make the best politicians; in turn, many Irish politicians are sure that they are above the law. Being the 1970s, the college political scene outside the law school was dominated by socialist groups, one of which would even chant 'Smash US imperialism' non-stop for hours on end. The notable haranguer of my time was Joe Duffy, nicknamed Joe Duffel because of his trademark working-class coat. It was said that he had a very active sex life, and that he came from Ballyfermot, then a very deprived though new-ish suburb, which I knew from working at its Free Legal Advice Centre. Imagine my surprise a decade later, on returning briefly to my home town of Leixlip, to hear that the celebrity star Joe Duffy was opening the town's summer festival and would shortly arrive by helicopter. He has become a much-loved and sympathetic agony uncle on the radio.

Socially, college had little to offer me. I found many of my fellow students immature, though pleasant, academically clever and hard-working. Probably I was more sexually experienced than most at the time, and I realized that I was used to a life that many aspired to. I recall having to explain to one that 'gay' people do not choose to be gay. He assumed that they were normal people who simply could not control their urges. As a result I tended not to join college societies though I attended the odd debate and won the first Mastermind quiz in the college. This success was based not so much on my masterly mind as in choosing the subject from a list that promised the shortest questions and answers, as there is a time limit. Fencing had been my school sport, being captain of the team in my last year at Winchester, and coming third and fourth in English championships. Having had this near-to-Olympic potential I found that Trinity's club was perhaps too relaxed and had too few members. My one foray into college rugby caused an injury to a hapless winger from my clumsy tackle.

My best friends were probably Ben O'Rafferty, Robert Power, Eddie Walsh and Nick Mulcahy. Like me, none was from legal families. Ben bravely set up on his own as a solicitor; Robert succeeded in insurance; Nick in publishing; Eddie as a barrister. We spent many hours in the Buttery righting the world's wrongs, usually over coffee, not beer. I still see them all but not often enough.

I left in the depths of a recession and despite my august-sounding moderatorship degree I could find no position in the law – those detractors that came from legal families had been right, up to a point. Given the aura of equality and meritocracy that emerged in the 1970s it was an unpleasant time for me until opportunities beckoned in America and then London. The 1980s' ethos of personal gain was exactly the opposite of the 1970s but it was perhaps more honest. In retrospect my time at Trinity gave me a good mental structure and a degree that has been useful in business. Almost all my memories are pleasant; those that are less pleasant are at least amusing.

Patrick Guinness (TCD 1975–80; Law) retrained for finance, married twice and has five children. Now a historian, he has sponsored genetic research on Irish origins. He is involved with the Iveagh Trust social housing organization in Dublin and lives amid a cluster of national monuments in County Kildare.

ROBBO'S NIGHTIE

nick mulcahy

SO THERE WE WERE chucking beer cans out the window of the hotel room in Brussels down onto the flyover below, when in walked the future president of Ireland. Standing there in her nightgown, her deep voice unusually shrill, Mary Robinson commanded her European Law students to behave less like delinquents and more in a manner appropriate to future officers of the court. It was a long nightie so it wasn't the sort of Mrs Robinson moment a young man would remember. Except that it was a good yarn to tell – 'I once saw Robbo in her nightie' – when our law professor progressed to inhabiting Áras an Uachataráin.

Mary Robinson wasn't the only future president to grace TCD's Law Faculty in the latter half of the 1970s. We law students were also lectured by Mary McAleese, another Áras incumbent. These days she wears contact lenses or has had her eyes lasered. Back then, this blow-in from the wee North wore huge horn-rimmed spectacles, which was a pity as this Mary was a real looker. I was so impressed that I got her to pose for a photo outside the Berkeley Library and we wrote her up as a pin-up in my student magazine, *Trinity Intellectual Times* (*TIT* for short).

Only two of my student peers would emerge as actors in the political arena. The late Brian Lenihan was in the class below me, and my abiding memory of young Brian is him pursuing my girlfriend with lascivious intent around a

Wicklow cottage. Also in Brian's class was Liz O'Donnell, later a Progressive Democrat minister. Liz worked her way through some of her college years so she had the edge over her classmates in cop-on and style. Her enthusiasm for good times gave no hint of the public-service calling that would emerge later on.

Most law students were not interested in politics. Though there was murder and mayhem occurring three hours up the road, I had far more intense pub discussions about the Provos in school than I ever had in university. Partly this was a familiarity thing. In college you're thrown together with a whole new bunch of people and it takes a few years to work them out. Trinity was the first time most of the boys and girls shared the same classroom, so scoring with the opposite sex took precedence over sorting out the national question.

The other reason nobody talked about the North was that most of the blokes you were drinking with were from there. Even as the Stormont state was imploding, its bright young things were being sent south for their education. The Law Faculty was stuffed with Northern students, fairly evenly divided between Prods and Taigs. As UK citizens, Northerners had their fees and accommodation paid for and they also had loads left over for drinking money. You were ten times more likely to hear a northern accent than a Dublin accent in the university located a stone's throw away from the capital's tenements.

One Dub who did sneak through was Joe Duffy, now one of RTÉ's most popular radio broadcasters. Joe and his duffle-coated disciples were in semi-permanent rabble-rousing mode, though their cause had more to do with college facilities than upending capitalism. Apparently we just missed the era of David Vipond, infamous for his Maoist credentials. From 1976 to 1980, the most revolutionary excitement we had on campus was the time some lefties shot and wounded a British car executive, Red-Brigades style. For the most part, Brits were thin on the ground, presumably because of the Troubles. However there were plenty of West Brits, mostly blokes who had been to public schools (the English variety) and were now back home for the cheaper alternative to Oxbridge. This crowd tended to stick together, hanging around Players to stage wretched dramas.

My favourite West Brit was Patrick Guinness, scion of the stout clan. He had a pad at the ancestral spread in Leixlip and his gate-lodge parties were always an adventure (how the hell do we get home from here?). Marianne Faithfull was at one of those parties, and she was famous at the time for her press-invented adventures with a Mars bar. Whatever I was smoking, I was convinced that her fine décolletage had broken out in mumps. Only later, after I barfed, did I realize that Marianne was wearing a lace top with little floral designs.

The mainstay of my Trinity social activity centered on the Northerners. While the southern convent girls played hard to get, at least in the Freshman years, the Northern girls had no issue with jumping you. Or you jumping them. The Northern blokes spent most of their time skulling pints in the Buttery and perhaps my biggest regret from my four years in Trinity was wimping out from attempting the 'Stations of the Cross'. This was a pub crawl of fourteen hostelries in and around Grafton Street, with a pint drunk in each bar. It obviously didn't take place on Good Friday but when the suffering kicked in the next day, no one could deny that it had been a form of penance. I can't recall the exact Stations' roll call of achievement though the name Stevie Rourke, an eccentric Northern history student, rings a bell.

Pop music defines an era and in our case it was a combo of disco and punk. We bopped to Earth Wind & Fire but for live music it was New Wave. Some highlights: sitting on the floor in the JCR with a few others to watch a forty-minute lunchtime set from U2, and The Stranglers playing the Exam Hall. Like John Peel, the Northern contingent was very excited about the Undertones from Derry, particularly as 'My Perfect Cousin' was supposedly inspired by a Northern guy in the law class above us.

After the pressure of school and the Leaving Cert., Trinity education was a doddle. While UCD taught a law degree in three years, the Trinity course proceeded for a more leisurely four. For the Legal Science degree, there were eight one-hour lectures a week. In the Freshman years, if lectures were scheduled for early in the morning, many students would head straight home afterwards or repair to the snooker room above the GMB. The enthusiasts who believed that a 2:1 degree would make a whit of difference to their legal career over a 2:2 would rush to the Library, though even the swots spent much of their time talent-spotting and chatting up.

One downside to being a law student was that you studied in the Berkeley Library and the Ussher Library, where the law reports were piled high. That cut you off from all the arts girls who populated the newer Lecky Library in the Arts Building, which was more of a meeting place than the Berkeley. The Lecky also housed a lively ESS (Economics and Social Science) crowd – guys like Eugene Bent, John Reynolds, Jonathan Westrup and Richie Boucher. The engineers, meds and dents were in their own zone down towards Westland Row and rarely the twain did meet.

Trinity's Law Faculty in the 1970s had a top-notch roster of lecturers. There was R.F.V. Heuston, the kingpin of Torts and Constitutional Law who spoon-fed his students by interspersing his lectures with regular 'commentaries', which we dutifully wrote down word for word. Dashing Patrick Usher, a silken-tongued Contract lecturer, just had to stand at the dais and flick his hair to make the ladies swoon. For the few students who signed up for Criminology or Human Rights studies, Aussie lecturer Mark Findlay treated us like we possessed a modicum of intelligence. Most of all there was the late Kader Asmal, who returned to South Africa in the post-apartheid years to become a government minister. Asmal was always enthusiastic, always engaging, always liberal, and always challenging students to stretch their minds.

And what a challenge that must have been. How do you educate nineteen-year-olds to appreciate the political nuances of UK labour law? Though we students were consumed with self-regard, in reality we were jumped-up children. And children like having fun, which we all did to a much greater extent than we ever managed in school. The college ethos was to facilitate enjoyment. The authorities didn't crowd you out. They provided good bars and had guys in black suits patrolling the place to keep out gougers. If you got a girl in the family way, the Students' Union would provide clinic addresses in the UK. If you wanted to publish a student magazine, they'd throw some money at you. If you wanted to import a celebrity speaker for a Hist debate, they'd fund the trip. If you wanted to organize a massive May blow-out days before exams began, the college would cobble together a security screen. And if after all that you wanted to learn something, then they would facilitate that too, and at a pace that didn't tax you too much.

There was no transition year or gap year. It was a straight path from school to university and out into the professions. This bourgeois production line certainly worked. Parents made their children understand and appreciate that the annual college fee was a financial stretch and there was never any question that you were going to drop out afterwards. The solicitors and barristers from that time enjoy large incomes and if very few have made their mark on society outside their profession, perhaps they were never meant to. And it's remarkable how many of the couples still endure from romances forged at a Trinity Hall disco or during boozy sessions in the Pav, The Bailey, The Lincoln Inn, Keoghs and O'Neills.

The class divide in Trinity, such as it existed at all, was somewhat evident on the playing fields. If you had a Dublin accent, chances were you played soccer. I played on the soccer team at the bottom of the AUL merit rung and for my troubles I got to visit northside dumps where the only post-match shower facilities was the rain that fell from the February sky. By contrast, the rugby players of that era were rather good. I remember one of those brutish monsters rounding on me at a Boat Club disco in Islandbridge, for some trivial reason, and ripping off my shirt with a swipe of his giant paw. And how we cheered those Neanderthals! An annual highlight was the Colours game when we would bombard UCD supporters with flour bombs, jeering 'Polytechnic!' An enduring source of pride is that because of our antics the game was switched from Lansdowne Road to Donnybrook.

Discipline, enforced by academics Trevor West and Sean Barrett, was really only an issue for students with rooms on the campus who overdid it in the Buttery or who turned up the stereo too loud when their friends came around. Most of these rooms were a throwback to the fifties, with their worn carpets, green paint and flimsy curtains. The rooms were allocated to students from outside Dublin and most Northerners got to sample at least one year of this important TCD heritage. Dubs couldn't afford them, anyway. In the summer breaks, we went to work in England, Germany or America because you had to if you wanted spending money for the next term.

My family background is magazine publishing so I tried my hand at college publications. My best idea was a student diary, which we gave away for free and stuffed with ads from banks, pubs and restaurants. Robert Power, who went on to make a fortune in the insurance arena, cut his salesman's teeth selling the space. The student magazine I published made a few bob but was much harder work. For typesetting we depended on an IBM golfball (thank you, Liz) and for headlines we needed a different sheet of Letraset for each font and point size. After a massive amount of effort with scalpels and cow gum, we would deliver our precious pages to a small printer off Pearse Street. When the reams of printed sheets came back, they had to be folded together manually to produce the magazine.

My approach to student journalism was in the tabloid style and at least one issue of *Trinity Intellectual Times* had to be pulped shortly after we started selling it. Students took the magazine's jibes very seriously, and some hold grudges to this day. One of our hacks, Barry McIlhenny, went on to become editor of *Smash Hits* and a big cheese in IPC Media. So it wasn't a complete waste of time for him. A peer publication with much more intelligence coursing through it was *TCD Miscellany*, where the prime movers included Damien Kiberd and Joe Mannix.

My best pal in college was Eddie Walsh, who was a year above me and is now an eminent senior counsel and proprietor of the wonderful Lissadell House. Eddie was one of the few students who had a car and he also had a mobile disco, a handy *entrée* to party action. Two other characters who stand out from that era are Ian Wilson and the late Gerry Ryan, who both went on to work in RTÉ. Wilson was a genuine Students' Union radical, distinguished by his long blonde locks. Ryan, who was in the Law Faculty orbit in a semi-detached sort of way, had an impish sense of fun and dated my future wife, Ann O'Neill, before I prised her away from his clutches. I'm still waiting for Ann to tell me exactly what happened at the overnight occupation of the Berkeley for some protest or other when she and Gerry sneaked away among the dusty stacks of House of Lords reports.

Another Gerry highlight: his glam rock staging of *Jesus Christ Superstar* in the GMB, in which I had a minor singing role. I took up the events torch ahead of the Trinity Ball in 1980, organizing a Yard of Ale challenge on the steps of the Dining Hall, a singing contest in the Buttery and a Trinity transvestite competition that packed out the largest lecture theatre in the college. After that May blow-out, it was heads down for finals and everyone being scattered into the big bad world, only occasionally to meet again. The real world of the eighties was fairly depressed in Ireland. Apparently the late-seventies economy was depressed too. But we never noticed in that isolated oasis in the centre of Dublin.

Nick Mulcahy (TCD 1976–80; Legal Science) unwisely decided not to pursue a legal career and became a journalist and publisher instead. He worked in three publishing startups – **The Sunday Tribune** (1980), **The Phoenix** (1983) and **The Sunday Business Post** (1989) before establishing **Business Plus** magazine in 1998.

LITERARY PILGRIMS

john conyngham

THERE WERE FOUR of us in a flat in Pearse Street. Through the window we could see the Academy Cinema, formerly the Irish Academy of Music, where James Joyce once sang. Around the corner in Westland Row was the Grosvenor Hotel, then derelict and boarded up, outside which in *Ulysses* Joyce has Leopold Bloom try to glimpse an elegant woman's stocking as she climbs aboard a horse-drawn cab, only to be thwarted by a passing tram. Behind our flat, and above ceiling height, was the track linking Greystones and Connolly Station, and beyond it the roofs of Trinity. Nearby in Pearse Street, where the railway line cuts diagonally above the traffic, was an enigmatic graffito, scrawled in huge letters across the brickwork: *Beware of Margaret, she could be dangerous.* Who was Margaret, we wondered, and why was there doubt as to the danger she posed?

As a lodging for Trinity students, 166 Pearse Street was extremely convenient even if it was maddeningly noisy, being wedged between the thunder of the trains and the drone of the traffic, which in those days was embellished by the castanet sound of the hooves of dray horses coming up from Ringsend, pulling carts filled with coal and grubby children. For a spell our unsympathetic landlord let the ground floor as an amusement arcade and through the floorboards would burst the electric clamour of pinball machines until mercifully a lack of patronage compelled it to close.

What had drawn the four of us to Dublin was the Postgraduate Diploma in Anglo-Irish Literature, Trinity's stroll through the works of Swift and Yeats and Joyce and Beckett, and assorted others like James Clarence Mangan, Dion Boucicault and John Millington Synge. My flatmates were Americans, graduates respectively of Harvard, Swarthmore and St Bonaventure, and I was a South African from the University of Natal. What had randomly brought us together in the hurly-burly of a new academic year was a note seeking flatmates on a noticeboard at Front Gate.

There were twenty of us on the course, all Americans except for two Irishmen, a young German woman, and me from south of the Equator. With its blend of Venetian palazzo and gentlemen's club, the Museum Building was our gathering point, and among our lecturers were names that resonated at Trinity in the last decades of the twentieth century. We had Brendan Kennelly for Yeats, David Norris for Joyce, Terence Brown for Louis MacNeice, and I remember tutorials with Anne Clissman, whose forte was Flann O'Brien. In our first term we had brief contact with the professor of English literature, James Walton, whose brother Ernest, a Trinity alumnus, had in 1951 won the Nobel Prize for splitting the atom, but he was on the point of retiring and seemed little concerned with our callow group. That there were only nine staff members lecturing Modern English gives an indication of the intimacy of Trinity in those days, with its several thousand students and its vestigial echoes of the ascendancy culture for which it had been founded.

Our routine was leisurely, with one lecture or seminar or tutorial each day. No sooner had we dashed down Pearse Street, looking askance for Margaret, and swung into the side gate, than we skirted the rugby field, burst into the foyer of the Museum Building and headed for a small lecture room on the right. And there, sitting at aged desks with their gouged hieroglyphics, we would find ourselves transported into a world of myth and allegory and romance, sprinkled with words like 'Houyhnhnms' and 'gyres' and 'riverrun', which must surely have enriched us for the rest of our lives.

After our daily encounter, a number of us would drift via Library Square and Parliament Square and Front Square to a room high in Regent House where we would drink coffee and read newspapers and talk as the traffic swept past in College Street outside. And then the group would fragment further, with some heading to libraries and others to Bewley's in Grafton Street for more refreshments and talk of literature until it was time to return to the Dining Hall for lunch under the gaze of the gilt-framed portraits. With afternoons less structured still, more hours were spent reading or talking, or browsing in bookshops like Greene's in Clare Street, or Hodges Figgis in Dawson Street, or Hanna's in Nassau Street.

As evening approached we would wander to a supermarket in Baggot Street to buy groceries, which we lugged homewards past Merrion Square, where Yeats had once lived, and Westland Row, where Oscar Wilde had been born. Even Pearse Street then was a source of provisions for it had two butcheries, one with an elfin butcher with a glint in his eye who struck our lamb chops so hard with a cleaver that we spent our suppers spitting out fragments of bone. Sometimes, as if to another country, we strayed north of the Liffey to Moore Street market for the banter and the vegetables.

In most of these perambulations my companion was Stephen Fenichell, a New Yorker who had excelled in English at Harvard and who with his erudition and his tweeds in many ways embodied the Ivy League ideal. Sustained by his sparkling flow of literary information, whether ferreted from Richard Ellmann's biography of Joyce, which I recall he had read with relish, or uncovered in his research for an article on Dublin that he had submitted to *The New Yorker*, we criss-crossed the city like literary pilgrims.

Once, after a particularly long odyssey, we found ourselves in Sandymount, where on the strand Gerty MacDowell thrills Bloom with a flash of her panties. As it was well into the afternoon and we were weary, we decided to catch a bus back to the city centre. With us among the rows of seats was one other passenger, a retired jockey who was garrulously drunk. What are we doing in Dublin, he asked. Studying Anglo-Irish literature, we replied. 'Anglo-Irish literature!' he exclaimed with a vehemence that surprised us, 'Now there you're flogging a dead horse.'

At some point in our course one of the Americans determined that someone famous was giving a tutorial nearby and that we could attend if we wished to. Several of us followed him down a corridor and into a room where a courtly, silver-haired man was already in discussion with a small group of students. If my memory is reliable, the pivot around which the deliberations revolved was the reference in a Greek text to a leopard where the animal was not known to have been found. Was the classical author ignorant, or merely indulging in poetic licence, and did it really matter, the maestro asked, and for nearly an hour we listened as he wove an answer. It was W.B. Stanford, for forty years Regius Professor of Greek and renowned internationally for his works on Hellenism, whose accomplishments had elevated him into a figure of veneration.

If R.B. McDowell was another academic who enjoyed cult status, so detached was our world as outsider postgraduates that I can only recall seeing him once. It was at the corner of Library Square, in the narrows between the Old Library and the Rubrics, where with a cluster of laughing companions he hurried past, dishevelled and voluble. Who is he, we wondered, before we learnt the answer.

No sooner had we completed our requisite number of assignments, which we typed on typewriters, than our day of reckoning loomed. In the exam paper, after the usual essays on specific works, almost as a final flourish we were asked to pose ourselves an intelligent question and then to answer it. If such a gesture seemed foolishly quixotic, I realize now that the examiners must have felt that they could detect anything suspiciously accomplished, or sense whenever a student sounded a discordant note.

But if our Dublin sojourn was steeped in literature, to the extent that it also included visits and readings by writers such as Seamus Heaney and John McGahern, there were other diversions. I remember memorable evenings in a variety of pubs, among them one in the now vanished Wicklow Hotel, and the musical Stag's Head off Dame Street, as well as concerts by Steeleye Span and The Bothy Band at the National Stadium. And there was a visit to the vaults below St Michan's Church to see the huge mummified crusader and the tiny mummified nun. One time, Bloomsday probably, David Norris had Ronnie Drew of The Dubliners sing and play at Trinity as part of a literary celebration and so linked our histories briefly to that legendary balladeer.

For foreigners like us there were also the obligatory outings beyond the city. On one occasion we headed north to Howth Head, where Bloom proposes to Molly, and walked along the hill path while far below us the Irish Sea shone like quicksilver. On another, we headed south into the Wicklow mountains, to marvel at the antiquity of Glendalough and at the grandeur of Powerscourt, the house a gutted silhouette but the gardens resplendent. And one wet and blustery day Stephen and I took the train to Belfast, then bristling with British troops and their Saracens, to see Queen's University and the Linenhall Library, and the battle-scarred Europa Hotel.

Late in our Irish sojourn, three of us hired a car to make a hurried pilgrimage to the west of Ireland to visit some of the places whose names had become so familiar. We visited Coole, with its lake and swans, and Thoor Ballylee, where Brendan Kennelly's voice on the pre-recorded audio-guide accompanied us as we climbed the winding stair. In that lull before the tourist invasion, Yeats's grave at Drumcliffe, with the bulk of Ben Bulben brooding beyond it, seemed appropriately austere and remote. Our final stop was Liss-adell, where in the light of an evening Yeats had immortalized Constance and Eva Gore-Booth, and while we were in the garden it was memorable that a window in that great grey house opened and Gabrielle Gore-Booth, the sisters' niece, engaged us in conversation.

As I had always been a jogger, I sought during our Pearse Street year various ways to keep fit. For a time at night I jogged through Merrion Square and around St Stephen's Green, like a spectre in the fog, but even after hours the traffic was too intrusive. And then somehow we heard of the Trinity Boxing Club and several of us joined. Under the benevolent tutelage of Fred Tiedt, who as a welterweight at the 1956 Melbourne Olympics had won a silver medal after controversially being denied the gold, we spent many hours exercising and sparring in the Trinity gym. Having once fought in Durban, sixty miles from the sugar farm that was then my home, and having fond memories of that city, Fred was keen to reminisce with one of its habitués and I found myself favoured, being chosen to represent Trinity in the light-middle-weight division. After a scheduled encounter with University College Cork was cancelled because snow had made the roads impassable, we prepared for the Irish Universities' Boxing Championships, which in 1978 were held in the Trinity gym, barely a stone's throw from our flat. With the three celebrated Christle brothers, who then so dominated Irish amateur boxing, pulverizing their opponents in the heaviest weight divisions, our team seemed invincible, but a number of our lighter team-mates lost, as did I in a split decision in the semi-finals.

When our course ended, each of us headed back to our respective home bases. As I flew south to the sombre prospect of two years of national service in the South African army, Stephen Fenichell returned to New York and for decades earned his living as a freelance writer. When he was in his mid forties, however, the financial demands of a growing family forced him to surrender to the formal job market, where he now holds a senior position at Merrill Lynch, now part of the Bank of America.

Even if Trinity has an abundance of architectural riches, with the Museum Building usually considered pre-eminent among them, there is surely nothing as awe-inspiring as the Old Library's Long Room. It was then accessed from the Berkeley Library forecourt, and as students we paid regular visits merely to marvel at its sheer size and beauty. And in the intervening decades since I left Trinity, on each of the three occasions that I have visited Dublin I have returned to pay homage.

On the first two, initially with my wife, and then with our son and daughter, I made forays through Front Gate, noting how little the sense of containment and timelessness had changed over the more than twenty years that I had been away, and on each occasion concluding with a visit to the Long Room. And on the third, a decade later still, while on a lightning stopover to research my Anglo-Irish forebears, I stayed for two nights in Goldsmith Hall and again made my customary pilgrimage to that cathedral of books. Standing once more in the towering vault, I gazed up at the curved wooden ceiling in its haze of golden light, and breathed in the dusty and resinous smell of centuries of learning, and was moved yet again by what must surely be the most awe-inspiring library in the world.

And on that last occasion, after wondering if the mythical Margaret was still alive, and if she might still pose a danger, if indeed she ever had, I wandered back along Pearse Street. The tailor who sewed leather patches onto the elbows of my sports jacket was gone, as were the two butchers. In the clotted traffic were no dray horses with their sooty cargoes. Yet the Academy Cinema building was still there, if in a more respectable guise. But opposite it, where 166 Pearse Street had once stood, was the shiny prow of the Naughton Institute, which, like a palimpsest, had erased all trace of its predecessor. As I stood there, with my reflection caught in the mirror of a new era, it was sobering to consider that my time was past and existed now only in memories.

John Conyngham (TCD 1977–8; Postgraduate Diploma in Anglo-Irish Literature) is author of three novels – the award-winning **The Arrowing of the Cane**, **The Desecration of the Graves** and **The Lostness of Alice** – and was for fifteen years the editor of **The Witness** (formerly **The Natal Witness**), South Africa's oldest newspaper. He has been a journalism fellow at the Poynter Institute for Media Studies in St Petersburg, Florida and at Oxford University. Married, with a son and a daughter, he works in the newspaper industry and lives near Pietermaritzburg, South Africa.

John Conyngham (left) and Stephen Fenichell on a Dublin bus, 1978.

ALANNAH

robert o'byrne

'I THINK I have always known about my memory,' wrote Lillian Hellman in her memoir *Pentimento*. 'I know when the truth is distorted by some drama or fantasy. But I trust absolutely what I remember about Julia.' And I, when reading those lines, I understand what Hellman meant. Because I feel the same way whenever I recall Alannah.

Last week I watched *Julia*, the film based on an episode in *Pentimento*. I hadn't seen it for more than thirty years, not since 1978 when I went to the cinema with Alannah. She'd already gone to see *Julia* the night before and was so enthralled that the following morning she bought a copy of Hellman's book and then persuaded me to skip a lecture and accompany her to an afternoon screening. Emphasizing the magnitude of friendship and loyalty, *Julia* struck a resounding chord with her. These were qualities imperative to Alannah and ones she sought in others. I hope she found them in me. Over the five years we knew one another, she was my most intimate friend, likely the closest I shall ever have, certainly the one I have loved best. And even after almost three decades I have only to think of her for a moment and she is restored to me as vibrant and entrancing as when we first met.

That was in September 1977 and the two of us were Freshmen reading History. We'd both grown up overseas – I in the Middle East, she in Southeast

Asia – and I suppose this might have given us an immediate reason to bond, finding somebody else who didn't possess the personal ties to one another that our college contemporaries seemed to have had since infancy. But maybe this is to seek more reason than is required for the origins of our friendship. It would have been impossible for me not to have wanted to know her. She was so vital, so full of enthusiasm and the kind of radiance ascribed by Henry James to Isabel Archer in *The Portrait of a Lady*. Like James's heroine, Alannah 'had a fixed determination to regard the world as a place of brightness, of free expansion … It was wrong to be mean, to be jealous, to be false, to be cruel.'

At least in part, personal history explained her buoyant cast of mind: in her teens she'd suffered acute renal failure and undergone several years of dialysis and a failed kidney transplant before a second operation proved successful. Unlike the rest of us, therefore, for Alannah death was no abstract concept but had been a real possibility. Hence the relish with which she approached each day, the gusto with which she tackled every enterprise. So many ventures, too little time. She was forever taking up projects, and then expecting me to embrace with similar passion whatever at that moment enthralled her. Sometimes it wasn't difficult to match the zest. I was more than happy to join her marching in a demonstration against Dublin Corporation's plans to build on Wood Quay, although somewhat less delighted with the loose approximation of Viking costume she proposed for us: we knotted sheets around our necks as cloaks, wore saucepans on our heads as helmets and carried their lids as shields.

The kitchen equipment had been temporarily purloined from one of her other interests at the time, operating an alternative lunch venue to the Buttery. The all-women Elizabethan Society, a genteel relic from the start of the century (it would be absorbed into the Phil a year after we graduated) seemingly served little purpose other than to organize an annual afternoon party in the Provost's Garden during Trinity Week, but it did have fine ground-floor rooms in Front Square. Alannah and a couple of the Society's other members decided to make some money by running a café on the premises, drafting everyone who knew her to help with the scheme. The menu wasn't ambitious, mostly sandwiches and soup, the preparation of which involved regular trips to Moore Street to buy cheap vegetables and then repetitious chopping of onions and carrots and parsnips. The scheme flourished for a while but finally folded, in part because her physical strength was limited, the years of illness having left a permanent legacy of tiredness. Regularly, whenever exhaustion outstripped enthusiasm, she took to her bed and slept for several days, insensible to telephone calls or ringing doorbells.

In any case, she lacked the kind of focus required to make the Elizabethan Society endeavour a long-term success. Despite sporadic spring cleans and ambitious intentions to be methodical, Alannah was chronically disorganized, her living quarters invariably shambolic. She told me that when sent as a girl to board at Newtown in County Waterford, having come from a home where staff took care of such things, the biggest shock had been to discover she was expected to pick up and look after her own clothes. In adulthood, the greater part of her wardrobe never reached that piece of furniture; it was left at best draped, at worst scattered about various rooms. At the start of our second year we attempted to share the house her parents had bought off South Circular Road. It proved an unwise idea and I moved out after just a couple of months, needing to live in a tidier environment than did she. Alannah drew up elaborate plans for the house's redecoration but these never progressed beyond the preparatory stage; one bedroom remained forever half-stripped of its wallpaper and half-painted in salmon pink.

Whether delivering an essay or meeting for tea, she always ran late. At the end of our first term, both of us bound overseas for Christmas, we agreed to have a final breakfast together at Bewley's on Westmoreland Street. Alannah never turned up; only at the start of the following term did I find out she had overslept and then made a frantic dash to the airport to avoid missing her flight. Her scattiness was on occasion maddening but so much a part of her persona she couldn't have been otherwise. In an era before the invention of mobile phones and email, she would regularly leave notes of contrition in her sprawling, exuberant writing, always with the promise of future punctuality. It wasn't a promise I ever expected her to honour.

The notes were pinned onto the Players noticeboard under the front archway. Early in second year, she'd decided acting was her metier and attended open auditions for a part in the first production of the season. I came along for support but in the event ended up getting a role – as one of the titular gentlemen in *Two Gentlemen of Verona* – and she was offered the opportunity to help backstage. Later she got the chance to appear on stage, her outstanding moment being a performance as fragile Catherine Holly in Tennessee Williams's *Suddenly Last Summer*.

For that role she cut her hair into a bob. Until then it had hung long and thick, her head seeming to droop under its luxuriant weight when she grew tired. Alannah's hair was a coppery chestnut that turned golden after exposure to the sun, just as her skin, sallow in grey-sky Ireland, would become tawny warm by the end of a summer in Asia. It was preternaturally soft and downy and plump and just as she never shed her full-cheeked baby fat, so she forever retained the delicious clean scent peculiar to the very young. She had a retroussé nose and a Cupid's bow mouth and her profile was as delicately drawn as that of Madame Récamier. Her eyes were dark and lively but sank into black pits at moments of exhaustion. Her laughter was Alannah's most alluring trait, a long low gurgle that finished in a whoop. It was always possible to trace her by listening out for that laughter. Instinct and early experience inclined her temperament to optimism, to thinking the best of others, to believing that right would always out. Though she relished gossip she was incapable of malice. Though sometimes angry her impulse was to forgive. Whereas we often disagreed on various subjects, over the five years we never had a serious argument and while our temperaments were fundamentally different – mine preoccupied with achieving order, hers a disordered jostle – I was never so at ease as when in her company.

Long before the end of our first term we had forged our bond. We went to every Trinity Ball together, in our second year attending in matching white boiler suits bought from an industrial clothing outlet on Capel Street; this was, after all, 1979, and neither of us was in a position to afford the Armani boiler suit we'd admired in Italian *Vogue*. That night, after an hour or so at the ball I lost my partner but eventually tracked her down to a Players dressing room where she had fallen asleep on an old velvet chaise. Alannah's capacity for alcohol was never very high and earlier in the evening I'd cooked us a dinner in which drink played the greater part. I covered her in a couple of costumes from the current Players production and went back to the ball; the following day a note of apology was waiting for me on the noticeboard.

Later that summer I flew out to spend a month with Alannah and her family in Singapore. Her father Duncan, a pilot with Singapore Airlines, was a big ebullient man whose children, Alannah and her two handsome siblings Sean and Fiona, provided the mainspring of his life. Her mother Zoe, a wiry New Zealander with a rasping voice, had a warier view of the world than did Duncan. They lived in an old colonial house with a capacious front portico, high-ceilinged rooms and no windows, only louvered shutters on the two floors. The first night there, disdaining mosquito nets, I was so badly bitten on the face that my swollen left eye wouldn't open the next morning.

While I recovered, Alannah spent the days showing me her Singapore, drinking cocktails in Raffles, ineffectually hunting for bargains in the Chinese quarter's markets, swimming at the club. Later we went on a couple of expeditions, first a short jaunt to the former Portuguese colony of Malacca, then a longer expedition to Chiang Mai in north Thailand. There we stayed in a guesthouse where our room was made of wooden planks with spacious gaps between them, and the bed was a couple of thin mattresses on the floor. We hired bikes and cycled everywhere around the flat landscape, to visit a celadon factory, to watch elephants bathing in the river and bathe there ourselves, to explore the outlying Buddhist temples. On our final night I contracted food poisoning and had to be nursed by Alannah during the long journey back to Singapore by bus and train. During a stopover in Bangkok, I lay retching on the cool stone floor of a temple while she mopped my forehead with a damp cloth; having once been so ill, she had infinite sympathy for sickness in others.

Though there were many later, shorter expeditions and regular discussions about future trips, we never again travelled together for so long or so far. When apart, as we were the following summer when I spent three months in France and Italy, contact between us was maintained by the constant exchange of letters, hers written with a fountain pen on blue notepaper in that big extravagant hand. Replete with illustrations to help explain some idea or other, the letters were habitually filled with schemes for the future because as much as she relished the here and now, Alannah believed what came next would be even better. And in her presence it was impossible not to believe likewise.

It's what we expected as the end of our time at college drew near; those closing months particularly privileged since ours was the last intake of students to sit final exams in the early autumn, permitting us to spend a summer living on campus supposedly devoting ourselves to revision. Post-exams I moved away from Dublin but she remained there, looking for employment at a time when there was little of it about. But her optimism remained undimmed, her confidence that something wonderful would turn up impossible to dent. And the following spring a job of sorts did materialize, work in a radio station with little or no pay and probably not a lot of prospects: in those days nothing in Ireland seemed to offer much of that. Her letters were as full of cheer and plans and hope as ever and when she came to spend a couple of days with me in early summer she was convinced, as was I, that a dazzling future in radio lay ahead of her.

A WEEK LATER her father Duncan telephoned me. Alannah was fatally ill. Because of her underlying condition nothing could be done to save her.

'But what can I do?' I asked. 'What am I supposed to do?' By this stage in our conversation both of us were crying so noisily it was almost impossible to hear the other.

'I don't know,' said Duncan, 'but you're her best friend.'

Did being Alannah's best friend make any difference at that juncture? I don't know, but I'm certain that had roles been reversed she would have behaved better than did I in those closing months. In fact, she behaved better than any of us, her family and friends, as we struggled to maintain a semblance of composure while tormented by the knowledge she was soon to disappear from our lives. And as death approached she came to resemble another Jamesian heroine, *The Wings of the Dove*'s Milly Theale, attaining a new serenity and beautifully, unobtrusively showing us how we ought to behave. The tone of her letters never altered, nor her voice on the phone, nor her manner when in her presence. Though confined to bed she remained as lively as ever, still talking of the future, still making plans for what it would hold. That she was terminally ill was not once mentioned. It was as though, having defeated death once, she was determined to do so again.

Alannah won many battles but not this one. My sister rang to say she had died and to let me know her funeral would take place in College Chapel. On the appointed day I came to Dublin, went to that familiar house off South Circular Road and then drove with Alannah's family to an undertakers' on

Thomas Street. She had been laid out in a room on the first floor. I climbed the stairs and looked into the coffin. Though the neatly arranged corpse had her outward form, it wasn't and never could be Alannah: that waxy, inanimate face did not belong to her. Her features had always been so full of movement, her mouth forever on the verge of laughter. None of the traits that had made her so special were apparent in the small inert form lying there. Nothing brought home the cruelty of her death so much as the uncharacteristic stillness.

I remember when, following the release of *Julia*, we read of other writers who argued Lillian Hellman had invented sections of *Pentimento*, that it was more a work of fiction than a memoir. In particular it was proposed her friend Julia had never existed, Hellman having borrowed aspects of the character from other people. Such speculation never troubled Alannah because she esteemed the concept of friendship that lay at the core of the book and of the film. Likewise do I because in her brief life she taught me the importance of cherishing friends both when they are with us and when gone. And so, even after all these years, I trust what I remember about Alannah.

Alannah MacLachlan 30 April 1958 – 6 September 1982.

Robert O'Byrne (TCD 1977–81; History) has had a varied career including curator of Damer House in Roscrea, County Tipperary; Mid-West Regional Arts Officer; founding director of the Music Network; and fashion correspondent of **The Irish Times**. He is the author of more than ten books, including a biography of Sir Hugh Lane, a history of the Irish Georgian Society and the **Dictionary of Living Irish Artists**. He is a board member of the Irish Georgian Society and the Alfred Beit Foundation.

THE CLASS OF 77

liz o'donnell

I WAS NOT your usual first year. At twenty-one, I was older and more worldly wise than my peers in the Law School. Or so it seemed. Friends recall a totally cool character, dressed in thigh-high red leather boots and tight elephant-cord orange jeans. My hair was short *à la* Annie Lennox. I looked like someone with a past and wore make-up, unlike my classmates in first-year Legal Science. Most were just out of school and some were dropped outside college by their dads! I had lived and worked in London and Dublin since I left school four years earlier. I had forgotten how to study; they were still high on their Leaving Cert. results, which to get into Trinity Law had been spectacular.

I had romantic notions about Trinity as a college and had never really considered going elsewhere. Growing up in Dublin's north inner city, I recall walking past Front Gate as a young child en route to Grafton Street, peering in at its strangeness. I knew nothing of it except that it looked mysterious, closed and foreign. None of my family had been to college. I was the first and it had taken me almost four years to be persuaded I should go further in my education.

I had been a bright but spirited student in my Limerick convent secondary school. I was constantly in trouble because of my tendency to question the status quo and the authority of the nuns. I was a 'messer', and must have been a pain in the neck for my teachers, who saw a bright girl who did little work and showed no ambition. The only exception was a passion for English literature, Art and Latin, at which I excelled in exams.

I was too young to matriculate at sixteen when I sat the Leaving Cert. In any event, my plan was to get out of Ireland and work in London. Armed with good typing and shorthand skills I headed off with two Limerick friends and enjoyed three years of work in a variety of jobs from the Press Office in Miss Selfridge to wearing the green polyester skirt of a junior bank official in AIB in Croydon. Though all great fun, I was intellectually bored and unfulfilled. To the delight of my parents, I eventually gave in and applied for college at home.

My first choice had been English in Trinity and I was accepted for this. My second choice was Law, at the suggestion of my former Latin teacher, barrister Antonia O'Callaghan, who cautioned against reading English as an indulgence. Mindful of my huge overdraft from London frolics, I plumped for Law as the more practical option. I knew nothing of the subject and had never met a lawyer. Later I discovered the only reason I was accepted was due to my A in Latin, which compensated for my otherwise mediocre Leaving Cert., which included failed Maths.

The first day of registration and familiarization was overwhelming. I knew nobody and felt out of place. My classmates appeared very young and I feared their intellectual superiority. Most were from the private Dublin schools and seemed to move in a different circle of confidence and privilege. Thankfully there were some older postgraduate students who shared our lectures, which was reassuring to an outsider like me.

The timetable was the biggest surprise: eight hours of lectures per week! This certainly suited my plans for part-time work to supplement what my father could send to me each week for rent and food. I was sharing a dingy basement flat on the South Circular Road with a good friend from school, Ann Keary, who, like me, was a late starter. She was studying for a B.Mus. and there were only a handful of people in her year. Her schedule was ferocious, with hours of practice on her instruments and then all the theory in the degree course. There were forty-four in my year, of which there was a good smattering of Northerners of both denominations.

The Library was frightening. Huge and unfathomable and lined with legal books and Irish reports. I spent little time there during the first term, and none during the rest of the year. Lectures were great. Everything was new, and I soaked up the knowledge. I loved the freedom to come and go as I pleased and drift around college taking in the sights. After years of atrophy, my brain was in gear again. I had not written anything of substance since school, apart from long and often maudlin letters to friends from London. Now I was at last among people who were as bright and more likely brighter than me. I was in my element.

Legal Science was very much part of the Humanities in Trinity, and we had a huge choice of subjects, practical and academic. My favourites were Constitutional Law and Torts, mainly due to the brilliance of Professor R.F.V. Heuston, who lectured in both. Reputed to be a descendant of Robert Emmet, to whom he bore a startling resemblance, he transfixed his students with his honed delivery. I hated European Law and Contract and can genuinely say I never attended one lecture on Land Law, such was my distaste for its dusty content. Mr Exshaw's notes were faithfully reproduced every year and that sufficed to pass. Family Law was a revelation with Professor William Duncan, an inspiring pioneer in the area. Professor Mary McAleese, who in retrospect must have only been a couple of years older than me, taught Criminal Law. Such was my interest in this subject, I managed to make her 9 am lectures in St Mark's Hall – quite an achievement for someone who was in the first throes of a love affair.

A chance meeting at the 54A bus stop in Dame Street was the start of a whirlwind romance with my future husband Michael Carson. He claims I picked him up with an innocent enquiry as to the location of the Irish Reports in the Library. As it was already late November, this ignorance on my part may have suggested a promising fecklessness, and he responded with an invitation to the International Bar, where we still occasionally repair to reminisce. Michael had read English at Cambridge and was doing the Bar exams at the King's Inns, which involved some Trinity lectures. As for the pick-up allegation, my story is that I always talk to people at bus stops.

My tutor was the late Kader Asmal, who lectured in Public International Law. His lectures were lively and intensely partisan affairs. Most days, they descended or ascended into polemic diatribes against colonial powers or the apartheid regime. Unfortunately, notes from his presentation meant little afterwards. It was pure theatre. He was a political refugee himself and founder of the Irish Anti-Apartheid Movement. He was a busy man, which suited me when I was looking for an extension for an essay. Waiting to see him in the corridor outside his office were far more needy and urgent cases such as people on the run, or about to be deported. My piffling request was waved through in a swirl of Rothmans smoke. Little did either of us imagine that twenty years later we would meet as equals in post-apartheid South Africa, when he was Minister for Water and I visiting Irish Overseas Aid Minister.

Before long, I found some like-minded pals, reluctant lawyers, who were up for long lunches and drinks in the Buttery, or better still the Berni Inn or The Bailey. I had easily acquired a surprisingly well-paid part-time secretarial job – certainly better than waiting tables, the fate of many of my classmates.

That class of 1977 was deemed a good year by the Law School. The academic standard was high but more importantly it was a good mix of personalities. The late Brian Lenihan, Senior Counsel and Minister, a sparkling intelligence then as he was until his untimely death, was the scholar in our year. Such was the standard that we had another scholar, Eanna Molloy, now a Senior Counsel. About a third of the class were from Northern Ireland and comprised a mixed bag of public-school Prods and middle-class nationalists. The strange thing, looking back, is that none had any interest in politics per se. They were all great craic and set on living it up on British grants in tension-free Dublin for the next four years.

But my best friend in the Law School was Ann O'Neill, an Alex girl, and now a leading family lawyer, whom I met on the first week as we tottered in high heels over Front Square. She was a tall busty blonde and hilarious. Bright as a button and with a photographic memory, she flounced through exams with a couple of weeks' revision. She and I were the glam girls of the class, except I was going steady so wasn't as flamboyant. She sang with a rock band and looked like a rock star; her family regularly fed me when I was broke and there was no food in the dingy basement flat. Mark Cawley, now an attorney in New York, was part of our flighty gang. He sang like an angel and was to give a memorable rendition of 'She moves through the Fair' at my wedding to Michael in Jesus College Cambridge in 1982. The late Gerry Ryan was at one point a boyfriend of Ann's although he was ahead of us in the Law School and involved with Ents (entertainments). Damian Collins and John Cronin, now senior partners in McCann FitzGerald Solicitors, and Fiona O'Neill, who was later to be John's wife, were also friends. Sinead Hanley, now a psychotherapist, counselled us from an early age. Michael Kealy from Derry, who was to become a brilliant libel lawyer, had rooms in college and there were parties thrown every time his grant cheque arrived. Robert Power, pensions guru, and Nick Mulcahy, publisher, were also mates. Nick was the editor of the *Trinity Intellectual Times* (*TIT*) and at one stage I typed the copy. There was surprisingly little social integration across faculties. The Law School had a self-contained feel to it. Engineers and scientists lived on another planet on the far side of the cricket pitch.

Those four years in Trinity were life-altering for me. It wasn't what I studied but the people I came to know and love during my college life that made the difference. It wasn't all fun. My father had a heart attack during my first year and had to retire at fifty-five from his job with Guinness. My brother Sean was just starting UCD at the time and financially it was a huge strain on the family to support us both in Dublin. My mum took in lodgers in Limerick to help out. My flat on the South Circular was disgusting and I spent a lot of the time in friends' houses or with Michael whose shared rented house was palatial compared to mine. There were grim winters spent shivering and fully clothed in bed. I remember transporting a bag of coal on the panier of my bike down the frozen Grand Canal during a fuel strike in 1979. There was a period when all we had to eat in the flat was porridge and tinned Carnation milk. At one stage I benefitted from a grant from the Trinity Trust when I couldn't pay my fees. I missed lectures and college activities because I had to work two days a week as a secretary. Student debating in the Hist or Law Societies was out of the question, and I was always behind in my work. Summers were spent labouring in Dutch bulb farms to pay off debts. When I graduated I was wholly owned by the AIB.

During my last year, I had worked as a waitress in the Unicorn Restaurant on Merrion Row, presided over by the famous Miss Dom. The tips were good and included a free pasta meal. It was then, as it is now, a haunt of politicians, poets and journalists. The contacts I made there were to serve me well later one when, as a young law graduate in a recession, I looked for work. My first job was with Vincent Browne, who was a Unicorn regular, flogging ads for *The Magill Book of Irish Politics*. Vincent was as scary then as he is now, wild-eyed and hair standing up on end. His key journalists in that grotty office on Merrion Row, which smelt of Kentucky Fried Chicken, were Fintan

O'Toole, Paddy Agnew and Gene Kerrigan. All in one room! The next job was as a production manager with Noel Pearson Productions, which I loved. After four years of law, the colour and energy of the theatre was a delight.

In light of my subsequent career in politics, my college days were surprisingly apolitical: on the contrary, I was unmoved by the strikes regularly organized by the Students' Union. I despaired of all that predictable left-wing rhetoric. One year, the ticket for the Student Union elections was Duffy/White/Hayes. The first was the yet-to-be-famous Joe of RTÉ. The second was the lawyer and senator Alex White. And the third was Liam Hayes, journalist, all duffle-coated socialists. I supported the campaign of the flamboyant James Mullen (who was a classmate in Legal Science) as an alternative and centre-right candidate. James had no policies. It was just a jolly and his handsome face looked great on posters. James went on to develop his family shirt-making business into the global Thomas Pink chain. But my real political awakening was to take place much later, when I noted with shock the dearth of women in the Dáil chamber when Mary Robinson addressed it as president elect.

At that stage I was a young mother of two on a career break. I had worked on the presidential campaign of my former Trinity lecturer and soon after, I was persuaded by a chance meeting with Mary Harney TD (also a Trinity graduate) to join her in the Progressive Democrats. After a successful first run in the 1991 local elections to Dublin City Council, I was elected in the snap General Election of 1992, and served as TD for Dublin South for fifteen years. For five years I was privileged to serve as a Minister of State at the Department of Foreign Affairs and was a member of the Government negotiating team in the talks leading to the Good Friday Agreement in 1998. None of my tutors would have predicted such a political outcome for the glamour girl in the orange elephant cords and high red boots. And none of it would have been possible without that A in Latin from the convent in Limerick and the vital force that was Antonia O'Callaghan BL, my Latin teacher at school. Sadly she died at a young age before my political career began, but she lived to see me reading Law at Trinity in line with her advice.

Trinity gave me the great gift of a liberal education, which in due course shaped my values in politics. Trinity introduced me to great friends of all religions and none. It taught me to embrace diversity and intellectual freedom and to challenge injustice. It gave me the confidence to trust my own judgment. It was the place that vindicated my earlier instinctive rejection of conservative Catholicism and narrow nationalism. It was the perfect fit for me. As my mother would say, 'It was the making of me.'

Liz O'Donnell (TCD 1977–81; Legal Science) was Progressive Democrat TD (Dublin South, 1992–2007). She was Minister of State at the Department of Foreign Affairs, 1997–2002, and played a role in Anglo-Irish relations and the multi-party talks leading to the Good Friday Agreement. She retired from politics in 2007. She wrote and presented a four-part TV documentary on Irish overseas aid, **Far Away Up Close**, in 2008, and now works in public-affairs consultancy and advocacy. She is a board member of the Chernobyl Children's Project International, is married with two adult children and lives in Dublin.

WORKING THROUGH COLLEGE

patricia quinn

MY FIRST experience of Trinity was the finals of a schools debating competition held in the Graduate Memorial Building, home of the Historical Society, in 1975. The motion ('*Dulce et decorum est pro patria mori*') stimulated neither side on the night, and the debate itself was desultory. We felt a little patronized by the tea and biscuits administered afterwards by the record recretary, George Birmingham, and treasurer of the society, Mary Harney, who despite their high office seemed barely older than we were ourselves. But the slightly chaotic atmosphere and the fizz of intellectually engaged youth in the room left a lasting impression. This was far from the orderly kind of setup that I was familiar with from schools debating, which, after all, is mainly a device for corralling querulous teenagers. It seemed to me that this was a place where people were excited by ideas.

I entered Trinity in 1977 from one of its established feeder schools, Mount Temple Comprehensive. This Dublin school had been established following the merger in 1972 of three long-established Church of Ireland institutions – the Bertrand & Rutland (girls), Mountjoy, and Hibernian Marine (boys) schools. I was far from a typical Mount Temple girl, having fetched up there late in my school career, a contrarian refugee from a Catholic establishment that had no use for principled, much less atheistic, dissent. Trinity seemed to me to be all of a piece with the kind of people I had recently met in Mount Temple – mostly Protestants with a sense of autonomy and personal responsibility, and a strongly defined, if somewhat diffidently expressed cultural identity. I saw it as a bastion of disinterested secularism, which strongly contrasted with the predominantly Catholic ethos that prevailed outside the walls. I liked this, and despite my atheism went so far as to join the altos of the Christ Church Cathedral Choir at the other end of Dame Street, then directed by Peter Sweeney, for regular doses of Tudor music and Jacobean English (*The Book of Common Prayer* was still in daily use), which sustained me with three services a week (and a small stipend!) throughout my college career.

Like many undergraduates, I had no idea what subject I would study. Initially I pinned my hopes on getting a place in English or, maybe, Music. In fact by great good fortune I fell into History. The Schools of Modern and Medieval History in Trinity in the late 1970s were in transition, with the recent or imminent retirements of a generation of prominent historians: 'The Ott' (Jocelyn Otway-Ruthven), Theodore Moody, R.B. McDowell et al., and their replacement by more culturally diverse figures with new research interests and different methodologies. The four-year course was then structured as two halves: the first two were mostly taught and covered general topics and periods, while the second two relied on primary sources and were structured more around small seminars and self-directed work.

The year I entered Trinity, it was a building site, with work on the Arts Block just coming to an end. In 1979, we moved from the temporary huts and the limestone and granite splendour of Deane & Woodward to the architecturally honest breeze blocks of Ahrends, Burton and Koralek. Until then, lectures and seminars were given in an assortment of available rooms of all shapes and sizes in venues throughout the campus – I never studied any English history, for example, because in those critical first weeks of term, I simply couldn't find the lectures in the bowels of the science block behind the cricket grounds. Instead, by good fortune, I took Early Modern Irish, thereby encountering the formidable Aidan Clarke, who delivered entire lectures in prose, without notes, while at the same time entertaining the silliest questions and interruptions with courtesy and erudition.

On reflection, I think that what we learned from that faculty was to listen, read and write. Lazy thinking, careless assembly of second-hand ideas, failure to attribute sources properly were first discouraged, then quite firmly censured. One of the new lecturers, the brilliant David Fitzpatrick, became so frustrated by the slipshod study habits of his undergraduate students that he actually brought a pack of 3 x 5 index cards and a shoebox to one of his tutorials, and set about, *Blue Peter*-like, to educate us in the basics of research methodology. Remarkable as it might seem now to students who enter college with a laptop or a tablet, essays were handwritten, and an IBM golfball typewriter was then the height of new technology.

I was an indifferent student, not least because I was very busy doing other things. I had left home on starting my college career – not the norm then for Dublin residents – and had a living to earn. At first I did the usual student things: delivering the Christmas post, gherkin-packing in Germany in the summer, and as time went on I picked up some of the more specialized work available to undergraduates, including a memorable stint in the State Paper Office and a long cataloguing assignment in the Long Room of the Old Library. I learned from John S. Doyle and David McKenna (publisher and editor respectively of *In Dublin* magazine, both now luminaries of RTÉ) how to be a journalist, and was for quite a long time the magazine's radio critic. My fee for a 750-word column every fortnight was £14 and my weekly rent was £7. Result: happiness, to quote Mr Micawber. My method was to fill a bath, which was the only source of heat besides a dangerous paraffin contraption in my tiny Fitzwilliam Square flat, turn on the radio, and not get out until I had enough material for an article.

All this should not suggest that I did not participate in student life. I believe there is a photograph still in circulation of Helen Roycroft, myself and two others (whose names I'm afraid I can't remember) playing string quartets (string quartets!) at a Trinity Ball, and I was a member for several years of the orchestras that assembled to accompany Joe Groocock's highly popular oratorio performances. These were thrilling events, in various ways, mostly because of Dr Groocock's boisterous enthusiasm for Bach, Handel and Haydn. I particularly remember sitting at the back of the cello section beside Joe Czibi who missed his cue and came in with a very showy trumpet voluntary *a bar early*. His eyes were almost closed, the veins stood out on his neck and his mind was clearly fully focused on the effort of performing his solo: short of stopping the show there was nothing the conductor could do to get him back on track, so the whole orchestra carried on, gloriously discordantly, to the end of the piece.

I thought I would study the cello seriously and took a gap year to work on scales and arpeggios. Fortunately, I was rescued from my delusions of professional musicianship by the late John Beckett, and once I joined his chamber-music class in the Royal Irish Academy of Music, learned to play the more forgiving viol, and joined the choir he assembled every year to sing Bach cantatas, I was firmly established as a musical amateur, to my great good fortune. The other vivid cultural memories of my time in Trinity were performances at Players (Robert O'Byrne was a splendidly camp Gentleman of Verona), and screenings at the College Film Society, presided over by the enigmatic David Lass, certainly a College Character.

In my first year, I fell ill with a fairly common gynaecological complaint requiring emergency surgery ('come back this afternoon with your nightie and a toothbrush, and we'll go in and have a look in the morning'), and encountered the Rotunda, yet another venerable Protestant institution. I mention it only because it gives me the opportunity to express my appreciation for David Thomas, the physician responsible for establishing the TCD Health Centre. Between them, he and George Henry at the Rotunda patched me up through a series of minor but disruptive surgeries and, perhaps mindful of my rather precarious means, never sent a bill. Moreover, I gained a very practical bird's eye view of the ethics policies of the Rotunda from a few stints in the public gynae ward.

As time went on I enjoyed my academic work more and more. I was lucky to hit the Department at a time when there were energetic lecturers who had both a passion for their subject and a capacity to make it interesting to undergraduates. I was also fortunate to have had as my tutor Ian Robinson, a most humane man who dragged me through my finals against my protestations of poor health (and fear of failure). Generations of history undergraduates owe a debt of gratitude to Ian and his wife Helga, whose walk from college to their home on the canal must often have taken many times its nominal duration as they encounter former student after former student, and stop for a chat. A long essay for Ian (on Erasmus's use of the printing press) started me on a lucky streak of topics about the dissemination or censorship of ideas in different historical periods and places, which happily preoccupied me for my last two years in college. I explained this in terms of a kind of work-avoidance racket to a fellow student, who mildly commented that he thought this was what was called a research interest.

But I was not snared by the academic life. By virtue of persistently appearing in the recently established state-of-the-art laboratory for conserving books and manuscripts in the attic of the Old Library, on some pretext or other during my time on the Old Library project, I got a two-year stint working as a trainee conservator in the lab. This began the day after my finals finished, and I happily became immersed in the crafts of paper, vellum, wood and leather-work, under the inspirational direction of Tony Cains. A non-academic, Tony had been attracted to set up the world-renowned conservation facility for the library, and if I could have stayed I sometimes think I would still be there. Certainly, working as a non-academic in Trinity gave me a further perspective on the institution, but that was in the eighties, and is a story for another time.

Patricia Quinn (TCD 1977–82; History). After graduating, she worked for two happy years in the book and manuscript conservation laboratory of Trinity's Old Library before moving to Cambridge to work for six months in the Cockerell Bindery. She came back to Dublin to take up the positions successively of music officer at the Arts Council, cultural director at Temple Bar Properties and executive director of the Arts Council. She is the founder and CEO of Irish Nonprofits Knowledge Exchange. Although she no longer sings, she still delights in playing chamber music. She lives in Dublin with her partner John and their two girls Ellen and Alice.

AN AMERICAN IN DUBLIN

stephan weinberger

I WAS twenty-two years old when I left Tulsa, Oklahoma, for Dublin in the fall of 1977 to enroll in the Anglo-Irish Literature Diploma course at Trinity College. I had never been outside of North America before leaving for Dublin and had no preconceived expectations. I had majored in English Literature at college and greatly enjoyed the Irish authors I read. My father had been to Dublin more than ten years before on a sales trip and came back enthusiastic about his time there including his tour of Trinity and the Book of Kells. Under the circumstances that was enough for me. It was a decided plus that the Irish spoke English (foreign languages not being a strong suit for me) and that the tuition, even with the 40-per-cent foreign-student surcharge, was affordable. I think for the full year it came to about £700 but it could have been dollars. So with a new passport, a full duffle bag, a sleeping bag and a fishing rod, I left for Ireland.

I was lucky from the moment I got to Dublin. On the bus from Dublin airport to TCD I met Andrew Whiteway, an incoming Freshman from Devon, England. After walking through Trinity's Front Gate together we made our way to the student housing office. Andrew wasn't provided with a room in college and decided not to take the off-campus accommodation he had been assigned. I was offered a room in Harold's Cross in a home owned by a man named

Padraig and Andrew chose to throw his lot in with me. And just like that we became room-mates and a lifelong friendship was born.

Padraig was a single man in his late thirties with a well-kept, clean house. Andrew and I shared a room upstairs with two beds and had the use of a room downstairs with a television and limited use of the kitchen when Padraig wasn't cooking or entertaining. Central heating was not commonplace in Dublin in the seventies and I was cold almost all of the time I was there. Making the cold worse in our room at Padraig's house was a jammed window that Andrew and I couldn't completely close for our first six weeks there. Years later when I saw Andrew again in London and we met for a drink he told me how much my offering him my sleeping bag in those first weeks meant to him. I think I slept in my clothes the entire time I lived in Dublin. I joined the boxing team more for access to the hot showers than for the exercise.

Padraig's house was too far from Trinity to walk every day and I took the bus back and forth, initially wondering at the women crossing themselves every few hundred yards. Then it dawned on me that we were passing churches along the way. Dublin was a much more outwardly religious city than any I had lived in before. I also soon learned that the last bus home was scheduled to coincide with last call at the pubs. I remember how safe I felt in Dublin at any time of night walking home from the bus stop alone. I felt that way, perhaps naively, because as far as I could tell no one in Dublin, including the police, carried a gun. I never thought for a moment that if I was robbed I was in danger of being shot. I was aware, of course, of the violence in Northern Ireland but never felt personally threatened by it and had decided not to travel there as a tourist.

Trinity College itself was a beautiful sight. From the moment you entered its gates and saw the porters and the arched stone entry where you collected your mail it was just as you might imagine what a great European university would look like if you were from America. I was happy to be here. Beyond the constant cold the most unsettling thing to me was the obvious poverty outside Trinity's gates. I hadn't expected to be surrounded on the streets of Dublin by children begging for money and trying to go through my pockets. I soon became aware that a large number of Irish people my age were leaving Ireland for better employment prospects, many of them heading for America.

There were twenty of us in the Anglo-Irish Literature Diploma course, almost evenly divided by sex, nine women and eleven men. Most of us were American but not all: Seamus Hosey was Irish and John Conyngham was South African. During John's time at Trinity he thought a lot about the military service that awaited him at home during a time of apartheid.

Our course work was light even by my state university experience. We met once a week for a lecture and once more for section in a smaller group. Our initial get-together as a group outside of class during our first week was arranged by Brendan Kennelly's wife at The Stag's Head, the only place in Dublin thirty years later that seemed darker and grimmer than I remembered.

We were spoiled with great teachers: Brendan Kennelly, Terence Brown and David Norris. My section teacher was Mrs Kennelly, née Margaret O'Brien. My recollection is that I was the only male in her small class and that Mrs Kennelly was a very pretty woman with long blonde hair. I was looking forward to reading and studying my favourite Irish authors: Yeats, Synge, O'Casey, Joyce, Beckett and Flann O'Brien. Eventually we got to all of them except Flann O'Brien, but we began with Maria Edgeworth's *Castle Rackrent* (previously unknown to me but as I found out a seminal historical novel concerning four generations of absentee landlords). And so began my introduction to a year of learning that Irish literature was inseparable from Irish history and politics. Looking back, Trinity was ahead of its time in teaching the now popular integrated curriculum.

There was no campus bookstore stocked with all the books we required of the kind I was used to or that exists at Trinity today. It took time to gather what I needed from smaller bookstores and I quickly learned to change gears to a different speed from what I was familiar with in America and adapt to my new environment. Some things were so much better than my experience in the US. Banking, for instance. I opened an account across the street from Trinity at the Bank of Ireland. They had a separate student office in a side room on the right of their magnificent building. The student bank office was decorated with a large poster of the English band The Police and staffed by a beautiful dark-haired blue-eyed teller named Clair, who always had a smile for us.

Our limited classes allowed for ample free time to study and explore Dublin and beyond. Looking back we were spoiled with an almost unimaginable amount of leisure hours to read and discover. We went to The Abbey Theatre and watched student plays on campus. I saw my first tiger at the Dublin Zoo and had a memorable fishing trip with classmate Terry Gallagher who lived in Howth. Terry and I travelled to Fore, County Westmeath, by bus and walked to a shop where we could rent a boat for the afternoon. Terry rowed and I fished and after a few hours without a rise we headed back to town and the pub. I can to this day remember sitting by the pub's window facing the road and watching a herd of cattle come towards us with blood streaming down their heads from where their horns had been cut. It was one of several visuals I'll never forget, another being a funeral procession down Pearse Street with the coffin held aloft on the shoulders of the pallbearers while bagpipes played somewhere off in the procession that followed.

In those days Trinity had three terms with long beaks between them. Classmate Betsy Skinner was travelling to Paris over Christmas break with some friends visiting from the United States and generously invited me to join them and stay at an apartment owned by her boyfriend's parents. During that same break, a housemate at Padraig's, Alfonzo, and I travelled together across Ireland in his car to Galway and the Cliffs of Moher, making a stop at Yeats's gravesite along the way. Alfonzo was from Austria and great company for a road trip.

Sometime during the first term Andrew met a girlfriend and wanted his own place after the break. I was ready to be closer to campus and what was meant to be a short-term stay on a couch in classmate Tom Strickler's room next to college at 166 Pearse Street before finding my own new room became my lodgings for the rest of my time there. Tom was an easy guy to get along with and needed the money. So for £6 a week, the couch was mine. Unfortunately, the heat was no better in the Pearse Street apartment but I had my sleeping bag and Tom had a small electric heater that you could sit in front of and singe the front of your clothes while your back froze. In addition to its advantageous location next to campus, three other classmates had rooms in the same building, and two of them, Stephen Fenichell and John Conyngham, remain good friends.

Outside of class time and required reading, often done at Trinity's beautiful Library, our time was our own and our day was whatever we chose to make of it. The bank manager remarked that we lived the life of Riley and looking back he wasn't all wrong. Coffee at Bewley's, a walk to St Stephen's Green, and for me and a few of the others practice with the boxing team. We had such a luxurious amount of time on our hands. Terry Gallagher organized a small group of us who got together to read *Finnegans Wake* out loud, trying make sense of it. And with the thought of going to business school the following year, I sat in on some maths and computer science classes.

As a group we had little money but we were students and Dublin was a poor place – you didn't need much money to get by and have a good time. For a few pounds you could drop off a bag full of laundry and pick it up later neatly folded. The food was modest but so were our tastes and you could eat relatively inexpensively. We often ate at the Dining Hall on campus. A year-end meal at Commons was a treat. Drink was widely available but I remember us all as moderate drinkers and perhaps the cost served as a check on that. One memorable evening a group of us went to see Martha Reeves and the Vandellas from Terry's home city of Detroit, with an opening act performed by the strongman Tony Brutus. Terry and Andrew went out to music clubs more often and came back one evening elated after seeing Mink DeVille, a group Terry and I saw again in New York a few years later at The Bottom Line. And somewhere along the way that year Andrew became friends with the guys who formed U2 and helped with their early management.

When I lived in Padraig's house I occasionally cooked, purchasing eggs and other provisions at small local stores. In the States I was used to large supermarkets but the shops in Dublin were either small general convenience stores or stand-alone butcher shops. The few times I ventured into a butcher shop hungry for a steak I left empty-handed. The hanging animal carcasses and overall presentation turned me back to dairy.

Going to Trinity gave me the opportunity to live in a foreign country that spoke a different sort of English, with 'yer man' this and 'yer man' that. Ireland was then and is today a rare country whose people embrace Americans. I had the time to read great literature taught by esteemed professors. I had the chance to see Europe on my breaks. And when it was nearing the end of my time there, as much as I enjoyed it, I was ready to go home. I learned much from my time in Ireland. I had great experiences and made lifelong friends. With all its beauty and open friendliness, Ireland also gave me a greater appreciation for home. For someone from a middle-class neighbourhood in America I was unprepared for the depth of its economic poverty.

I have clear memory of walking through the inner courtyard of Trinity after completing my final exam. It was a rare warm spring day and Professor Brown was walking towards me, surprised that I had finished my exam with nearly an hour of allotted time left. I had prepared for the exam, including memorizing a long section of the poem 'Nightwalker' by Thomas Kinsella, and when I was done writing, having said what I wanted to say, wished to be outside in the warm weather. I told him how much I had enjoyed my time at Trinity and that I would never forget it but was ready to go home.

Bono says that America isn't just a country, it's also an idea. And the Anglo-Irish Literature programme at Trinity in the late seventies wasn't just a year of graduate school for me. It was an adventure and a marvellous bridge to the rest of my life and the more serious business I faced, when it was over, of going to professional school and then on to a regular job.

IN NOVEMBER 2009, after a more than thirty-year hiatus, I went back to Dublin and Trinity College to meet my daughter who was on a short break from university in France and invited me to join her in Dublin for five days. My overnight flight from New York arrived in the morning and she wasn't due in until later in the afternoon, giving me a chance to wander on my own for a few hours. On the bus in from the airport I wondered how things had changed since I had left in 1978. After checking into the Westin Hotel, the old Allied Irish Bank building across from Trinity, and getting a room with a view of the college I headed out to Grafton Street for a cup of coffee at Bewley's. The streets were crowded and despite my absence for many years it was easy to find my way. Grafton Street had changed. I found that it was now closed to automobiles and had become a pedestrian mall. I walked into Bewley's and waited for a seat to open by the window on the second floor. It was, believe it or not, a mild sunny November day (fifty degrees or so) and as I sat there it started raining, the biggest raindrops I've ever seen, while the sun was out. It was like something choreographed for a movie and felt unreal. When I looked up from watching the passing crowd below, there was a rainbow. And I thought, are you kidding me?

I met my daughter Skye later in the afternoon and for the next five days we had as good a time as a father and daughter can have together. I was reliving my youth and she was seeing Dublin as it is today, a magnificent, beautiful European capital. The poverty I remembered was nowhere to be seen. The people looked healthy and the girls were beautiful. Every building seemed to have been given a fresh coat of paint in the last week. I can't remember a cleaner city and the friendliness was just as I remembered. Dublin is a great walking city and Skye and I walked for five days. We did all the tourist things, starting with a tour of Trinity, where the excellent guide told us that the student population was now about three times what it was when I was there. We saw the Book of Kells. We went to St Stephen's Green and the statue of Oscar Wilde and walked up O'Connell Street to the Post Office and on to the Writers' Museum. We went to the National Gallery and to the Chester Beatty Museum at Dublin Castle where we had a great and relatively inexpensive meal at the Silk Road Café. In general we ate surprisingly well, though not cheaply. One thing we missed was a meal at Commons because it was booked for Commencement. My daughter and I agreed that we would eat there the next time. I knew then that Ireland was beginning to face hard financial times again and we saw some protests against cuts in government spending. But the full force of the hard times ahead was yet to come.

Before going home I stopped by the Alumni Office, gave them my current address and picked up a brochure and application. I have a fifteen-year-old son. Who knows? He could do worse.

Stephan J. Weinberger (TCD 1977–8; Diploma in Anglo-Irish Literature). While at Trinity he joined the Boxing Club and attended computer science lectures. He went on to earn his Master's in Business Administration at the University of Chicago. In the early 1980s he worked in London and reconnected with TCD room-mate Andrew Whiteway. He is now a partner at an investment management firm in NYC. He is married to Linda Frazer and they have two children.